Christi

Contemplation

Simplified

~ • ~

Opening the Heart and Mind to Divine Love

Donald James Giacobbe

Miracle Yoga Services

The overall cover design, graphics, and interior layout of the text were created by Donald James Giacobbe.

Published by Miracle Yoga Services
— miracleyoga@gmail.com —
Cottonwood, Arizona

Printed in the United States of America

BISAC Subject Codes and Headings:

OCC010000 Body, Mind & Spirit—Meditation

REL012080 Religion: Christian Life—Prayer

REL012020 Religion: Christian Life—Devotional

Library of Congress Control Number: 2015911254

Giacobbe, Donald James
Christian Contemplation Simplified:
    Opening the Heart and Mind to Divine Love

ISBN 978-0-9843790-5-7

CONTENTS

~ o ~

PREFACE

~ o ~

Christian Contemplation Simplified is a condensed version of the 568-page book titled *Christian Meditation Inspired by Yoga and "A Course in Miracles."* Because some chapters are almost identical in both versions, it may not be wise to purchase both books. The longer version is suggested for seekers who already have some experience with meditation. This shorter version is recommended for beginners. Unlike the longer version, this brief meditation manual makes only some references to yoga and makes no reference at all to the philosophy of *A Course in Miracles.* The longer meditation manual teaches "Christian Yoga Meditation," which combines six techniques. Because this simplified version is written for beginners, this book emphasizes a simple and easier meditation practice called "Progressive Meditation," which includes four techniques used in sequence.

The purpose of the meditation techniques is to learn how to focus the mind and increase receptivity to the Holy Spirit. The practice of meditation prepares you for entering a deeper level of receptivity called "contemplation." Christian contemplation is an overshadowing of the Holy Spirit in which the mind becomes still without needing a focusing object, such as a sacred word or words. Through your practice of wordless contemplation, the Holy Spirit can gradually lead you to a greater degree of integration and unification that will transform you. Your goal is to open to divine love and allow that love to flow through you to others.

The seeker who is committed to following Christ will be guided from within by the Holy Spirit and will be shown ways of inwardly and outwardly living a life patterned after Jesus. How this applies to his prayer life will change from time to time as he makes progress spiritually. Consequently, a series of progressively more advanced techniques is offered here for the seeker's consideration of how to grow toward becoming more Christ-like. As the seeker's meditation experience deepens, he will gain greater responsiveness to the inner promptings of the Holy Spirit. His inner guidance will show him with increasing clarity what techniques to use and perhaps how to create his own methods of meditation that will best meet his individual needs. Eventually, the time may come when he is able to leave behind meditation techniques and experience deep contemplation as a gift from the Father.

Realistically speaking, not everyone is called to advance beyond meditation methods and into contemplation, since this is a divine calling. But each and every Christian seeker is called to do God's Will and allow the love of Christ to flow through him to touch the minds and hearts of every person that he meets. Therefore, the Christian seeker must remember that the primary purpose for him in practicing meditation is that it will make him a better instrument to manifest Christian love in the world.

In regard to using the techniques described here, I recommend that each seeker test these methods of meditation through practical application and firmly hold on to an attitude of purity of purpose and openness to the divine influence. There is no right way of meditating that is suitable for everyone. But everyone has within himself a right way that is an inner spiritual prompting. I trust that the Spirit within you has guided you to read this book. That same Spirit will continue to guide you to apply whatever would be most beneficial for your spiritual growth and will help you to set aside whatever would not benefit your growth. I request only that you pray to God for His guidance and remain sensitive and open to His spiritual promptings.

ACKNOWLEDGMENTS

I am very grateful for the support and encouragement of my sister Lillian Blackburn and the help of my friend Stuart Dean in preparing a previous version of this beginner's meditation manual. My thanks go to Tina Hardy for her professional copy editing assistance. I am grateful for the service of proofreading provided by John Francis, Janet Dews, Marta MacDonald, Donna Lock, Janet Dews, and Lillian Blackburn.

Other Books by
Donald James Giacobbe

Memory Walk in the Light (autobiography)
Christian Meditation Inspired by Yoga and "A Course in Miracles"
An Overview of "A Course in Miracles"
The Two-Month Bridge to "A Course in Miracles"
"A Course in Miracles" Seven Keys to Heaven

INTRODUCTION

~ ● ~

Since this book is an instruction manual for Christian meditation and contemplation, a good starting point would be to define each of these terms. First, the word "Christian" can be defined as referring to anyone who is a follower of Christ. A follower of Christ may belong to a group, such as a traditional church of a particular denomination, or a less structured nontraditional group. Of course, Christians who participate in group worship invariably recognize the importance of a private daily prayer life. There are also followers of Christ who do not belong to any group form of worship, but are concerned solely with developing a personal relationship with God based upon being alone with Him. For many Christians the word "Christ" is exclusively related to Jesus, Who perfectly embodied Christ, so He is known as Jesus Christ. Yet this book takes the broad view that you, too, can identify yourself with your true nature as part of the universal Christ.

Although there will never be a common Christian theology, there is a *common experience* of the divine within. Fortunately the focus in this manual is on this common experience, rather than theology, which can be divisive. Although there are no dogmas in this book, a fundamental premise of this manual is that the universal Christ is within and can be experienced. Hopefully you will not allow your theology, whatever it may be, to become a stumbling block to your experience of the universal Christ within.

Instead of believing a rigid theology, you may be one of the many "alienated Christians" in our society. These are individuals who were raised as Christian churchgoers, but who left organized religion for one reason or another. In some cases, the reason for leaving was that their church seemed only to make them feel increasingly guilty. In other cases, they could not accept a particular dogma that was integral to their church's teachings. Sometimes this dogma was a zealous and narrow-minded viewpoint that taught that if you do not worship God in a particular way, there would be no salvation for you.

Often these alienated Christians have linked their image of Jesus Christ with the dogma of their former church, so they feel a need to reject Jesus along with rejecting their former church. If you are one of these alienated Christians, you may not realize that Jesus Christ is not a judgmental figure that requires His followers to hold certain set beliefs about Him. Jesus loves you unconditionally, regardless of your beliefs or shortcomings. Your relationship with Jesus is entirely based on His love for you and your openness to loving Him.

On the other hand, there are many alienated Christians who are not alienated with Christ Himself. Often these individuals still would like to follow Christ and are receptive to finding a closer connection with Christ within. If you are one of these alienated Christians, you are, of course, encouraged to use the techniques you will find herein to deepen your inner life with Christ. Also, if you do not currently consider yourself to be a follower of Christ, but if you are at least open to exploring that possibility through learning to meditate, hopefully this manual will be helpful for you.

Your goal in meditation is to open to "divine love" and allow that love to flow through you to others. This experience of divine love may be called the "divine embrace," which is another way of describing the goal of yoga, meaning the goal of union. The words "divine embrace" specifically convey the connotation that you want a personal encounter with the divine within. Accomplishing this goal of the divine embrace involves inviting the Holy Spirit not only into the mind, but into all aspects of yourself. This includes inviting the Holy Spirit into every part of the body in order to remove inner obstacles to the divine embrace. The divine presence is embracing you even now, but you can only become consciously aware of the divine love within you by removing inner obstacles that are blocking your awareness. Some of the meditation techniques in this manual include focusing on a specific part of the body to help center the mind, to invite the Holy Spirit into that part of the body, and to release inner blocks related to that part of the body. Removing inner blocks replaces tension with positive energy and brings about an increased openness to the divine within.

The words "prayer" and "meditation" are often used as terms that indicate communication with God, but may have a variety of meanings for different people. For the purpose of this meditation manual, prayer is defined as *expressive communication* with God. In prayer we use the expressive nature of the mind and consciously direct our thoughts and feelings toward God. For some people the word "meditation" means to think about a spiritual topic, such as choosing a scriptural passage to mentally consider its meanings in a prayerful manner. However, for this manual the word meditation will have an entirely different meaning. In contrast to prayer in which we express different thoughts and feelings to communicate with God, meditation may be defined as *receptive communication* with God, in which we assume a passive state of mind. Meditation always involves focusing on one object or on one thought, such as a sacred word or words. Focusing on one thought allows you to let go of all the other distracting thoughts. How to actively relate to God in an expressive manner in prayer is important for our spiritual growth, but is only a secondary goal of this book. The primary purpose of this manual is to provide a step-by-step approach on how to produce the inner receptivity of meditation.

When the many thoughts of the mind are stilled by focusing on one thought during meditation, the mind becomes calm and open to the influence of the Holy Spirit. This peace of the mind resulting from meditation serves as a preparation for a much deeper form of spiritual receptivity, which is called "contemplation." During the experience of contemplation, you release even the sacred thought and the focusing object of meditation, and you enter a wordless inner silence. The goal of this book is to help you to first experience the peace of mind gained by meditation with words and to then experience the inner silence of contemplation. During contemplation you learn to open your heart and mind to the Holy Spirit and increasingly experience the divine love within you.

Through contemplation the Holy Spirit can lead you to a greater degree of integration and unification that will transform you. The transformation process that begins with meditation techniques and that is taken to a deeper level with contemplation is essentially a process of releasing darkness and accepting the light. Unacceptable thoughts and emotions, such as unresolved grievances or traumatic past experiences, are hidden in the darkest corners of the mind through the defense mechanism of denial. You will need to be willing to allow your hidden shadow side to be uncovered and to be surrendered to the light. This takes pure faith, requiring receptivity and courage. Through facing your dark side and letting go of selfish attachments, you are able to increasingly reveal and accept your true nature in Christ.

Meditation is sometimes mistakenly thought of as a nebulous and airy endeavor, when it is actually both a science and an art, which can be learned only through determined daily application and growth over time. Meditation, as it is presented in this manual, is a doorway leading to contemplation, which brings you into *His World*, an inner world with its own laws and way of being. There are doors within you that are closed. Meditation in coordination with the Holy Spirit helps to open these inner doors, creating a doorway to His World. This sacred inner world needs to be approached with earnestness, respectfulness, and consistency. This book provides a step-by-step approach to entering His World and going to deeper levels of His World. Coming into His World is a journey of discovery and transformation. The meditation methods provided here will help build a solid foundation for making this journey of transformation.

However, these meditation techniques leading to contemplation only represent a part of your transformation. Your transformation will involve changes in your inner meditative life as you become immersed in His World, but your transformation will also involve changes in your outer life manifested in the everyday world. Your goal will be to find balance between living in His World and living in your everyday world.

The word "integration" can be helpful to describe the wholeness you are seeking by reconciling your inner meditative experience and your outer experience of the world. In general, the word "integration" can be defined as the coordination of all aspects of yourself working together to bring about wholeness, which in a spiritual sense could refer to the ultimate goal of union with God. In addition to this general definition, the word "integration" can be defined with a more specific psychological meaning. Therefore, integration can be identified as the coordination of perception, behavior, and personality to bring about harmony with others and with the environment. In this sense, integration can refer to not only the universal goal of divine union, but also simultaneously to the more specific goal of harmony in everyday living in the world. Thus integrated spiritual living is the manifestation of a harmonious interrelation between His World and your everyday world. This is the hope of the prayer, "Thy Will be done on earth as it is in Heaven"— letting the outer expression in the world come forth from His World as a reflection of inner divine peace.

Since this is a meditation and contemplation "manual," it is designed and presented in a systematic way that includes many specific techniques. Although the techniques that are described in this manual may help experienced meditators, they are designed primarily to meet the needs of beginners and to serve as a secure foundation for future growth. This handbook is divided into two very distinct parts, as follows:

PART ONE: HOW TO START PRACTICING MEDITATION

Part One describes how to make a twenty-eight day commitment to deepen one's spiritual growth and learn meditation through practical experience.

PART TWO: GUIDELINES FOR DEEPENING MEDITATION

Part Two provides alternative methods for deepening meditation. The practical guidelines offered in this section prepare the meditator to be receptive to God's grace that will allow him to advance beyond methods and be drawn into contemplation.

PART ONE

~ . ~

HOW TO START PRACTICING MEDITATION

1

WHY MEDITATE?

≈ ० ≈

A. Your Motivation for Meditation

The first question you may want to ask yourself is, "Why do I want to meditate?" You may not be satisfied with your prayer life and seek to discover if meditation would help. On the other hand, you may feel good about your communication with God through prayer, but would like to enhance your spiritual life with meditation. Perhaps you may already practice meditation and would like to deepen your meditation experience in order to lead you to contemplation.

Regardless of your background or your experience, the most basic answer to the question "Why meditate?" is that you wish to deepen your relationship with God. This desire for a deeper relationship with God usually originates from a realization that there is a "void" in your life. You can fill your life with activities to fill this void, but you will only be able to temporarily *avoid the void*.

This void is a feeling of incompleteness. You may seek satisfaction and completeness in accumulating money and possessions, in sexual activity, in finding the right partner, perhaps in raising children, in your vocation, in travel, in recreation, and in creative outlets. You understand that all these activities of your life are important, but they are like pieces in a puzzle that do not quite fit together to make a complete picture. It appears to you that there is a major piece of the puzzle that is missing. You may even go to church and adopt all the concepts of your church and not find the missing piece there, either. Because you feel incomplete, you also feel alone and isolated. Perhaps you feel no one loves you, or even if you feel loved by others, you may still feel incomplete.

All these ways of seeking to fill the void in your life are attempts to find the missing piece to the puzzle by looking outside of yourself. All such attempts will ultimately fail. But in that failure comes a grace. There is a Voice inside you that is unlike the many voices, the many desires within you, shouting for your attention. This is a quiet Voice that is whispering, "I love you. Look inside, and you will find Me." When you give up seeking completion outside of yourself, you can begin to listen to this Voice, not with your ears, but with your heart. This is where seeking to deepen your relationship with God begins. You may try to pray by speaking to God, or if you wish to go deeper within, you may want to enhance your ability to listen to God.

Meditation can help you to listen to God, but needs to be viewed properly. Meditation can be defined as *receptive communication with God*, which may be facilitated by the repeating of one thought in order to quiet the mind and increase your awareness of the divine presence. The holding of one thought in the mind, such as the repeating of the Name of Jesus Christ, is merely a technique. It is not a magic formula that creates an awareness of God. What makes it work is your faith, your intentions, your commitment, and, most of all, God's grace.

There are two elements that may be considered the keys to spiritual growth. The first is *desire* and the second is *application*. You can have spiritual growth to the degree that you both *want* it and are willing to put that wanting into *practical application*. You have been told in scripture that if you seek, you will find, if you knock, the door will open, and if you ask, it will be given. God, for His part, is always willing to give you more blessings than you are willing to receive. Consequently, it is your responsibility to open yourself to receive those graces, which He would so willingly give to you.

Your receptivity begins with your desire for God, and the desire to deepen your relationship with Him is already in your heart, planted there by His grace. Your desire for God is like a seed within you, and, as with any seed, you cannot force it to grow. What you can do is simply allow yourself to become aware of the presence of that seed of your desire for Him and water it by paying careful attention to it. You may think of meditation as this act of "paying careful attention" to the desire for God within you that increases your receptivity to Him. If you put your desire for God into practical application by taking the small amount of time needed each day to contact this desire, your meditation will be effective in opening your heart and mind to Him. But if you do not take the time to find within yourself this true wanting, then your meditation will most likely become just another temporary self-improvement activity.

B. Entering His World

Those who meditate from a real desire to be closer to God have found that drawing closer to Him involves leaving your own world and entering His World. Your world revolves around you. If you want an outer symbol of your world, you can pull out your driver's license and look at it. You will see a picture of your face, your birthday, your height, your weight, your sex, your address, and your driver's license number.

Your driver's license is a symbol of your world in two ways. First, it shows that you are the driver of your world. Your world is a world of "doing," and you are the doer. Second, if you look at your driver's license, whose image do you see on it? It is not the image and likeness of God that you see there, but only an image of your body. Your world of doing centers around your "doing self," which is your thoughts about your body and your mind. The single thought that you are only your body and only your mind contained in your body may be called the "ego." All the other thoughts you have built around the ego can be called the "doing self," your "self-image," or just the "self." All your daily activities, thoughts, feelings, and relationships orbit around this self, which is the focus of your doing world. You are so attached to this self that you consider it to be your personal identity that tells you who you are.

To want a closer relationship with God means you must be willing to leave your doing world, which revolves around you, and enter a "being world" that revolves around God, the source of all being. In His World, you can find your "being Self," which may be called your "true Self," or simply your "Self," made in His image and likeness. What is this image and likeness of God? Since God is Spirit, the image and likeness of God, which is your Self, is your spiritual nature in God. But there are various ways of conceptualizing this spiritual nature in God. Here is one way of describing your true Self in God:

Generally Christians believe that everyone is a child of God and a part of the "body of Christ." Your Self can be thought of as your "part," "place," or "participation" in the body of Christ, yet these words are inadequate to define your role in the body of Christ. The overall concept is that all seekers participate in divine oneness with God as well as with each other as parts of the body of Christ.

The Christian viewpoint is that in divine union, the individual identity based on the ego is released. However, from the Christian perspective, the seeker does not lose all of his or her individual identity. Rather, a radical transformation in consciousness occurs in which the ego identity is replaced by a divine individual identity that is centered in perfect oneness with Christ, joined with God and with the Holy Spirit. It is the seeker's part, place, or participation in the body of Christ that provides that seeker with an individual identity. In this manual your true identity will be called your "Self," but it will be important for you to understand that this means your *Self in Christ.* For greater clarity, sometimes this manual will refer to your Self as your "Christ Self," which means your identity in Christ. Your true identity, your Christ Self, is already established in His World. Your Christ Self has been created by God the Father and therefore is unchangeable. Nevertheless, you can choose to be aware of your true identity, your Christ Self, or you can choose to allow your true identity to remain hidden from your awareness.

Jesus became fully aware of His true identity and is the example for others to do likewise. Jesus became so identified with His true identity that He became perfectly one with the universal Christ. Therefore, He is rightly acknowledged as the "Christ." Following Jesus means much more than just acknowledging and celebrating His accomplishment of perfect oneness with the universal Christ. Truly following Jesus means at least attempting to reveal the Christ Self that is already within you in His World. Whereas your world of doing is based upon the idea of separation, His World of being is based upon oneness that reveals to you your Christ Self united with God and with the Holy Spirit.

You will probably have your own way of describing your spiritual identity and the role of Jesus, which may be very different from the above description. Nevertheless, please do not let theological differences in either concepts or terminology be a stumbling block to drawing closer to God through practicing the techniques of meditation recommended in this manual. There is certainly no need for you to adopt the above description or terminology in order to benefit from this book. You are encouraged to retain whatever concepts you feel will help you to draw closer to the divine within. If you have conceptual differences with the above ideas regarding your identity in Christ, perhaps a more basic premise will be easier to accept. For example, since "God is Love" and you were made in His image and likeness, you may want to accept the premise that you are a being of love. Or you may want to simply accept the very basic premise that you are a being within the Being of God.

Yet how do you get in touch with your being within the Being of God? To discover your being within the Being of God as an experience rather than merely as an intellectual idea requires that you proceed by a way of being. To proceed by a way of being requires letting go of reliance upon doing. This means not only setting aside physical doing, but also includes setting aside intellectual doing in order to enter into a way of being. Normally, you cannot immediately stop doing and just be. Your world contains habit patterns and belief systems that you have been building for years and that are not easy to leave behind. Making the transition from doing to being is the purpose of meditation. If you truly desire a closer relationship with God, then meditation will allow you to make this transition in a gentle and graceful way.

You may think of the transition from your world of doing to His World of being in the same way that you think of the transition from loud noise to quieter sounds and then finally to silence. If you wish to experience the silence of His World, all you need to do is empty yourself of the sounds of your world. The sounds of your world are your thoughts that revolve around you. Your thoughts clutter up your mind, creating noise that prevents you from dwelling in the silence that is at the core of your being. Meditation is a way of growing toward silence through emptying your mind of your noisy thoughts that make you a captive of your world. The upcoming chapters will describe various procedures and practices of meditation that will help you to empty yourself.

Chapter 2 describes a specific series of procedures for meditation. In addition, this chapter and also Chapter 3 will provide information to help you choose a spiritual ideal, such as Christ, and a mental attitude, such as doing God's Will, in order to focus your spiritual and mental intention to grow toward God. The Twenty-eight Day Demonstration of daily meditation is recommended to increase your awareness of God's presence within you and to serve as a firm foundation for future growth. Chapters 2 through 6 will provide all the information necessary to conduct this Twenty-eight Day Demonstration of your desire to draw closer to God and begin the process of entering His World.

The fact is that God is already calling you to enter His World and leave your own world; otherwise you would not have been prompted by His grace to open this book and seek to deepen your relationship with Him. And your response to His call of love will in itself draw you closer to Him, because your response will be a union of your will and His Will. In your Christian practice of meditation you are not seeking an object or end result that you can possess. Rather, your meditation experience is an ongoing process of uniting your will with God's Will. In that union of wills, you are opening yourself to recognizing the being state of your Christ Self in God. Thus, in meditation, your intention is not to possess something or achieve something or make something happen, as it would be if you were in your world of doing. During meditation, you are still doing something, but it is a doing that is an "undoing"—an emptying of the self. You are letting go of the self to become aware of what is already truly at the core of your being.

The general process of letting go of the self is the same for a beginner and an experienced meditator, but each one's challenge is quite different. If you are a beginner, your challenge is to begin the process of inwardly letting go of the self. If you are an experienced meditator, your challenge is to let go of the self at a deeper level and to increasingly reveal God as the source of your being. In either case, as you read the next five chapters and put them into practice, your act of faithfully seeking God will in itself increase your awareness of His presence within you, or, more accurately stated, of your being within His Being.

However, it is best not to approach meditation with any judgments or preconceived ideas about what you want or expect to get out of the meditation experience. To do so would be to retreat back into your world of self-seeking, rather than to proceed to His World. You can be sure that your loving Father will demonstrate His Love for you, but what you cannot know is just how He will show forth His love. By letting go of these preconceptions, you can be fully open to His Will and know that whatever response He gives to you will be for your own highest good and will meet your deepest needs at the time and in the way that is most appropriate for your growth.

Meditation has been described as a way of leaving your world of doing and entering His World of being. But it would be an unfortunate error if you assumed that the purpose of meditation is to escape from your active world of doing and from your responsibilities in your world. With experience, you will discover that the entering of His World of being that occurs in meditation will help you to come back to your world of doing and perceive and also experience your world in a new way.

Your world will remain a world of doing, and you will still be the doer of your world. However, your perception of yourself will change so that you will see yourself as one who is being guided. You will recognize that your world of doing does not have to be controlled solely by you in order to ensure that your needs are met. You will understand that you can let go of some of that control and allow your decisions and actions to be guided by God because your meditation experience has shown you that God is at the center of your being.

Just as you have learned to become aware of His presence in His World during meditation, you will also learn to sense the influence of His presence in your world. You will allow your doing to flow forth from your being in Him, rather than from self-will. Instead of denying the everyday world or seeking to escape from its responsibilities, you will gradually learn to allow your doing world to be an outer expression of your being in His World. As you allow your world of doing to be a divine reflection of His World, you will discover that your investment in your meditation practice bears fruit both inwardly and outwardly, providing consistency and integration to your life.

2

PROCEDURES FOR MEDITATION

~ • ~

A. Options

In this chapter and subsequent chapters, a structured approach to meditation is offered for your consideration. In many places, the word "optional" is used to indicate that a particular structure is not essential and can be included or excluded according to your choice. But for the sake of clarity, it needs to be emphasized that in this book *everything is optional*.

There is only one thing that is definitely not optional and that is your true relationship with God. Your true relationship with God is that He created you as part of Himself, and He loves you. Consequently, you do not have the option of changing your relationship with God. However, you do have the option of being aware of that relationship or not.

The story of *Sleeping Beauty* is well known as a children's fairy tale, but it can also be interpreted as a story about your relationship with God. The Princess is asleep and in time the Kingdom has been overgrown by wild vegetation. The Princess is waiting to be awakened by the Prince, and then the Kingdom will be restored. In the story, the Prince comes and kisses the sleeping Princess. She awakens and immediately all the wild vegetation recedes, revealing the Kingdom.

Just as the Princess in the story is asleep and waiting to be kissed and awakened by her beloved, you are asleep and waiting to be awakened by God. In some way you have already been kissed by the Holy Spirit. Otherwise you would not be interested in learning about meditation. Perhaps you have been blessed with a sudden spiritual experience, giving you a foretaste of your true beauty as a child of God. Maybe the Spirit has simply stirred your heart in faith that the divine can be found within you.

But unlike the immediate return of the Kingdom in the fairy tale, one kiss cannot awaken you all at once. The wild forms of vegetation that have overgrown the Kingdom are the many thoughts and desires that you have woven around your true Self, thus hiding your true relationship with God. Since you exerted your free will to create these thoughts and desires, you need to participate in the work of removing the inner blocks you have created. Since your goal is freedom from inner obstacles, you need the freedom to learn how to let go in your own time and way. In addition, you need to establish a certain amount of self-discipline in order to break away from your inner obstacles.

The structures provided here are meant to be options for you to con-sider in your process of letting go. These structures are the means to an end, not the end itself. Thus these structures are designed as a suggested way to approach meditation, but with an understanding that everything is optional. You need to be constantly looking within and asking the Holy Spirit to guide you and confirm that you are choosing structures that are right for your spiritual development. Also, some structures that are useful in the beginning of your spiritual journey may not be needed as you make progress. Consequently, you will need to exercise your option to let go of these outgrown structures. The way you meditate and the depth of your attunement will change as you grow spiritually, and you will need to make adjustments along the way on your journey of self-discovery.

B. The Purpose of Meditation

Before meditating it is good to remind yourself of the reason why you are meditating. Meditation is simply a process of purification in which the self and the cares of the world are being emptied so there may be greater receptivity to the Spirit. It is important for you to understand that you are embarking on a purification process. Some meditators perform a physical action as a symbolic representation of the inner cleansing that takes place in meditation. For example, some meditators drink a small cup of water or take a shower as a symbolic cleansing. However, there is certainly no need to express this purification process outwardly through some form of physical cleansing.

Although meditation in general is a purification process, you need to decide upon a specific purpose for meditating to which you can make an inner commitment. To do this you need to answer the question, *What is my highest spiritual ideal?* Your highest spiritual ideal is the ultimate spiritual destination toward which you would like to grow. In other words, your spiritual ideal would be your way of symbolizing Ultimate Reality. It is not a goal that can be reached and then possessed, such as something that you would like to do or accomplish in the world. Your spiritual ideal needs to be your highest spiritual aspiration, which forms a direction toward which you choose to live your life.

Your spiritual ideal may be represented by a name for God or a word that reminds you of God. "Love" and "oneness" are good examples since these are attributes of God's nature. You may choose a name as your spiritual ideal, such as "God" or "Jesus," so you can grow in that direction to be like God or like Jesus. Eventually you will discover your own spiritual nature not by possessing the spiritual ideal as though it were an object of attainment, but rather through uniting with the ideal to produce a state of oneness. Your spiritual ideal is only a symbol you choose to represent a spiritual reality. Therefore, uniting with your spiritual ideal means uniting with the *reality* of your spiritual ideal and discovering your own true reality in Ultimate Reality, which your ideal represents.

When deciding upon a spiritual ideal, it is best to choose one word or a few words that represent the highest aspiration that you can have for living your life. Your spiritual ideal represented by one or more words helps keep you focused on your spiritual destination. Because of the type of meditation techniques that will be recommended, it would be helpful to limit your choice to as few words as possible, perhaps one or two, or at the most four words. The choice of your spiritual ideal is a personal decision based upon your highest level of understanding.

In choosing your ideal, you need to realize that your ideal is not merely a perfect moral code or standard toward which you are growing. Viewing your spiritual ideal as just a perfect outer standard creates impossible expectations for you from your present ego perspective. As you attempt to live up to an ideal that is a perfect outer standard, you will, of course, fail in your attempts. Since your ideal creates unrealistic expectations of perfection, you will be unable to accept yourself. Thus you may be tempted to either pridefully pretend to live up to your ideal or condemn yourself for your failure to live up to your ideal.

To avoid this pitfall, you need to remember that your ideal is a name for God or a reminder of God. God is not merely an outer moral code or standard. He is a living and loving presence that is within you as your source and substance. Therefore, your ideal most of all represents that loving, divine presence that is living within you. Because of your ego condition, you are identified with the self that feels separate from the divine presence of God. However, you choose a spiritual ideal to help you form a deeper, more conscious identification with your true Self that is united with God. For your ideal to serve this purpose, you need to choose an ideal that is personally meaningful to you.

The words "purpose" and "meaning" are often used interchangeably, but they do not mean the same thing. A purpose has to do with a goal that you set out to achieve. Once it is reached, you can choose another goal. Yet the question arises, *How important is the purpose to you?*

In other words, what is its meaning to you? You can have a meaningful purpose or a meaningless purpose. You may choose a spiritual ideal that becomes your purpose. This happens when you decide that you want your purpose, your goal, to be to grow toward that spiritual ideal. You may never fully accomplish that goal, but even growing toward that ideal can be your purpose. The crucial question is not, *What is your purpose?* The more relevant question is, *How meaningful is your purpose to you?* If it is not a meaningful purpose, you will lose your motivation and give up on your purpose. This is especially true of a spiritual ideal, since it is such a lofty goal that you may be tempted to give up because it is a difficult goal to reach. Therefore, it is absolutely imperative that you make your purpose as personally meaningful as possible. Thus if your spiritual ideal is to be the reason for your purpose, it needs to be one that gives meaning to your purpose.

Christian seekers often choose the word "Jesus" as their spiritual ideal because He is personally meaningful to them. Jesus can be perceived as the person who lived two thousand years ago and who is now united with God. Of course, Jesus is a perfect outer role model to emulate, but more importantly His divine presence is within you. His divine presence helps you to recognize your own true Self made in the image and likeness of the Father. If you choose Jesus as your spiritual ideal, it would be unwise for you to view Him solely as a perfect outer standard that you can never hope to fully live up to. Instead, you can choose Jesus as your ideal to increase your awareness of your own divine nature and to deepen your personal relationship with Him as your guide to the Father. In time, you can learn to call upon Him as you would call upon your closest friend and know you are loved just as you are in your present ego condition with all of your flaws.

Just as the word "Jesus" can have a personal meaning related to the person Jesus Christ and a universal meaning related to reminding you of your own divine nature, the word "Christ" as your chosen ideal can also have a dual meaning for you. Consequently, the word "Christ" can refer to Jesus Christ, who guides you to the Father, and it can also refer to the universal awareness of your true Self, your Christ Self. However, some Christians like to use the words "Jesus" and "Christ" with a singular meaning rather than with a dual meaning. In this case, the distinction is usually made for the sake of clarity that "Jesus" refers to the person Jesus, and "Christ" refers to the universal Christ.

The meaning of the words you choose to represent your spiritual ideal is not just a theoretical consideration because your choice can affect your inward practices. For example, some Christians feel that calling upon "Jesus" nourishes their personal devotion. Other Christians feel that affirming the word "Christ" supports their universal devotion and helps to awaken their awareness of their own divine nature. You will need to choose the specific words and assign the meaning of these words that will be most beneficial for you and best represent your spiritual ideal.

Before you decide upon the exact word or words that you would like to use to represent your spiritual ideal, you may want to read the next chapter, which will provide a wide variety of specific choices for your consideration. It is necessary to choose one ideal as your primary spiritual ideal, but you may have several secondary ideals. If "love" is not chosen as your primary ideal, then you may want to consider "love" as a secondary ideal. All spiritual growth is a matter of learning how to love at deeper and deeper levels, as will be discussed in Chapter 10.

After choosing your ideal, the question you need to ask yourself is, *What is the most important mental attitude I can have that will help me to grow toward my spiritual ideal?* The spiritual ideal may be thought of as your ultimate destination, while the mental attitude is that which will help you to take each step on the path toward your destination. Although final and complete union with your spiritual ideal will always be beyond your reach until the end of your journey, the mind can be used as an instrument of the Spirit to lead you in the direction of your destination. The mental attitude is the specific way you choose to use the mind along the path toward your spiritual ideal.

To further illustrate the distinction between the ideal and the mental attitude, you can think of life as a journey on a sailboat. You can choose a destination that you would like to reach at the end of the journey, and by analogy this would be your spiritual ideal. The sailboat, which is your traveling vehicle, would be the mind (and also the body), and the sail itself would be the mental attitude. The wind would be God's Spirit. Just as the sail must be filled with the wind to reach its destination, the mental attitude is that particular way of using the mind that would allow you to be filled with the Spirit and to grow toward your spiritual ideal. If you don't have a mental attitude that turns the mind toward your spiritual ideal, you won't be able to be guided by the Spirit. Consequently, you won't make progress toward your destination, just as a sailboat, without its sail being up, cannot catch the wind and will flounder aimlessly.

If your chosen spiritual ideal is "God" or "love," then you may choose a mental attitude that would help you to maintain the direction of growing toward God or love, such as "I wish to serve and be a channel of blessings to others." The mental attitude is expressed in the form of a brief statement that would be most appropriate to you. As another example, you may choose the ideal of "Jesus." In this case, you may choose a mental attitude, such as "Thy will be done," since this was the mental attitude He chose to become one with the Father. Most Christian seekers choose doing God's Will as their primary mental attitude.

Of course, there are many different mental attitudes you can have, but it is best to choose just one to be your primary mental attitude. This single mental attitude can form the foundation for the way in which you choose to direct your mind toward your spiritual ideal, and any other mental attitude can be a helpful secondary influence. Choosing your mental attitude does not mean that you will always be able to direct the mind in that way. For example, if "Thy will be done" is your chosen mental attitude, it will help you to express God's Will, yet it does not mean that you will always be able to express God's Will. It does mean that it is your sincere desire to do God's Will. Having this mental attitude will serve as a way of guiding your mind in this direction, and this will help you to be open to God's grace so you will make progress toward your spiritual ideal.

As an optional practice, both your spiritual ideal and your mental attitude can be stated to yourself once before meditation begins and, if desired, once after meditation. This practice serves as a reminder to you of your spiritual and mental commitment to grow toward God. Your commitment, expressed in the form of a dedication before and/or after meditation, can give you not only a direction for your meditation, but eventually it can also give a direction to your whole life.

C. The Place

Where you choose to meditate is important. You will want to choose a spot that is private and quiet. Ideally it will be a place that is not used for any other purpose. An example may be a space in front of a window in your bedroom or in front of a wall. It is best to use the same place each time you meditate because this will help as a way of conditioning yourself to establish the habit of meditating. Most meditators who choose to meditate in the evening prefer a dimly lit room rather than either bright lights or complete darkness.

D. Timing

The best times to meditate are in the early morning before eating breakfast and at sunset before dinner. A third option is at night just before going to bed, but the drawback of evening meditation is that the mind may not be as alert as it is earlier in the day because of fatigue. Also, some meditators discover that they expand their awareness so much during evening meditation that they have trouble going to sleep.

It is important to avoid practicing meditation immediately after eating because your digestion will prevent your meditation from being effective. Your digestion will not interfere with your meditation if you wait at least one and a half hours after a light meal or two hours after a heavier meal before meditating. It is not wise to meditate if you are overly hungry or are extremely tired. Your meditation practice will be more effective if you meditate at the same time every day. This consistency of timing serves as a conditioning device that will help your meditation practice.

If you decide to conduct the Twenty-eight Day Demonstration in meditation, which will be described in subsequent chapters, you will need to set aside at least one twenty-five-minute period each day for this purpose. However, it is recommend that you set aside two twenty-five-minute periods each day, preferably one in the morning just after waking and one at some time in the afternoon. You may prefer to have your second meditation period in the evening as long as you are not tired or drowsy at night. Another option is to meditate one time per day on the weekends and two times a day on Mondays through Fridays when more interior time is needed to counteract the stress of a weekday work schedule. Once you have set a schedule for yourself, it is important to stick to it. Being persistent and consistent will help your practice of meditation. The effects are cumulative, so if you start skipping days or changing times, it will not be nearly as effective.

It is recommended that you set a timer for your twenty-five-minute meditation, so you won't have to be distracted by being conscious of the time element. Digital timers that are available in most stores have a fairly loud ringer. You may have to go to an electronic specialty store or go to an online website to find a digital timer with a quiet ringer. Also, there are applications that allow you to use your cell phone as a timer. If the sound that your timer makes is a little too loud, you can put something over it to muffle the sound. If you don't want to use a timer, you may have a watch or clock within view that you can look at after you think twenty-five minutes have elapsed.

After you gain some experience in the practice of meditation, you will probably develop an intuitive sense of timing. When this happens you won't consciously think about the time while you are meditating, but you will have an inner sense of when the twenty-five minutes is completed, and your eyes will open at just about the right time. Yet this ability may eventually disappear as your meditation experience deepens and you become totally unaware of time. When you are in deep meditation, a twenty-five-minute meditation may appear to you as only five or ten minutes. Obviously you will require a timer, rather than a watch or clock, when your meditation deepens.

E. The Posture

For sitting meditation, your posture is very important. Having your spine in the proper alignment allows a free flow of energy, which will rise upward to enhance your meditation practice. It is recommended that before beginning your meditation practice, you check to make sure that your spine is straight, but not rigid. The center of balance in the body is the lower abdomen. It helps your meditation to relax the abdomen and have it slightly protruded. Some meditators will gently rock the upper body backward and forward to find their center of balance and then rock the upper body from side to side to center the spine properly.

Another way to make sure the spine is in the proper alignment is to imagine that a string is attached to the very top of the head and the string is being pulled straight up. Imagining this string being pulled up can help you to mentally check to make sure the neck and head in particular are properly aligned. To align the head, the chin needs to be drawn in very slightly. The chest needs to be held slightly up and out. If the chest slumps down, the head will move forward out of alignment. If your spine is properly aligned, the side view of your body will show the tip of the nose in line with the navel and the ears in line with the shoulders. Before beginning your meditation practice, you can remind yourself to mentally check to make sure that you have a good posture in which the spine is straight, but relaxed.

Most people prefer meditating in a chair. The illustration shown on the opposite page depicts the recommended body posture for meditation practiced while sitting in a chair. You place the legs about a foot apart in line with the shoulders. You place the feet flat on the floor and have the legs relaxed. When using a chair, you sit with the spine erect so that your back does not lean against the chair. Leaning your back against the chair prevents the spine from being in the proper alignment for establishing correct body balance. Also, placing your back against the chair inhibits the subtle energy within your body that becomes activated during meditation. If you have a back problem that is relieved by leaning against a chair, then you need to sit in whatever way is most comfortable for you.

Any solid chair with a flat surface can be used. Typically this is the type of chair used for sitting at the dinner table rather than a soft chair usually found in the living room. You can place a cushion on the chair both for softness and to adjust the height so you are not sitting too high or too low. Although the cushion can be flat, you can give yourself a significant additional advantage by placing a folded towel under the back of the cushion. This is intended to raise the back portion of your

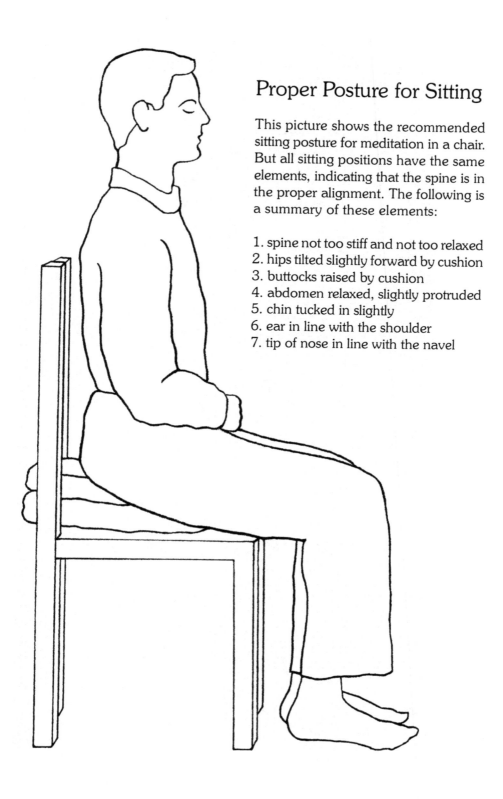

Proper Posture for Sitting

This picture shows the recommended sitting posture for meditation in a chair. But all sitting positions have the same elements, indicating that the spine is in the proper alignment. The following is a summary of these elements:

1. spine not too stiff and not too relaxed
2. hips tilted slightly forward by cushion
3. buttocks raised by cushion
4. abdomen relaxed, slightly protruded
5. chin tucked in slightly
6. ear in line with the shoulder
7. tip of nose in line with the navel

Hand Positions for Meditation

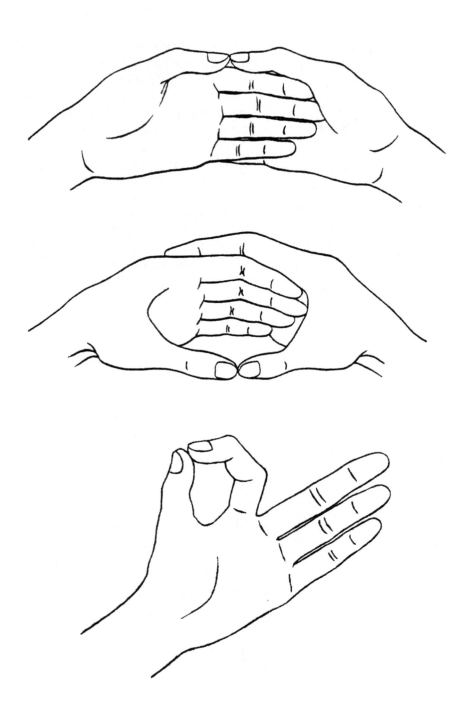

sitting surface so your hips are tilted just slightly forward. The purpose of the forward tilt is to keep the back straight and to place the hips in the ideal position for raising energy within the body. Having the back portion of the sitting surface raised helps to spread and raise the buttocks. Spreading and raising the buttocks also help to place the abdomen in a slightly protruded position that aids the posture and the body balance.

Sitting in a chair is recommended for most beginners, but some meditators prefer sitting on the floor with the legs crossed, although at first it may feel uncomfortable. One option is the full lotus position, in which each foot is placed on top of the opposite thigh with the soles of the feet turned upward. This is not a realistic sitting position for most meditators because it requires a great deal of flexibility. Others use a half lotus, which requires a moderate degree of flexibility to place just one foot on top of one thigh. Most meditators who sit on the floor just cross their legs in the usual way. If you are not used to sitting with the legs crossed, it may take a while to stretch the muscles and the ligaments of the legs and to get out the stiffness.

For sitting on the floor, you use a folded blanket or a firm cushion. Sitting on a raised seat is recommended not only because it is easier on the legs, but also because it helps to keep the spine erect and to maintain the body balance. Instead of sitting with the legs crossed, some meditators prefer the kneeling posture, in which the legs are folded underneath the body. In this posture, a blanket or cushion is placed under the buttocks to relieve the pressure of the body weight upon the legs. In addition, there are special meditation benches that are available commercially for sitting meditation.

It is best to keep the hands resting in the area just below the navel because this is the center of balance for the body. However, if this is not comfortable, you can lower the hands to the place where they feel most relaxed and where the body balance can be most easily maintained. You may want to experiment with different hand positions until you find the one that is the most comfortable for you.

In considering a hand position, it is most important to find a relaxed position for the hands. You can choose to use any relaxed and unstructured hand position. There are also specific and structured hand positions that you can use. You can see in the illustration shown on the opposite page that there are three specific hand positions that you may want to consider. The top hand position in the illustration is sometimes used by Buddhist meditators. For this hand position, you place the left hand on top of the right hand with both palms facing upward to form the lower half of a flattened circle. In this hand position, the tips of the thumbs of each hand are gently touching each other. In this case, the thumbs of each hand are placed against the index finger of the left hand. The hands rest in the lap with the little fingers touching the lowest part of the abdomen.

The middle hand position shown in the illustration is a variation of the hand position above it and is used by Zen Buddhist meditators. As with the previously described hand position, the left hand is still placed over the right hand with both palms facing upward. However, by repositioning the thumbs away from the other fingers, this variation changes the lower half of the flattened circle into a full flattened circle. For this variation, the thumbs are raised upward, away from the other fingers, so the index fingers and the thumbs create an oval shape. The tips of the thumbs are placed together. The thumbs are gently touching each other and are located against the abdomen just below the navel.

Another popular hand position is to place the hands on the legs with the palms turned upward or downward. Some meditators prefer to place the hands upward or downward on the knees. The bottom hand position in the illustration is a structured way of placing the hands on the legs. For this hand position, you place the right hand on the right leg and the left hand on the left leg. The tip of the thumb and the tip of the index finger of each hand are gently touching each other. The touching of the thumb and index finger creates a circle out of each hand. The other three fingers of each hand are separated from each other and extended away from the thumb and index finger. This is a yoga hand position called the *jnana mudra*.[1]

These structured Hindu and Buddhist hand positions may appear as only ritualistic expressions, but there is actually a functional reason for these particular hand positions. The life force that emanates from the body and gives it life is constantly flowing through the body. Much of this energy exits the body through the hands and feet. These hand positions tend to draw energy back into the body and encourage the flow of energy upward toward the head. This upward-flowing energy creates a purifying and spiritually revitalizing effect. Any one of the three structured hand positions described above may be used by Christians. On the other hand, these hand positions may be too rigid and formal for most Christians and for most beginning meditators. You are welcome to experiment with using a structured hand position, or you may want to use an unstructured hand position of your choice. But your most important consideration is to choose a hand position that is comfortable for you.

You may also wonder why many forms of Eastern spirituality place such an emphasis on sitting with the legs crossed. This sitting position, like the hand positions, tend to draw the energy inward and upward toward the head. Yoga philosophy would identify the crossing of the legs as a unifying of the male (right leg) and female (left leg) energy. The full lotus position is the most well-known posture associated with meditation. This posture is not recommended for most Westerners because it is too difficult to maintain for extended periods. Although the full lotus position is the most effective posture for focusing the mind, it is the most difficult to maintain. The half lotus position, in which only one foot is placed over the opposite thigh, is more commonly used than the full lotus. Any position that includes crossing the legs will be helpful unless there is discomfort that distracts you from your meditation. Nevertheless, using a chair is generally recommended because it is easier and more relaxing, and therefore more effective for most Westerners.

If sitting for meditation is not possible or if it is too uncomfortable, then as a last resort you can meditate lying down. Sitting meditation is more effective at raising energy in the body than lying-down meditation, which inhibits energy from rising up the spine. Although, in general, sitting meditation is more effective, lying-down meditation may be the only possible way for some people to meditate. If you normally practice sitting meditation, you may occasionally employ lying-down meditation when you require an increased degree of physical relaxation. However, if you find that you tend to fall asleep in the lying-down method, you should practice sitting meditation exclusively. A good time to practice lying-down meditation is the late afternoon before the evening dinner, because that is a time when the body may need a rest and yet the body will not be so tired that it will fall asleep.

For lying-down meditation, it is best to lie down on the floor with a blanket underneath the body. Another folded blanket or pillow can be used to raise the head an inch or two off the floor. If no other alternative is feasible, then you can simply lie in bed. In the lying-down position, you place the hands over the area just below the navel. You position one hand over the other. The tips of the thumbs are gently touching each other and are placed just below the navel. Place the legs slightly apart.

This lying-down position is designed to relax the body for meditation and yet provide just enough structure to discourage sleeping. Instead of using the structured position described above, you may spontaneously place the hands and the feet in any position that is comfortable for you while lying down.

F. Relaxation (Optional)

Relaxing the body is a good way to prepare for meditation. Perhaps the easiest way to do this is to just give the body a mental message to relax by saying the word "relax" to the body, and then consciously feeling the body relax completely. Some meditators use an expanded form of mental suggestion for relaxation. This is done by saying the word "relax" to each of the body parts individually. The usual procedure is to begin by mentally relaxing first the feet, then moving upward one part at a time all the way to the head. This form of relaxation may be done while sitting or lying down.

Many meditators prefer to use the simple *Head and Neck Exercise* for relaxing the body in preparation for meditation. For this exercise, you move the head forward three times, backward three times, to the right three times, and to the left three times. Then you roll the head in a wide circular motion three times one way and then three times the other way. The Head and Neck Exercise is recommended in the readings of Edgar Cayce.[2] He has been called the "Sleeping Prophet" because he went into a trance to provide health recommendations and other information for spiritual seekers in the first half of the nineteenth century.

Taking a few deep breaths before meditation is another option for helping the body to relax. You may want to practice *Yoga Deep Breathing*. With the inhalation, you can expand first the abdomen, then the lower chest, and then the upper chest. With the exhalation, you can contract the upper chest, then the lower chest, and then the abdomen. Though described in parts, the breathing is actually done in one flowing motion. By inhaling from bottom to top and exhaling from top to bottom, your breathing is very deep and calming.

Establishing a daily routine of hatha yoga body postures (*asanas*) and breathing practices (*pranayama*) can be very helpful to prepare the body for practicing meditation. Hopefully you will be able to attend a typical hatha yoga class given by a hatha yoga instructor who is not affiliated with any religious group. Such a class may be an hour or an hour and a half one day per week for six to eight weeks. However, the real benefit of taking such a class is in learning methods that you can incorporate into a daily practice at home. Practicing yoga every day will not only serve as a relaxation method, but also as a means of supporting health and as a purifying practice preparing you for deepening your meditation experience.

Stretching, listening to music, and devotional chanting or singing are also helpful methods of relaxing and preparing for meditation. You may want to experiment with different methods of relaxation to find out what works best for you. While not essential to meditation, a relaxation method is recommended as a good way to prepare for your meditation experience.

G. Preparatory Prayer (Optional)

In addition to your statement of your ideal and attitude as a dedication of yourself prior to meditation, you may want to offer a preparatory prayer to place yourself in the proper frame of mind before beginning your meditation practice. There is a fundamental difference between prayer and meditation. Prayer uses the expression of thoughts or the imagination to reach out to God. In contrast to prayer, meditation uses the reduction of thoughts and setting aside of the imagination to quiet the mind in order to contact the Spirit at a deeper level.

Before offering a preparatory prayer, you can pause briefly to feel yourself becoming inwardly quiet. Then you may choose, for instance, to simply ask God in prayer to surround and protect you from distracting influences during your meditation. Some meditators choose to use a spontaneous preparatory prayer, while others prefer repeating a formal prayer, such as the Lord's Prayer. The optional preparatory prayer should only take a minute or two and serves as a way for you to prepare for shifting the mind and heart toward the direction of deepening your relationship with God. Prayers may likewise be offered after completing meditation.

Why use a preparatory prayer? There are three reasons. First, it prepares the mind to be quiet. Second, it is an invitation for the Holy Spirit to enter in and show you how to commune with God. Perhaps you may even want to put this invitation to the Holy Spirit into words and have it be your preparatory prayer itself. Third, it is a protection against negative influences.

In addition to the choices of preparatory prayer that use words, there is a wordless form of preparatory prayer that relies upon the imagination of white light. You simply imagine that a white light from above the head comes down over the outside of the body and surrounds it. Then you imagine a white light coming down from above the head, filling the head, and continuing downward to fill the entire inside of the body. Imagining white light can be done briefly in this manner or in another way of your choosing.

This imagination of white light is a protecting influence, and you may think of this light in either one of two ways. The white light may be considered as the light of God, since "God is light."[3] Or the white light may be considered as the light of Christ, for Jesus says of Himself, "I am the light of the world."[4]

The use of the imagination usually involves imagining something that is not real and yet the seeking of God is the seeking of Reality. Thus the imagination would not normally be used for the seeking of God. But the imagination of white light is an exception to this rule because when you are imagining white light, you are imagining something that has a reality behind it.

Saints who have experienced illumination invariably bear witness to their encounter with a supernatural light that is a reality. However, under normal circumstances, the reality of this supernatural light is hidden from conscious awareness and for most people is accessible only through the imagination. After imagining white light to be real, the reality behind that imagining begins to shine through so you become increasingly aware of the presence of that reality. In this case, white light is first imagined so you can become aware of the reality of God's light or Christ's light.

Visualization is one way of using the imagination and if you choose to do so, you can use visualization to imagine the white light. Yet you may just as easily and just as effectively imagine the white light without using any visualization. While imagining white light is an option for your preparatory prayer, the imagination and in particular visualization are generally not used during meditation itself.

H. Thoughts in Meditation

A variety of meditation techniques will be described in subsequent chapters and all of these techniques will involve the challenge of dealing with the fluctuating thoughts of the mind. Meditation is a process of inner purification in which the mind is silenced so that you can become increasingly receptive to the Spirit, which transcends rational thinking. The mind is constantly filled with many thoughts that are centered upon yourself. In order to redirect the mind from being self-centered to being God-centered, it is best to take up one thought in the mind and repeat this one thought mentally. This one thought will dominate all the other thoughts in the mind. Many thoughts may appear during meditation, especially for a beginner. However, by holding one thought, these other thoughts have no power, and they disappear as quickly as they have arisen.

When any other thoughts appear, you do not hold on to them and examine them, and you do not try to push them away. These other thoughts are like a visitor who comes to your door at a time when you are busy working on an important project that must be done at that moment. You can hear the ringing of the doorbell by the visitor, but you do not even go to the door to talk with him. If you do open the door and talk with him, there is no telling how long your conversation will last. Before you know it, he will be inside the house, and you will have no time to do your work. Even if you open the door just to tell him to go away, he may still draw you into a lengthy conversation. It is best in such a case to not even go to open the door. The visitor will ring the doorbell a few times, and when no one comes to the door, he will go away.

Just as you do not open the door to an unwanted visitor, you do not open the door to distracting thoughts that come as visitors to the mind. You neither invite them in nor tell them to go away. Distracting thoughts will go away if you ignore them and just continue with your project. The project, in which you have become absorbed, is the holding of just one thought firmly in the mind.

In the beginning, you may find that you can hold one thought only for a very short while, and then your mind wanders. When you realize that your mind has wandered, you can gently bring the awareness of the mind back to the one thought. This process of holding the one thought, losing it, and then returning to the one thought is called *concentration*. Through the practice of concentration, you gradually begin to practice *meditation*. From the perspective of technique, meditation may be defined as the sustaining of any one thought in the mind continuously. Through the practice of meditation, the mind is purified of self-centered thoughts, and you become increasingly aware of the divine presence within. However, inner receptivity to the Spirit is not an automatic result of holding one thought in the mind. Meditation that is reduced to merely a mental device alone would be ineffective. To be truly effective, meditation is not only a *focusing of attention*, but also a *focusing of intention* in which you express your sincere desire for God.

For the sake of clarity, a distinction needs to be made here between meditation and *contemplation*. Contemplation is a form of internal communication with God in which the soul is overshadowed by the Holy Spirit. This communion with the Spirit is a state of heightened awareness in which the normal rational thinking process is set aside. Contemplation is resting in God produced by divine grace and is not itself a technique, but techniques can lead to this experience. Meditation, on the other hand, is a method of reducing self-centered thoughts in order to increase receptivity to the Spirit. By maintaining one thought in the mind during meditation, you cannot manufacture contemplation, yet you can prepare yourself to be receptive to that gift of the Spirit.

The one thought that you choose for meditation may theoretically be any one thing that can be used as a focus for your attention. For example, some meditators focus solely on observing the breath. Others count the inhalations and/or exhalations. However, most meditators prefer choosing one thought in the form of a word or combination of words. This choice of a word or words creates a sound vibration that the body and the mind become in tune with through repetition. This one thought still remains vibrating in the mind long after the meditation period is over and gives stability to the mind even when it is employed in outward activities. Retaining any one thought in the mind will calm the mind to a certain degree. Nevertheless, there are certain words that have more power and effectiveness than others, because these words work at a deeper level of consciousness.

The best word to repeat for your meditation practice is one that will affect your total being at the deepest level. In order to find a word that will work at the deepest level within, you need to find a word that is more than just a sound vibration. It is true that repeating any one word will calm the mind. For example, even the word "tree" will work to a certain degree. Nonetheless, it is best to use a word that will draw you to the secret place within yourself where you are touched and moved most personally at the center of your being. You can find such a word in the roots of your own religion, whether you are practicing the outward form of that religion or not. This word that will enable you to go to the very center of your being is the *Divine Name*.

The Divine Name, regardless of what form it takes, is a name for God or a name that serves as a reminder or symbol of God. Therefore, you may want to choose a form of the Divine Name to represent your spiritual ideal. The practice of calling upon the Divine Name has been widely recognized as a means of invoking a greater awareness of the divine within. The use of Divine Names and choices of other words to repeat during meditation are elaborated upon in the next chapter.

The words you repeat during meditation may be called *affirmations* because you are affirming and even building within yourself the nature of those words you have chosen. Just as listening to music can create in you a vibration and feeling related to the type of music chosen, likewise this affirming is actually building within yourself the vibration and feeling of the words chosen. Therefore, the words for the affirmation need to be chosen wisely. They must be of a spiritual nature so that when repeated during meditation they will affirm the divine within and actually increase your awareness of the divine presence. For this reason, it is best to choose an affirmation that points directly (or at least indirectly) to your spiritual ideal. Consequently, a spiritual ideal, preferably in the form of the Divine Name, is recommended for your choice of an affirmation or to be used as part of your affirmation.

Nonetheless, affirmations, even those of your spiritual ideal including the Divine Name, have a built-in limitation. They are all only symbols. They are useful symbols because they represent your desire for the divine. They help to focus your intention to be one with your spiritual ideal, and meditation after all is a focused intention. But doesn't your intention itself go deeper than words? Isn't your intention a yearning that cannot be limited by words?

Learning to repeat an affirmation in order to build these words that represent your intention into your consciousness is only part of your task. The other part is learning to let go of the affirmation and rely on your intention itself beyond words. By practicing the methods recommended in this manual, you will learn how to use an affirmation along with body awareness to help you focus on your intention to be receptive to the Holy Spirit. In addition, you will learn how to let go of repeating the affirmation and to center your mind only on body awareness in order to focus on your intention. Finally, you will learn how to let go of both the affirmation and body awareness so you can focus on your intention in silence and be led into contemplation.

Before making your choice of an affirmation, you might want to read the next chapter that elaborates upon the use of Divine Names and other affirmations. Then, after you read three additional brief chapters, you will have all the information you will need to begin your practice of meditation with the goal of becoming increasingly receptive to God's presence within.

I. Completing Meditation

After your meditation is completed, it is best not to get up quickly. You can just remain sitting quietly for a brief time. This time at the end of your meditation can be used for prayer. In your prayer, you can reaffirm your dedication to your spiritual ideal and purpose, or you can pray for others or for yourself, perhaps expressing gratitude for this time spent in divine communion.

Some meditators like to complete their sitting period with a gesture of bowing forward. If you are sitting in a chair, the hands can be located at the chest in a prayer position with the palms and fingers placed together, and you can bow forward slightly from the waist. Another option is to omit raising the hands to the chest and instead simply bend forward from the waist. After the energy has been raised up into the head during meditation, a gesture of bowing forward helps to absorb this energy into the abdomen, creating an inner balance of energy stored for future use.

You can also use the expression of bowing forward described above if you had been sitting on the floor rather than in a chair. But if you are sitting on the floor, you may choose to use an alternative bowing gesture, which is actually a yoga posture called the *Yoga Seal*. For this gesture the arms are placed behind the back with the right wrist being held by the left hand. With your hands behind the back, you bend all the way forward, relaxing and allowing gravity to exert its force over the body. During your practice of meditation, energy rises upward and into the head. After your meditation is completed, bowing forward into the Yoga Seal allows the energy that had arisen into the head to descend into the chest and heart area and then into the abdomen to be available for future use.

If you have been sitting on the floor for your meditation practice, you may discover after your meditation is finished that parts of your legs have become numb. The numbness is caused by your sitting in a body position that produces a restriction of the nerves going to the legs. Because of the numbness you may not be able to immediately move your legs as you normally would, but no physical harm has actually occurred to your legs. If the numbness does occur, you do not need to be alarmed. You can simply stretch the legs or move the feet with the hands. You will notice the legs returning to normal within seconds.

After your meditation is over, you may find that you need to urinate. This may be due to the relaxation produced by your meditation practice. Another reason is that meditation, as a purifying practice, not only cleanses the mind but also the body. Your meditation practice can throw off toxins that have previously been stored in the body, and urination helps to release these toxins. Also, meditation affects the endocrine glands, especially the pituitary gland. Your meditation can result in the pituitary gland releasing hormones, which regulate the bladder functions and result in your need to urinate.

After your meditation, you may have a greater feeling of peace and well-being because of inviting the divine presence, but also because of a wide variety of both physiological and psychological benefits. Meditation increases the release of neurotransmitters, including dopamine, serotonin, oxytocin, and endorphins. These brain chemicals are linked to different aspects of happiness. The Mayo Clinic identifies these emotional benefits from daily meditation: "gaining a new perspective on stressful situations, building skills to manage your stress, increasing self-awareness, focusing on the present, and reducing negative emotions."[5]

1. Swami Rama, Rudolph Ballentine, M.D., and Alan Hymes, M.D., *The Science of Breath* (Honesdale, PA: The Himalayan International Institute of Yoga Science and Philosophy, 1979), pp. 126-127.

2. Harold J. Reilly and Ruth Hagy Brod, *The Edgar Cayce Handbook for Health Through Drugless Therapy* (Virginia Beach, VA: A.R.E. Press, Copyright 1975), p. 113 (#3549-1 of the Edgar Cayce readings).

3. First letter of John 1:5.

4. John 8:12.

5. http://www.mayoclinic.org/tests-procedures/meditation/in-depth/meditation/art-20045858.

3

DIVINE NAMES AND OTHER AFFIRMATIONS

~ • ~

A. Names for God used as Affirmations

One common practice found in most religious traditions is to repeat the Divine Name of God. Instead of a Divine Name for God, a quality of God may be repeated as an affirmation. Any word or words may be chosen that remind you of God or in particular remind you of your relationship to God. The sacred word or words that you choose gain their strength not from the words themselves, but rather from your willingness to allow them to summarize your intention to be open to God's presence.

B. The Jesus Prayer of the Heart

If your heart moves you to say the Name of "Jesus" as an affirmation, then stick to it. You will not find a sweeter or more powerful Divine Name than this. Repeating the Divine Name of Jesus is called the *Jesus Prayer* or the *Prayer of the Heart*. The complete form of the Jesus Prayer is, "Lord Jesus Christ, Son of God, have mercy on me, a sinner." This long form may be employed. However, this book does not recommend using the word "mercy" or "sinner" because these words can contribute to building a negative self-image. A shortened form of the Jesus Prayer is recommended for a Christian affirmation. Here are some examples:

Lord Jesus Christ
Jesus Christ
Christ
Jesus

The Name "Jesus" (or any of His other Divine Names) is a declaration that you trust that all your needs of grace will be met in that Name. Christian Divine Names allow you to express your divine and true nature in Christ, your "Christ Self." At the last supper, Jesus gave His own Divine Name as a new invocation. But He did not do so to replace devotion to God the Father. Jesus did not say, "Ask for anything of Me in My Name, and I will give it to you." Instead, Jesus said:

> Truly, truly, I say to you, if you ask anything of the Father, he will give it to you in my name. Hitherto you have asked nothing in my name; ask, and you will receive, that your joy may be full.[1]

When you call upon the Name of Jesus, you are not devoted to Jesus alone since Jesus is one with the Father. Therefore, your calling upon the Name of Jesus enhances your devotion to God the Father. Some individuals are reluctant to call upon the Name of Jesus in meditation because they think that doing so will detract from devotion directly to God the Father. This is an unfortunate misunderstanding of the role of Jesus. The role of Jesus is to always be an open doorway directly to the Father. Instead of blocking your relationship to God, calling upon His name assists in revealing your true relationship with the Father. Jesus, as the Son, reveals your own Sonship with the Father. Jesus is the first to completely awaken to His Sonship in the universal Christ. But Jesus, having become the Christ, wants nothing more than for you to awaken to your Christ Self in union with God and with the Holy Spirit. Thus all devotion offered to God in the Name of Jesus helps you to become receptive to the Holy Spirit. Through receptivity to the Holy Spirit, you will learn to allow God's Love to flow through you, and your mind and heart will increasingly open to the awareness of your own true loving nature, your Christ Self.

The focus of the Jesus Prayer is in the heart so early Christian monks called it the "Prayer of the Heart." They believed that holding one's attention in the heart area cut through the rational thinking process and enkindled their deepest feelings of love, which enabled them to reach the core of their being far beyond the superficial self. To repeat the Name of Jesus Christ in the heart evoked their innermost loving faith at the ground of their being and invited the Holy Spirit to dwell therein.

It was purity of heart that these early monks sought above all else. Their focusing upon this simple prayer of faith was intended to awaken their single-minded desire for God alone. Their secret for purifying the heart was holding their awareness in the heart in order to leave behind the distracting thoughts of the mind and cleanse themselves from egotism and selfish desires. Through prayerful attention in the heart, they were able to focus upon and intensify the most important quality of their prayer life, which was devotion focusing on divine love.

Whether you choose the words Jesus, Jesus Christ, Christ, or another form of His Name, the most important reason for the effectiveness of the Jesus Prayer is in the divine grace that flows from Jesus Himself, whose Divine Name is being invoked. However, it is through its repetition as an affirmation that His Name gains a mastery over the mind and the ego. To understand the power of the Jesus Prayer as an affirmation, you need to properly view the mind and the ego.

Your mind is a vehicle through which your spiritual nature flows to express thought. But your rational mind cannot directly perceive its spiritual source, because thought is its only instrument of awareness and thought of the rational mind cannot penetrate Spirit. Therefore, you use your rational mind to define yourself with a thought about yourself. Since your rational mind can only perceive thoughts and bodily senses, you come to the false mental conclusion that says, "I am the rational thinking mind and the body," and this single thought is the "ego."

Since the ego is just a false thought, it would appear to be a simple matter to change the thought, but the problem is greater than that. Unfortunately, all the other thoughts you have about yourself revolve at the subconscious level around this one false thought of the ego to create a whole belief system of thoughts and habit patterns. This collection of thoughts that form a belief system is called the "self," and is the false world you create around yourself. The ego, which is at the center of this fabricated belief system of the self, is represented in the mind as the word "I." The ego represented by "I" is identified with your physical and mental nature, but does not identify with the reality of your spiritual nature. This false perception of yourself symbolized by the word "I" dominates your subconscious mental patterns of the mind. If you doubt the mental dominance of the ego, just attempt to go one day without saying the word "I."

Through repeating the Jesus Prayer, the conscious mind is impregnated with the spiritual ideal of Christ. Gradually His Divine Name becomes a dominant mental pattern that sinks down into the subconscious mind where it helps to release the attachment to the "I" of the ego. Letting go of the subconscious attachment to the "I" allows your true spiritual nature in Christ to shine through and manifest not only temporarily during meditation itself, but also as an aftereffect in your daily living. The result is that instead of living a self-centered life, you live a life centered in Christ.

The affirmation of the Divine Name of Christ not only disempowers the ego so you can live in Christ, but it also affirms a deeper truth, which is hidden by the ego. That truth is that your true Identity is the Christ Self— *even now.* In your world it may not appear to be so, but in His World, you are a Son of God, made in His image and likeness. If a light bulb is turned on and then is painted black, it will outwardly appear to be black and without light, even though its light is in fact still shining. Since God turned on your light in your creation, He has never withdrawn His Life and Light from you, so you are still shining just as brightly as always, yet unaware of your true divine nature.

The ego condition of your everyday world says that you are separate from God. In reality, at the core of your existence you are one with the Father, the source of your existence. It is your oneness with the Father that is your true Self, your Christ Self. But because you are not aware of your oneness with the Father, an intermediary is necessary to help you discover your true relationship with God. The Holy Spirit plays the role of this intermediary and divine Teacher for all of God's children. Yet Jesus, being already awakened Himself, serves as a personal intermediary in direct coordination with the Holy Spirit to assist you in uncovering the image and likeness of God that is your true nature, your Christ Self.

Thus, through the action of the Holy Spirit, Jesus Christ is the way to the Father, and as such you repeat His Divine Name as a reminder of your oneness with the Father. You do not repeat His Holy Name as a reminder of His miraculous earthly deeds. In your prayers you can rightly dwell upon His passion, death and resurrection. But, for your meditation upon His Name, you are not focused on past events. Instead, you seek to abide in His loving presence and in the presence of the Holy Spirit. In His presence you have the assurance that you are not indulging in a form of hero worship, and you are not seeking something foreign to your own nature. Instead, as you approach Jesus, you are actually entering His World, which you discover is your own true Home as a Son of the Father.

When you choose an affirmation, you need to consider what words most remind you of your oneness with God. As was mentioned in the previous chapter, some Christians make a distinction between the words "Jesus" and "Christ," such that the former refers to the *human* nature of Jesus Christ and the latter refers to the *divine* nature of Jesus Christ. These individuals may decide not to repeat the word "Jesus" since it may remind them only of a person. Yet these same individuals may choose "Christ" as an affirmation because this word reminds them of the divine nature that is in Jesus Christ and is likewise in everyone.

The word "Christ" as an affirmation is a wonderful choice for your meditation because it encompasses in just one syllable both a personal Divine Name for the one who is your guide to the Father and also the name for your own divine nature, the Christ Self. The term "Christ Self" is used here to convey that all God's children share the same oneness with the Father. Nevertheless, even the word "Christ" can be so identified with the personality of Jesus Christ that you may find yourself only affirming the personhood of Jesus outside of yourself and failing to affirm your own oneness with the Father. If you feel you may be strong in affirming Jesus, but weak in affirming your own inherent oneness with God, you may want to combine the Divine Name of Jesus Christ with a word that would help you to affirm your own oneness with God. For instance, you may want to use the word "One" to affirm your oneness with God. Consequently, an example of an affirmation of the Divine Name that would affirm your oneness would be "Christ, One."

Obviously, differing ideas about the meaning of the Name of Jesus Christ will affect your affirmation choice. Nonetheless, you can be certain that repeating His Divine Name, in whatever form you may choose, will have a profound impact upon you. The effect of letting the Jesus Prayer penetrate deep within you is summarized in the following quotation from an enjoyable book titled *The Way of a Pilgrim*:

> Many so-called enlightened people regard this frequent offering of one and the same prayer as useless and even trifling, calling it a mechanical and thoughtless occupation of simple people. But unfortunately they do not know the secret which is revealed as a result of this mechanical exercise; they do not know how this frequent service of the lips imperceptibly becomes a genuine appeal of the heart, sinks down into the inward life, becomes a delight, becomes, as it were, natural to the soul, bringing it light and nourishment and leading it on to union with God.[2]

Probably the earliest form of the Jesus Prayer sprang forth from the lips of Bartimaeus, the blind man of Jericho, who repeatedly cried out, "Jesus, Son of David, have mercy on me!"[3] Although this scriptural quote may have inspired the Jesus Prayer, no one knows when it was first used as a meditation technique. The recorded knowledge of the Jesus Prayer goes back as early as the third and fourth centuries when it was used by the early monks of the Christian church who lived in the desert. The following quotation by one of these monks, St. Macarius, will serve to summarize the merits of the Jesus Prayer:

> There is no other perfect meditation than the saving and blessed Name of our Lord Jesus Christ dwelling without interruption in you, as it is written: "I will cry out like the swallow and I will meditate like the turtledove!" This is what is done by the devout man who perseveres in invoking the saving Name of our Lord Jesus Christ.[4]

Obviously a name for something and the thing itself are two very different things. The name is a symbol for what it represents. It is not the thing itself. For example, the name "stone" is not a stone itself. It is only a symbol used to call to mind the reality of the stone itself. All names are symbols. Even a Divine Name of God is not the Reality of God, but only a symbol of that Reality. Yet a Name of God is helpful because it calls to mind the reality for which it stands. The name "stone" can only call to mind a stone, which is merely an inanimate object. However, a Name of God calls upon awakening your awareness of the Reality of God, but more importantly invites God to actively interact with you.

The Divine Name, and in particular the Name of Jesus, is only a symbol, yet it can carry you beyond all symbols by helping to open your mind to Reality itself. Calling upon the Name of Jesus is not a time to ponder philosophy, theology, or dogmas. Rather, you are seeking a direct existential contact with the Ground of Being. You are seeking a personal experience of the deepest truth about your identity in God. Finding the presence of God expands your capacity to know His Will and has the aftereffect of guiding you to do His Will. This is something much more basic to your inner being than making petitions for beneficial external concerns. To rest in the ground of your being is to experience the unconditional Love that created you and keeps you in existence. To be fully aware of His Love is the deepest yearning of your heart. Nothing can completely satisfy this yearning except God Himself. Thererfore, you call His Name in order to listen for his Word that says, "I love you. You and I are One."

While calling on the Name of Jesus seems generally accepted by most Christian groups, these groups have very definite and different ideas about the nature of Jesus. It would be impossible and unnecessary to homogenize these ideas into one universally accepted picture of Jesus. In regard to my own ideas about Christ, the only certainty is that my ideas are too small to contain Him Who is one with God, the Incomprehensible. If the ideas about Christ that are shared in this manual are different from your own, hopefully you will not let this be a stumbling block to proceeding with Christian meditation. Intellectual ideas, including both yours and mine, are only "about" Christ and cannot encompass Him and cannot enable you to feel His presence or the presence of God the Father.

Your intellectual knowledge about Christ (and about God) is very helpful at the start of your spiritual growth and is appropriately expressed in your prayers. However, when you switch from prayer to meditation, you change from thinking about Christ prayerfully to stilling the mind in order to experience the divine presence at a deeper level. The fact that Christian seekers have different theological understandings is of little importance in the practical application of meditation. It is your theological ideas, as well as all other ideas, that must be set aside during the practice of meditation. Consequently, in meditation you do not think about Christ with your ideas, but rather repeat His Divine Name and open yourself to the grace of the Holy Spirit that will enable you to experience the divine presence within. The deepest level of your relationship with Christ is not primarily based upon your theological beliefs, but rather upon His Love for you and your love for Him. Through the stillness of meditation, you are seeking to awaken your awareness of your loving relationship with God.

C. The Ideal as an Affirmation

As was stated earlier, each meditation is dedicated to your chosen ideal, which is the spiritual destination toward which you would like to grow. Similarly, each meditation is dedicated to your mental attitude because this is the specific way you are using your mind in order to grow toward your chosen ideal. You may choose to acknowledge this dedication simply by stating the ideal and mental attitude once before meditation and, if desired, once after meditation.

However, you may choose to use part or all of this dedication as an affirmation for meditation itself. You may choose to repeat the spiritual ideal as an affirmation. For example, if Christ is your ideal, then, of course, the affirmation of His Divine Name would be appropriate. You may also choose to use your mental attitude as an affirmation. For instance, if Jesus is your chosen ideal, you may choose a mental attitude, such as "Thy will be done," for your affirmation. An affirmation may include both the ideal and the mental attitude. An example might be: "O Lord, I wish to be a channel of blessings to others." It is recommended that affirmations be condensed into as few words as possible.

Using your ideal and/or mental attitude for an affirmation is a way of increasing your dedication to the highest within. Meditating on your ideal helps you to build within yourself the awareness of that ideal toward which you are growing and helps you to become like that ideal. Meditating upon your mental attitude helps you to focus your mind in the right way to help manifest your ideal. Meditating upon both the spiritual ideal and the mental attitude helps to create an inner harmony of spirit and mind working together to manifest through the physical. The physical body is the vehicle through which the spiritual ideal is expressed. That spiritual ideal is made manifest by the proper application of the mental attitude.

Of the choices of affirmations that have just been mentioned, the most highly recommended is the use of the spiritual ideal alone, especially in the form of the Divine Name. The reason is that your spiritual ideal focuses directly on what you have chosen to be the center of your spiritual life. Meditating on the spiritual ideal itself has the effect of imprinting the focus of meditation upon the very structure of the physical body so that the body itself becomes the carrier of the ideal. When this happens through meditation, then the thoughts, the feelings, the actions, and the words that manifest through the body begin to carry more and more of the divine influence. That's when the ideal is truly your ideal, not a theory or idea, but rather a living reality that is actually being applied in your life.

D. Other Affirmations

If you desire a Christian affirmation and none of the ones already mentioned appeals to you, then you may find a word from scripture that appeals to you personally. For example, you may want to use the word "Amen," which is normally translated "truly" or "so be it." Another possibility is that you may choose a very brief scriptural phrase or a statement, such as "Be still, and know that I am God."[5] You may want to employ a form of the Divine Name in combination with another word or words of your choice. For example, you may want to choose "Christ Light," "O Christ," "O my Jesus," or "Come Christ Jesus." You may want to repeat the Divine Name with a virtue or quality. For instance, you may want to say "Jesus, humble" or "Jesus, peace." For your choice of a virtue or quality to combine with the Divine Name, you would want to choose an attribute that you feel you need. In so doing you can be assured that you will acquire that attribute. You may possibly want to express praise by repeating the affirmation "Jesus, thank you." Since so much of spiritual growth is based on learning to love, two of the affirmations recommended most highly are "Jesus Christ Love" and "Christ Love." You can allow your choice to be guided by the Spirit within.

E. Invoking the Holy Spirit

The role of the Holy Spirit is very important to your spiritual growth. Unlike God the Father, Who is Reality itself, the Holy Spirit has one foot in the reality of His World and one foot in your world. Acting as a bridge between these two worlds, the Holy Spirit, with the assistance of Jesus Christ, leads you back to the Father in Heaven. It is your free-will choice to direct your own life or to allow the divine influence to motivate your thoughts, words, and deeds. Like God the Father, the Holy Spirit will not violate your free will, so if you want assistance or guidance, you must pray and ask for help from the Holy Spirit. In addition to a direct request in prayer for the Holy Spirit to come into your life, meditation is a means of inviting the Holy Spirit to come upon you and transform you.

Meditation involves letting go of self-centered thoughts and developing receptivity to the incoming of the Holy Spirit. Your spiritual growth in general, both expressed inwardly in communion with God and outwardly in relation to your brothers and sisters, is a continual opportunity to set self aside and be responsive to the prompting of the Holy Spirit. Your practice of meditation is an opportunity to focus on invoking the Holy Spirit. This invoking can be done directly or indirectly. All the affirmations that have been suggested thus far are indirect ways of inviting the Holy Spirit. An example of a direct invocation is the asking of the Holy Spirit to enter as a part of your preparatory prayer before meditation. Another direct invocation is choosing an affirmation for meditation that includes the invoking of the Holy Spirit. A possible choice of an affirmation is "Come, Holy Spirit." Another possible affirmation is simply "Holy Spirit" repeated with the feeling of welcoming that spiritual presence.

Whether you choose to invite the Holy Spirit directly or indirectly, this invitation is central to a proper understanding of meditation. While meditating, you may repeatedly be distracted by your thoughts, but this does not make your meditation fruitless. Although your own efforts to control the mind may be weak, you need to realize that you are not relying on your own skill. Instead, you are relying on the fact that you have invited the Holy Spirit into your inmost being. It is not your technique, but rather your purity of intention that opens your heart and mind so the Holy Spirit may enter. You know by faith that your invitation is being answered each time you practice meditation with a pure intention.

Even though you may not feel the presence of the Holy Spirit as a conscious experience during meditation, your invitation allows God to have free reign in your subconscious mind. There beneath your conscious awareness, the Holy Spirit has a healing effect that removes inner obstacles to your spiritual growth. The obstacles that the Holy Spirit removes may be desires, thoughts, habit patterns, and emotions, which you have suppressed into the subconscious mind and never completely resolved and released.

Sometimes the Holy Spirit will assist you by bringing your inner obstacles to your conscious awareness so you can then give them back to the Holy Spirit for their release. At other times the Holy Spirit will produce a spontaneous inner healing without the aid of your conscious awareness of the nature of the obstacle that was removed. Gradually your cooperation with the Holy Spirit can bring about a transformation of consciousness because of your daily meditation practice that opens you to receive God's grace. As you allow the Holy Spirit to transform you at the subconscious level, you become more willing to likewise allow the Holy Spirit to affect your conscious experience of everyday living. Thus your thoughts, your conversations, and your dealings with your brothers and sisters increasingly convey the divine influence so you become a greater expression of Christ's love in the earth.

F. Counting Meditation

Counting Meditation is a way of focusing the mind without using an affirmation. For this method you count mentally from one to ten and then return to the number one and repeat this process of counting for the entire meditation. If you forget the count or count past ten, simply start again by returning to number one. The counting is coordinated with the breathing. Number one and all the odd numbers are inhalations. Number two and all the even numbers are exhalations.

If you regularly meditate with an affirmation of your ideal, you may choose to use Counting Meditation briefly as a way to aid your ability to reduce stray thoughts. The way you can do this is to begin your practice by first using Counting Meditation as a means of clearing away the cares and concerns of daily life. After a short while of focusing on counting, you can gain greater mental clarity and then you can switch to using an affirmation of your ideal in your regular form of meditation.

Another reason for employing the counting method is that initially meditating on an affirmation of your ideal may create unwanted mental pictures or thoughts. For example, if you meditate on the affirmation of "Jesus," you may see mental images of Jesus and think about Him. This would be very good as a form of prayer, which involves using both the imagination and thoughts to communicate with God. But in meditation you seek to set aside the imagination and thoughts—even if they are holy thoughts. Therefore, having mental pictures of Jesus or thoughts about Him during meditation would be a distraction, which would prevent the stilling of the mind. Thus you may choose to temporarily use the counting method in meditation to remove these mental pictures and thoughts. Then when the mind becomes more still, you may return to repeating the affirmation of "Jesus" without creating any mental pictures of Jesus or thoughts about Him. The purpose for using an affirmation of the Divine Name of Jesus Christ is not to mentally intellectualize about Christ, but rather to experience and feel the divine presence within as a living reality.

---

1. John 16:23, 24.
2. *The Way of a Pilgrim and The Pilgrim Continues His Way*, translated from the Russian by R.M. French (New York: Seabury Press, 1972), p. 203. Originally published by the Seabury Press; rights owned by Winston Press Inc., Minneapolis, MN.
3. Mark 10:47.
4. From Amelineau, quoted by Resch in *Doctrine Ascetique des Permiers Maltres Egyptiens*, p. 151. In turn, quoted by Thomas Merton in *Contemplative Prayer*, cited from the paperback edition (New York: Image Books, 1971), p. 21. The original, hardcover edition was titled *The Climate of Monastic Prayer* (Kalamazoo, MI, and Spencer, MA: Cistercian Publications, 1969).
5. Psalm 46:10.

4

BODY AWARENESS MEDITATION METHODS

~ o ~

A. Body Awareness and Distraction

Many of the meditation techniques presented in this manual employ body awareness as part of the meditation practice and are intended to lead toward contemplation that does not employ body awareness. Before describing the specific techniques of inward seeking recommended in this manual, it may be helpful to discuss issues related to body awareness during meditation.

Meditation is a helpful means of becoming increasingly receptive to the Holy Spirit. Developing receptivity to the Holy Spirit is a gradual process, and body awareness can be a stumbling block to that process. When beginners attempt to meditate using the Divine Name without incorporating a technique of body awareness, they discover they are distracted from meditation by their own body awareness, which cannot be ignored.

Body awareness can be compared to a child. Anyone who has worked with children knows that children want attention. To the child, getting attention is an outer demonstration of a person's love for the child. If a child cannot get a person's attention through positive behavior and if a child is ignored, he will find a wide variety of negative ways to get that person's attention. If that person is wise, he will give the child a task that will occupy his time positively and enable him to get the attention he wants in an appropriate way. In addition, the task performed by the child may prove to be very helpful to that person.

Just as a child seeks attention in this example, body awareness is constantly seeking to get your attention during meditation. If body awareness cannot get your attention positively because it is ignored as part of your meditation technique, then body awareness will become a negative attention getter. This will take the form of all sorts of body sensations and feelings that will be presented to the mind as a reminder that the body is being ignored. These reminders are sometimes gross and sometimes subtle. Their effect is to distract you from focusing on the affirmation and prevent meditation from deepening.

On the other hand, if body awareness is given a positive task by being incorporated into your meditation technique, it becomes an asset rather than a liability. This will not eliminate body awareness as a distraction altogether, but it will greatly lessen this distraction and deepen meditation.

To understand specifically how to incorporate body awareness into your communication with God, you need to understand the mechanics of the vehicle God has given to you for this communication. The body is constantly receiving stimuli and recording these in the brain. You selectively choose to become aware of only a very small portion of these. Some body stimuli present themselves to your awareness spontaneously without your seeming to have any choice in the matter. For example, you may hear an airplane fly overhead without choosing to hear it. This may be considered involuntary awareness. However, from the viewpoint of meditation, it is more important to discuss where you place your awareness voluntarily.

When you voluntarily bring your awareness to a part of the body, your entire awareness does not remain in your conscious mind. Your awareness will actually go to the part of the body where you choose to place your awareness. A certain kind of energy will accompany your awareness and therefore also go to the part of your body where you are focusing your mind, as will be explained in Chapter 8. In relation to preventing distraction, the key element to consider here is the fact that your awareness becomes localized in the part of the body where you have placed your awareness.

If you feel the big toe on your right foot, for example, and hold your awareness there, you cannot feel the thumb on your right hand unless you decide to move your awareness to that thumb. Once you move your awareness to your thumb and hold it there, you cannot feel your toe anymore. In order to feel any part of your body, you need to make a voluntary choice to bring your awareness to that body part. If you decide to hold the awareness of the mind on any one part of the body, the other parts of the body are not in your awareness consciously because you choose not to bring your awareness to them. (The exception to this is when an experienced meditator can hold the awareness simultaneously in several parts of the body or even be aware of the body as a whole.) The significance of this is that you can hold the awareness in one part of the body to prevent the distraction in meditation caused by allowing the awareness to wander from one part of the body to another.

It is important to keep in mind that during meditation you do not visualize or *think about* the part of the body in which you are holding your attention. Rather, you actually bring your awareness into the physical location of the part of the body you are focusing on. Holding the awareness in one part of the body is one example of a general ability of the mind, which can be called *selective attention*. This type of attention involves focusing on a specific aspect of something and ignoring other aspects. Selective attention can be unconscious or conscious. If you look at a green field with a single yellow rose, the rose will initially receive more attention. This is an example of unconscious selective attention. You may think that you are absorbing the whole scene all at once, when actually you have taken in only the area where you are placing your attention and merely have a general sense of the remainder of the scene. You are using a conscious type of selective attention when you make a mental decision to bring your awareness to something and ignore other aspects of that thing. Practicing meditation involves a conscious form of selective attention since you hold your attention on one thought in the mind while you ignore all other thoughts. All variations of meditation rely on conscious selective attention. Focusing on one part of the body to ignore the rest of the body is one particular type of selective attention that makes meditation more effective, especially for beginners.

Usually conscious selective attention involves placing your attention on an interesting task or object rather than an uninteresting one. A very common example is watching television instead of looking at a bookshelf. I recently watched an informative television show that illustrated how we use our attention selectively. The moderator asked the audience to watch two teams of basketball players. The specific task was to count the number of passes made by the team wearing white outfits. I completed the task along with the studio audience. Afterwards the moderator asked if anyone had noticed anything unusual. Only one person in the studio audience had seen that the moderator had run onto the court, done a spin of his body, and then left the scene. The rest of the studio audience and I had been so focused on the passing of the ball that we had entirely missed seeing the moderator come onto the court. A replay of the passing scene allowed me to see the moderator come onto the court. The moderator explained that the inability to see him initially was an example of "selective inattention," which can also be called "inattentional blindness." Selective inattention explains why meditators often don't hear noises in their environment when focusing inwardly during meditation. It also explains why focusing on one part of the body (selective attention) allows you to ignore other aspects of the body (selective inattention) that might otherwise draw your attention.

When the inexperienced meditator makes a choice not to exercise the ability of selective attention, the awareness tends to move from one part of the body to another, subject to the attraction of outer stimuli that affect different parts of the body. This causes distraction and makes meditation less effective. If your mind is distracted in this way, you can literally say that you have a "wandering mind," because the awareness actually changes locations as it wanders through the body that is distracted. However, you can choose to develop your ability to hold the awareness in one part of the body and thus prevent the distraction in meditation caused by allowing the awareness to wander from one part of the body to another.

At first it may be difficult to hold the awareness in one part of the body, but gradually with daily practice this ability to maintain the awareness in one place will increase and the awareness will be less likely to wander to other parts of the body. When you have developed the ability to hold the awareness in one place, you will find that distractions occur less frequently, and when they do occur they are less intense and less likely to disrupt the meditation process.

There are other ways to include techniques related to body awareness as a part of meditation. Breathing is a body process that is important to meditation. Breathing is an involuntary process that goes deep within, but it also can be a voluntary process that can be affected by your conscious thoughts. There is a strong link between breathing and the mind. Calming the mind will automatically calm the breathing, and calming the breathing will automatically calm the mind. Hence, by simply observing the flow of the breath without manipulating the breath, you can calm the mind. In fact, some meditators use this as a meditation technique in itself without using any affirmation for meditation.

Those who choose to use an affirmation such as the Divine Name find that coordinating the affirmation with the natural flow of the breath will deepen meditation considerably. Some of these meditators choose not to focus on any single part of the body, because they are satisfied with focusing on breathing alone in coordination with the affirmation as an effective means of using body awareness to aid meditation. This manual emphasizes focusing on a part of the body in addition to awareness of breathing, because awareness of a part of the body reduces distraction.

Generally speaking, when Christians are taught meditation they are not taught to include body awareness as part of their meditation technique. The concept of letting go of body awareness sounds like a simple and easy approach. However, it is actually quite difficult to put this into practice because it presupposes that the meditator can exclude body awareness from the meditation process. Generally speaking, beginning meditators do not have the ability to meditate deeply enough to allow them to leave behind body awareness altogether. Consequently, if you are a beginning meditator, you may want to first use a meditation technique that includes body awareness as part of the method. After successfully using methods that include body awareness, you can set aside a short time at the end of your practice to experiment with using a technique that does not use body awareness. If you feel comfortable using this technique at the end of your practice, you can gradually increase the time for methods that do not use body awareness.

B. Body Awareness for Receptivity

In addition to reducing distraction, there is another, more important reason for holding the awareness in particular parts of the body. By focusing on certain body parts, you can increase your receptivity to the Spirit in a variety of ways. An example that illustrates this principle is the holding of your awareness in the chest area, which can help you to become increasingly receptive to developing the spiritual quality of devotion.

Early Christians recognized this fact and indeed referred to the Jesus Prayer as the "Prayer of the Heart." This heart-centered meditation is the origin of the method that is described below, called "Heart Meditation." It is primarily based on the techniques of early Christian desert hermits, who repeated the Name of the Lord while holding the awareness in the heart. This method evolved into a very definite technique of coordinating the breathing with the heartbeat. The writings of these early Christian hermits were collected in a book called the *Philokalia*, which became a manual of spiritual discipline and meditation technique.

While the popularity of using the Name of Jesus for meditation has been growing here in the West recently, the importance of the body in meditation that was known by early Christians has been largely ignored. Generally when the Jesus Prayer is taught today as a form of meditation, meditators are instructed to repeat the prayer without focusing on any part of the body and without coordinating it with the breathing. Many seekers have been helped in this way by simply repeating the Divine Name, but it is unfortunate that so many are missing out on the benefits that nourished the spiritual life of the early Christians.

Meditation that focuses on the *heart area*, in addition to encouraging openness to devotion, also helps to develop "emotional receptivity." This kind of receptivity opens you to both letting go of negative emotional tension and building a base of emotional stability. The heart is not the only beneficial focusing area in the body. By focusing on the *navel area* you can develop "physical receptivity." This will assist you in releasing physical tension and help to redirect sexual energy in a way that will enhance your meditation experience. Another important focusing area is the *brow area*, which may include the forehead. By focusing there you can be assisted in developing "mental receptivity," which will help you release mental tension and enable your mind to be increasingly focused.

Meditation is a *focused intention*. Your focused intention in practicing meditation techniques that use body awareness is really a combination of a general intention and a specific intention. The general intention is your desire to grow toward your spiritual ideal, expressed in a word or words by your affirmation. Your general intention also includes your desire for the Holy Spirit to enter your consciousness to assist you in growing toward your spiritual ideal. However, in the practice of body awareness techniques there is a specific intention for receptivity related to the parts of the body that serve as a focus. The release of tension described above is not solely the result of focusing on parts of the body. It is a result of your intention for receptivity, which is your openness to the Holy Spirit to come into you to bring about an inner transformation. With your invitation to the Holy Spirit, you are cooperating with the Holy Spirit to release inner tension as part of your transformation process.

You always retain your general intention, but your specific intent varies depending on the method you use. When you focus on the navel area, your specific intention is your desire for physical receptivity, which is your openness to a physical transformation. When you focus on the heart area, your specific intention is your desire for emotional receptivity, which is your openness to an emotional transformation. When you hold your attention on the brow area, your specific intention is your desire for a mental transformation through mental receptivity.

All of these kinds of receptivity open you to increasingly allow the Holy Spirit to facilitate changes in you that will help to integrate and unify the physical, emotional, and mental levels of your being as a preparation for contemplation. Meditation methods that do not include body awareness can lead you to the experience of contemplation. But such techniques are more effective after you have already used methods that include body awareness to increase your physical, emotional, and mental receptivity to the action of the Holy Spirit.

Incorporating body awareness into your meditation practice helps to reduce distraction and increase receptivity as described above, but there is another significant reason for employing body awareness. By focusing on a series of areas within the body, you can dramatically assist a natural process that occurs as you invite the Holy Spirit into your consciousness and open yourself to inner spiritual transformation. This natural process is explained in the next chapter, which describes *Progressive Meditation* and includes focusing on a series of areas that follow a sequence from bottom to top within the body. Progressive Meditation is a combination of four different meditation techniques. The first three of these techniques use body awareness. Focusing on particular parts of the body helps you contact spiritual centers of awareness associated with these parts of the body. These three spiritual centers of awareness are the navel center, the heart center, and the brow center. Holding the awareness in these three spiritual centers can be beneficial to your experience of meditation and can serve as a preparation for contemplation, which does not use body awareness.

Instruction will be provided below in how to use body awareness as an aid to meditation, as well as how to gradually develop the ability to let go of body awareness techniques in order to become receptive to experiencing contemplation. Contemplation is not a technique, but rather a gift of the Spirit. The techniques described here will help to prepare you to receive this gift by aiding in producing receptivity to the Spirit within.

C. Choosing and Using your Affirmation

The three meditation techniques described below will show you how to combine repeating an affirmation with focusing the awareness on various parts of the body. These methods produce physical, emotional, and mental receptivity to the Holy Spirit. For these kinds of meditation techniques, you will need to choose a Divine Name or other affirmation that represents your spiritual ideal or reminds you of your spiritual ideal. Your affirmation represents your intention to grow toward your spiritual ideal and your desire to be open to the divine presence.

It is best to have only a short affirmation, preferably one word. But you may choose to use two, three or four words for your affirmation. After you choose one word or a very brief combination of words, it is important to remain with this one choice without making the mistake of continually changing from one affirmation to another. Using just one affirmation increases the potency of its effect. In the following explanations, however, several different affirmations will be used as examples. Three separate methods of meditation that use body awareness are explained in this chapter. Then the next chapter explains a fourth method, which is called "Inner Silence Meditation," that does not use body awareness. The next chapter also describes how these four methods may be combined into one technique, called "Progressive Meditation."

For the following techniques, the affirmation will be coordinated with the breathing so that the first half of the chosen affirmation is mentally repeated on the inhalation and the second half of the affirmation is mentally repeated on the exhalation. For example, if you have chosen the Divine Name of "Jesus" to represent your spiritual ideal and you would like to use this as your affirmation, then "Je" would be repeated on the inhalation and "sus" would be repeated on the exhalation. If a one syllable word is chosen for your affirmation, the same single syllable word can be repeated on the inhalation and then again on the exhalation. Some meditators prefer to repeat the single syllable affirmation only on the exhalation, but not on the inhalation. Other meditators prefer to repeat the one syllable affirmation only on the inhalation, but not on the exhalation. Although a specific way of coordinating the affirmation with the breathing is recommended below, you may choose to repeat the affirmation and be aware of the breathing in any way that feels comfortable to you.

There are two different ways to use an affirmation. One approach is to use the affirmation strictly as a yoga mantra that is continuously repeated throughout the entire meditation in order to build that affirmation into your consciousness. The benefits of continuous repeating of a mantra are supported by the long history in India of using Hindu mantras. The benefits can also be found in the traditional Christian usage of the Jesus Prayer, and the contemporary practice of "Christian Meditation," which has been advocated by John Main and which will be described in Chapter 8.

The other approach is to use the affirmation to counteract distracting thoughts, and then after the affirmation has successfully calmed your mind, you can let go of it. This manual follows this second approach because meditation is being taught here as a practice that leads you in the direction of contemplation. When your meditation has done its work of leading you into the restful state of contemplation, there is no need for an affirmation. Indeed, the activity of mentally repeating an affirmation during contemplation would itself draw you out of the silence and the rest of contemplation. Therefore, all of the techniques described below will show you how to use the affirmation and also how to let go of it. Your affirmation affirms your intention to be aware of the divine presence within, but by letting go of your affirmation you can carry forward your intention to a deeper level—a level beyond words, where you are guided by pure faith.

Although only the intermittent use of the affirmation is mentioned and recommended in each meditation technique described below, this is not intended to be a hard and fast rule without flexibility. For example, if you are a beginner, you may find yourself becoming discouraged in your meditation practice because you are constantly becoming distracted by stray thoughts. In the event that you are having a great deal of difficulty calming the mind, there is a possibility you may find more success initially by repeating your affirmation continuously. If you choose to employ the approach of continuously repeating the affirmation to help learn how to calm the mind, you can, of course, change that approach at a later date. After learning how to calm your mind, you will be better prepared to use the affirmation and then let go of it for increasing intervals of time in order to experience the inner silence of contemplation.

However, some seekers do better with continuous repeating of the affirmation as an ongoing practice, even after becoming an intermediate meditator. If you want to make this your permanent practice, the major benefit is the building of your affirmation into your consciousness at a deep level. The continuous repeating of your affirmation is a more active practice than the passive approach of using the affirmation and then letting go of it. Thus the active approach of using the affirmation continuously is best suited to those who have a very active, physical, emotional, and mental disposition. As an experiment, you may want to practice using your affirmation continuously on a daily basis for an extended period of time, and then switch to using the affirmation and letting go of it for an equally long period of time. These two periods of time to experiment with each approach will give you a frame of reference based on experience to determine which approach works best for you. It is important to find a method that feels comfortable and that will best help you deepen your awareness of the divine presence within you.

The first three techniques of Progressive Meditation, which will be described in detail below, can be successfully practiced with the option of continuously repeating the affirmation rather than the recommended method of letting go of the affirmation when the mind is calm. But Inner Silence Meditation, the fourth technique of Progressive Meditation, can only be practiced by using the affirmation and then releasing it in order to experience the objectless and wordless awareness of contemplation. Instead of employing Inner Silence Meditation as your fourth technique of Progressive Meditation, you can practice "Christian Meditation," as taught by John Main. For this practice you repeat your affirmation continuously and let go of body awareness. However, this option is not recommended if you want to experience wordless contemplation.

What if you prefer to repeat your affirmation continuously, but would also like to experience contemplation? The fundamental drawback of continuously repeating your affirmation is that this practice prevents you from entering the inner silence of contemplation in which there is no holding on to thoughts, not even holding on to the single thought of your affirmation. Is there a way to repeat your affirmation and still experience the resting in God of contemplation in which thoughts are silenced? Yes, you can apply the continuous repeating of the affirmation only for the first three techniques of Progressive Meditation, but not for the last technique. For the final method, Inner Silence Meditation, it will be necessary to implement this practice just as it is described below in order to lead you to the experience of contemplation. Your practice of the first three techniques of Progressive Meditation will allow you to hold on to your affirmation continuously for the vast majority of each meditation session. Then your practice of Inner Silence Meditation at the end will still give you the opportunity to have a short period of time to let go of your affirmation and hopefully enter the restful state of contemplation.

D. Centering Meditation

The first technique that will be described is *Centering Meditation*. This method helps you to find your center of balance and to establish a calm breathing pattern. The major benefit of this technique is that it helps develop *physical receptivity* to the Holy Spirit. Consequently, practicing Centering Meditation will enable you to let go of physical tension in the body and also free the natural physical energy of the body. This physical energy is what we normally call sexual energy, but it actually would more properly be termed "creative energy." This creative energy can become sexual energy if it is directed toward sexual purposes. Yet this same creative energy can become a purifying energy that rises upward if it is dedicated to spiritual purposes. Through focusing on the navel area, Centering Meditation produces physical receptivity to the action of the Holy Spirit that allows the creative energy of the body to rise upward. The rising energy releases physical blocks in the body and produces a purifying effect. When the creative energy is rising during meditation, it is normally a subtle energy that usually cannot be felt as a conscious experience, especially by beginning meditators.

After having done the preparatory work of sitting, relaxing the body, and completing the preparatory prayer, you are ready to begin meditation. While sitting erect with the eyes closed, you observe the area stretching from the navel to three-finger widths below the navel. You can feel this area just below the navel as the center of balance within the body. You focus the mind on the navel area not by using visualization, but rather by actually bringing your awareness into the navel area. You can be aware of the breathing in this area, but without trying to manipulate the breath in any way. The mouth is closed during meditation, so naturally you are breathing through the nostrils.

If you observe the breathing of a baby, you will notice the pronounced expanding and contracting of the baby's abdominal area. This abdominal breathing is the most natural and relaxed means of breathing. Thus it is the best form of breathing for meditation, regardless of what technique is used. Ideally during meditation the body is kept as still as possible, and abdominal breathing occurs automatically with minimal expansion and contraction of the chest.

To help you focus on the area below the navel during Centering Meditation, you observe this area expand outwardly with each inhalation and contract inwardly with each exhalation. At first it may be easier to focus on the surface of the skin at the navel area, but gradually it will become natural for you to hold your awareness underneath the surface of the skin. In Zen Buddhism this navel area is called the *hara*, which is the focusing area employed in the Zen practice of sitting meditation, called *zazen*.

Your chosen affirmation is divided in half. You mentally repeat the first half of the affirmation on the inhalation and repeat the second half on the exhalation. With "Jesus" as the sample affirmation, you keep the awareness in the area below the navel and mentally repeat "Je" with each inhalation and extend the sound "jjjeeee" for the entire inhalation. Then with the awareness still just below the navel, you mentally repeat "sus" with each exhalation and extend the sound "sssuuusss" for the entire exhalation. It is important to be relaxed and for the breathing to be natural and not manipulated in any way.

This practice is very simple and effective. In fact, it is so easy that it may seem absurd to some. But by participating in this practice, you will experience the benefits for yourself. It is important to pay no attention to stray thoughts. You do not want to be attracted to any thoughts, and in particular you do not want to indulge in any form of evaluating yourself during your meditation practice. If thoughts come, your only reaction needs to be to hold more firmly to "Je" on the inhalation and "sus" on the exhalation, while continuing to focus your awareness on the area below the navel. Though the awareness is focused just below the navel, it is actually the whole abdomen that naturally expands with each inhalation and contracts with each exhalation. As meditation deepens, the breathing will naturally become slower and more relaxed. In fact, the breathing may become so slow that you cannot feel the navel area expanding and contracting at all, yet the awareness can still be focused on that area.

In addition to holding the affirmation, there is also the opportunity to let go of your affirmation. When your mind becomes calm through using your affirmation, you can release repeating the affirmation yet retain your focus on the navel area. After letting go of the affirmation, focusing on the breathing is not required. But if you find it helpful, you can temporarily focus on both the breathing and the navel area by noticing the expansion of the navel area with each inhalation and the contraction of the navel area with each exhalation. After a while you can also let go of focusing on the breathing and just hold your awareness on the navel area alone. Thoughts will probably continue to present themselves to your conscious mind during most of your meditation, but you can let go of the affirmation if these thoughts are not distracting you. Thoughts only become distracting if you allow your awareness to follow these thoughts by participating in creating a succession of new thoughts. At those times when you can allow thoughts to float by without being concerned about where these thoughts are coming from or going to, you can let go of the affirmation.

If your mind becomes calm by ignoring thoughts as they float by, you do not need your affirmation. Instead, you can focus just on the navel area alone, as long as you do not become attracted to any stray thoughts and as long as you do not push away any stray thoughts. But if you become distracted again by allowing your attention to be carried away by stray thoughts, then you can gently return to repeating your affirmation. When your mind becomes calm again, you can let go of the affirmation and return to focusing on the navel area. In this process, the holding of the affirmation helps you to focus on your spiritual intention in words, and letting go of the affirmation allows you to take your intention to a deeper level beyond words.

If you are a beginner and find that initially your mind is constantly distracted, you may feel it is necessary for you to continuously repeat your affirmation for the entire meditation period. However, as you make progress and calm your mind, you will notice that your thoughts can come and go without you becoming preoccupied by them. When you find that thoughts can float by in your mind for short intervals of time without you being distracted by them, you can then learn to let go of the affirmation for increasing amounts of time. The same process of holding your affirmation at times and then letting go of it for short intervals of calmness is used for each of the next meditation methods that will be described in the sections below. Each of these techniques has a different focusing area in the body for meditation. For the method called Inner Silence Meditation, you can let go of both the affirmation and the body awareness. This method allows you to enter inner silence, leading toward contemplation, as will be described in detail in Chapter 6.

It is important not to confuse Centering Meditation with another similarly named practice called "Centering Prayer," which has been popularized by Thomas Keating and Basil Pennington. Centering Prayer, described in Chapter 8, does not advocate focusing on a part of the body as does Centering Meditation. Actually the practice of Centering Prayer is very similar to Inner Silence Meditation, which will be described in the next chapter.

E. Heart Meditation

The second method is *Heart Meditation*, in which the awareness is held in the chest area. The major benefit of Heart Meditation is the development of *emotional receptivity* to the Holy Spirit, which enables you to release emotional tension and to increase devotion. Emotional receptivity is particularly important because tension and stress can build up over time, creating emotional anxiety. This emotional anxiety can become a stumbling block that hinders your ability to learn how to be open to divine love. By focusing on the chest area, you develop the emotional receptivity that gives permission for the Holy Spirit to assist you in releasing the stored up emotional tension within you. Releasing this emotional tension produces a deeper level of emotional stability and openness to love that is necessary to make progress in your spiritual growth.

If you are a beginning meditator, you will not initially experience this release of emotional tension as a conscious and dramatic experience. Instead, you will simply feel calmer and more peaceful at an emotional level as a result of your meditation. Thus the ups and downs of daily life will have less of an effect on you. Likewise, if you have emotional moods swings during meditation itself, these too will tend to level off. As you become more experienced in your meditation practice and as your emotional receptivity increases, you will be able to open yourself at a deeper level to the action of the Holy Spirit.

For the practice of Heart Meditation, you can focus your awareness either on the left side of the chest in the location of the physical heart or in the center of the chest. If the location of the physical heart is chosen as your focus for meditation, you may find one very small area on the left side of the chest that draws your attention more readily than any other area. Then you can allow your awareness to remain focused in that area. If the center of the chest is chosen, you may find one area (higher or lower) that attracts your attention, and the awareness may be focused in that area. As with the previous method, the first half of your chosen affirmation is repeated mentally and extended for the entire inhalation, and the second half of your chosen affirmation is repeated mentally and extended for the entire exhalation. For example, if "Jesus Christ Love" is your chosen affirmation, "Jesus" would be repeated on the inhalation and "Christ Love" on the exhalation. Again the breath is observed without manipulating it in any way.

As with Centering Meditation, you follow the same process of holding and letting go of the affirmation. You repeat the affirmation to counteract stray thoughts. If your mind becomes calm so you can ignore stray thoughts, you can let go of repeating the affirmation and hold your awareness only in the heart area or in the center of the chest. After you let go of the affirmation, you no longer need to focus on the breathing. Nevertheless, if you find it helpful, you can continue for a short time to be aware of the breathing while holding your awareness on a focusing area in the chest. But after a while you can let go of being aware of the breathing and be aware of only a focusing area in the chest. If your mind wanders because of stray thoughts catching your attention, you can allow this to be a gentle reminder for you to return to repeating the affirmation in coordination with your breathing. At first most of your practice may be just repeating your affirmation. But gradually you will be able to let go of your affirmation for short intervals and then later for longer periods of time. You are led in this process by your intention to grow toward your spiritual ideal. You do so first by holding your affirmation and then by letting go of it to allow your intention to go to a level deeper than words.

While the focus of awareness remains in the chest area, you may experience a feeling of energy or a feeling of warmth. Also, you may feel a tingling sensation, or you may feel the heartbeat. Feeling the heartbeat or any of these other sensations in the heart area can be employed as a way of helping to focus the awareness. Nonetheless, these feelings do not occur to everyone, and they are not necessary for this method of meditation. If awareness of the heartbeat or some other sensation does occur, this should not draw the attention away from repeating the affirmation. More information about coordinating the heartbeat with the affirmation is explained in Chapter 9. Generally this manual does not recommend coordinating the heartbeat with the affirmation unless you feel intuitively guided to do so. Most meditators who practice Heart Meditation simply coordinate the affirmation with the breathing and maintain the awareness in the chest area without coordinating the heartbeat.

With Heart Meditation there is the possibility of side effects caused by an accumulation of too much energy in the area of the physical heart. If you feel a slight pain in the chest or if your heartbeat suddenly becomes faster while practicing Heart Meditation, you need to temporarily switch to another technique. These side effects may be caused by concentrating for too long on the heart area, resulting in excessive energy being released. Sometimes this energy is reabsorbed by the pericardium (the fibroserous sac that surrounds the heart), causing the heart to beat faster. This may also lead to difficulty in breathing or to pain in the chest. Therefore, it is wise to temporarily use another method of meditation, such as Centering Meditation, if you begin to feel pain in the chest or a rapid heartbeat.

These symptoms are not common, but are more likely to occur when you choose to focus on the area of the physical heart for long periods of time. If such symptoms do occur, then you may find that these symptoms do not recur when the focus is held in the center of the chest instead of the location of the physical heart.

Although symptoms are less likely to occur while meditating with the awareness held in the center of the chest, there is no attempt here to discourage you from holding the awareness in the location of the physical heart. If you feel guided to focus on the physical heart, you are certainly encouraged to follow your intuition, as long as none of the previously described negative symptoms occur. Beginning meditators may not notice any significant difference between holding the awareness on the physical heart and holding the awareness in the center of the chest.

However, many intermediate meditators prefer focusing on the physical heart because they discover that doing so awakens a deeper devotional quality than focusing on the center of the chest. As meditation deepens you may have a feeling of the divine presence in the location of the physical heart or even a feeling of both love and light in the heart. After first focusing on the physical heart and feeling light and love in that area, some intermediate meditators switch to focusing on the center of the chest to facilitate the expansion of love and light into the whole chest area. More information about feeling love and light in the physical heart and in the center of the chest is provided in Chapter 11, which describes a technique called *Inner Light Meditation.*

F. Brow Meditation

The third method of meditation is *Brow Meditation*, in which the awareness is held in the *brow area* slightly above the space between the eyebrows, but within the head itself. The practice of holding the awareness in the forehead area during meditation increases your ability to focus the mind. Brow Meditation specifically encourages *mental receptivity*, which gives the Holy Spirit permission to guide your thinking process. Your openness to the Holy Spirit's mental guidance helps you to stay on track in your process of learning how to let go of stray thoughts during meditation as well as learning how to hold on to the one thought of your affirmation.

Your increased mental receptivity not only aids you in letting go of stray thoughts in meditation and focusing the mind, but also assists you in releasing mental tension. Old habitual thinking patterns are stored in the subconscious mind. These ego-based thinking patterns may have been placed there from childhood and can produce tension in your mind. Your increase in mental receptivity due to bringing your attention to the brow area gives permission to the Holy Spirit to help you let go of these old discordant thinking patterns that are not in harmony with your spiritual growth. The result is a release of mental tension and a reorientation of your thinking process that changes your perception of yourself and others as well as your perceptions regarding spiritual matters. Gradually this brings about a change in your basic belief system, but you will generally not be aware of any change taking place as an inner conscious experience during meditation. You will instead become aware of the effects of your increased mental receptivity in your daily life. You will notice that you will have a greater willingness to look at yourself and your life in a new light. With a clearer mental picture of yourself, you will find that your mind is calmer and you will also feel a deeper sense of dedication toward manifesting your spiritual purposes outwardly through service to others.

For practicing Brow Meditation, you may hold your awareness just above the space between the eyebrows. However, the exact location may vary depending upon finding the place along the center of the forehead that feels intuitively right for you. Some meditators prefer the space between the eyebrows, but most meditators prefer an area slightly above that in the middle of the forehead. Feel free to meditate at whatever area you feel intuitively guided to bring your awareness. Just as with the previous methods, the affirmation is coordinated with the breathing. For example, if "Christ, Light" is the chosen affirmation, then "Christ" would be repeated on the inhalation and "Light" would be repeated on the exhalation.

With each of the previously mentioned methods of meditation, it is important to not think intellectually about the meaning of your chosen affirmation during meditation. You will need to rely on repeating the words themselves, rather than on an intellectual analysis of the words. This does not mean that the affirmation should be repeated mechanically. On the contrary, you repeat the affirmation with your wholehearted attention and desire for God. Allow all of your innermost being to be summed up and expressed in just these few words you have chosen. By repeating these words without intellectualizing, you will be brought beyond the level of conceptual thinking.

Your mind will become calm by repeating your affirmation, so your thoughts will pass by in your mind without attracting your attention. When you can hold your focus without being distracted, you can let go of your affirmation and focus solely on holding your awareness in the brow area. You can release being aware of the breathing when you let go of the affirmation. However, if you find it helpful, you can temporarily continue to be aware of the breathing while also focusing on the brow area. Then after a while, you can let go of being aware of the breathing and focus only on the brow area.

After letting go of the affirmation, you may notice the mind wandering because of stray thoughts. If stray thoughts grab your attention, you can then allow this to remind you to bring your focus back to repeating the affirmation again. Your meditation can be a continuous repeated process of holding your affirmation and then letting go of it. Whether you are using your affirmation or letting go of it, you can maintain your intention of growing toward your spiritual ideal.

5

TECHNIQUES LEADING TO CONTEMPLATION

~ • ~

A. Inner Silence Meditation

After learning how to use an affirmation along with focusing on body awareness, as was described in the previous chapter, you may want to consider using a technique that does not rely on body awareness. One such method is *Inner Silence Meditation*, which will assist you in learning how to let go of body awareness in order to experience the inner silence of contemplation. For this method you repeat your affirmation without focusing on any part of the body. When your mind becomes calm, you can let go of your affirmation and allow yourself to be open to the divine presence in silence. If your mind becomes distracted by stray thoughts, you then return to the stabilizing influence of repeating your affirmation. Your meditation during Inner Silence Meditation consists of alternating between times of using the affirmation and times of letting go of the affirmation in order to rest in silent receptivity to the divine presence.

The goal of meditation is to silence the mind so that the Spirit can shine through. Normally an affirmation is used for this purpose. But some beginning meditators decide to learn meditation without using any affirmation and attempt to go directly into silence. A few may succeed at this, yet most beginners fail to experience inner silence because of being assailed by numerous stray thoughts.

The problem of overcoming distracting thoughts is addressed by the use of an affirmation to help silence the mind. Initially in meditation you will have difficulty in controlling the tendency of the mind to wander. Then through repeating an affirmation, you will notice a gradual improvement in your ability to reduce stray thoughts. The affirmation calms the many thoughts of the mind by turning the awareness toward the one thought of the affirmation.

Nevertheless, that one thought of the affirmation is itself one step away from complete silence. Your affirmation is like a physical ladder that helps you to climb one step at a time to the top of a roof. Once you are on top of the roof, it would be foolish to pull the ladder up and carry it around. Similar to a ladder, the one thought of the affirmation does its work of lifting you up to a higher state of having a quiet mind. Then you can let go of this one thought so you can rest on the rooftop of your awareness, which is the inner silence of contemplation.

Using Inner Silence Meditation is an ongoing process, which alternates between two activities. The first activity is to hold the affirmation without focusing on the body and to let go of the thoughts that pass through the mind. When the mind becomes calm because you are not distracted by stray thoughts, you can practice the second activity. This second activity, which is more of a non-doing than a doing, is to let go of the affirmation and enter inner silence. There are deep states of inner silence that can potentially be reached in which there are no thoughts, but invariably thoughts will appear during your experience of inner silence. These thoughts that float by in your mind do not in themselves have the power to disturb the silence of your contemplative practice. However, if you have some sort of reaction to these passing thoughts, you give these thoughts the power to distract your mind. Your goal is to let thoughts float by without paying any particular attention to them. Your approach is to follow a path between the extremes of aversion and attraction, so you do not push any thought away and you do not attract any thought. This is a process of continually letting go and surrendering to the Holy Spirit. You rely only on pure faith without the support normally provided by your reason, memory, or imagination.

After being absorbed into inner silence briefly, you may find yourself distracted by wandering thoughts that have captured your attention. When this occurs, it would be a mistake to judge yourself adversely for having become distracted. Evaluative monitoring of yourself will only add even more distracting thoughts to an already distracted mind. Instead of evaluating yourself, you gently pick up your affirmation again and focus on your choice of a sacred word or words. You continue to hold your awareness on your affirmation, until your mind becomes calm again and you are ready to let go of your affirmation and again enter inner silence.

This process of letting go of discursive thinking, entering silence, and relying on pure faith in the Christian tradition has generally been called "contemplative prayer." But the term "prayer," as it is used in this manual, refers to expressive communication with God, while meditation refers to receptive communication with God. Therefore, in this book, instead of using the term contemplative prayer, the process of entering into contemplative silence is called "Inner Silence Meditation." A similar process of going into inner silence is commonly taught today under the specific name of "Centering Prayer," as it is described in Chapter 8.

The term "contemplation" by itself is the best way to describe the overshadowing of the Holy Spirit that tends to occur when practicing the technique of Inner Silence Meditation. Contemplation is both a restful and dynamic state of inner absorption, in which your mind has an inner focus that allows stray thoughts to pass by without causing distraction. This inner absorption has no object that serves as a focus.

You do not "manufacture" the state of communion with the divine in contemplation because your union with God is already a pre-existing condition of your true nature. This condition of union is hidden from your awareness, but you can assist in letting go of the blocks to your awareness that prevent you from recognizing your union with God. Since your self-centered preoccupation with your own thoughts is your major stumbling block, you can use the affirmation to help you let go of your thoughts, which will assist you in revealing deeper and deeper levels of awareness. You do not think about the meaning of your affirmation because this would only add more discursive thinking and increase your preoccupation with your thoughts, rather than reduce your self-centered preoccupation. The affirmation can help to reduce thoughts and increase your awareness of the divine presence by being used in different ways depending on the needs of the seeker.

The affirmation is a way of leading you toward union with your spiritual ideal. The affirmation consists of both the form and the content of the affirmation. The form is the actual word or words used. The content is not the literal meaning of the words, but rather your intention to awaken your awareness of the divine presence. If you are a beginner, you may initially rely on using the form of your affirmation as a means of leading you to the content of your intention. Then, as your experience deepens, you can learn to rely less on the form and more on the content itself. Relying on the content of your intention will then lead you through faith to the experience of the divine presence in contemplation.

The next pages provide a list of four phases of using the affirmation in the practice of Inner Silence Meditation. These four phases can be used one after the other in sequence during one meditation session, but usually your awareness will fluctuate back and forth between these phases. This list starts with the most structured, gross, and form-related usage of the affirmation. Then it proceeds to less structured, and more subtle and more content-related usages of the affirmation. The more structured, gross, and form-related usages are most helpful for beginners, and with progress these will be less needed and can be reduced or omitted altogether.

The goal is to *internalize* the affirmation because in doing so you are internalizing your spiritual ideal. The word or words of the affirmation that represent your intention for a closer relationship with God are first used and then are left behind and replaced by the fulfillment of your intention—your communion with the divine presence. Each individual phase is only a stepping stone to the next, culminating in the experience of contemplation.

Four Phases of Using the Affirmation in Inner Silence Meditation

1. Mentally Pronouncing the Affirmation

For the first phase, you repeat the affirmation, pronouncing it in your mind only, not with your lips as an outward verbal expression. You do not think about the literal meaning of the word or words of the affirmation. You understand that the word or words are an external form-related representation of your inner spiritual ideal of God and your intention to unite with your spiritual ideal. You mentally repeat each syllable of the affirmation in whatever way feels most natural to you, yet there is no focusing on any part of the body. You do not coordinate the repeating of the affirmation with the breathing. Nonetheless, if you find that you are having unusual difficulty with very distracting thoughts, you may occasionally coordinate your affirmation with your breathing just to overcome this temporary difficulty.

This repeating of the "word form," the mental sound of the word or words, is done only to counteract distracting thoughts. When the mind is calm enough to go to a deeper level, you can let go of repeating the affirmation in the form of a sound pronounced mentally. In addition to overcoming distracting thoughts, the repeating of the sound of the affirmation is a way of affirming your desire for God. The next phase is a more receptive and less structured way of expressing your desire. As a beginner you can learn how to use the first phase of mentally repeating the affirmation and then you can switch to the next phase. However, you have the option of omitting this first phase altogether and starting with the less structured and less form-related second phase described below.

2. Allowing the Affirmation to Deepen your Awareness

The second phase lets the thought of your affirmation bring you to deeper and deeper levels of awareness by letting that thought come to your mind in whatever way it presents itself. You allow the thought of your affirmation to be an unstructured reminder of your intention to be open to God's presence. Consequently, the thought of the form of your affirmation becomes a symbolic reminder of the thought of your intention, which is the content of your affirmation. Your affirmation serves as an expression of your desire for God and your choice to give permission to God to come into your awareness. You let the affirmation come to your mind however it presents itself in order to lead you to your awareness to God's presence and activity within you. Since the affirmation is only a reminder of your desire, you do not have to repeat the affirmation in a structured way during the second phase. You just let your affirmation enter your awareness as a transition point to your intention for God, which your affirmation symbolizes. This phase occurs prior to actually experiencing God's presence and instead is primarily about your desire for God and your willingness to become aware of His presence.

You do not try to control how the affirmation "should" come into your awareness. You gently remind yourself of the affirmation when you are distracted by stray thoughts, but you allow the affirmation to be clear or indistinct in whatever way it may come to your awareness. Your affirmation is just a symbol of your intention, so you can allow the form of the affirmation to come to you in any way. For example, when you recall your affirmation, it may come to you spontaneously as the sound of the affirmation. Also, it may come as the thought of the word or words of the affirmation, without the accompanying sound, and, of course, without conjuring up the intellectual meaning of the word or words. It may come to you as a vague thought, an impulse of the will, or a feeling.

You allow the affirmation's form to be whatever it is and to lead you to your intention itself, which the form symbolizes. Thus the form of your affirmation can fade away as your intention itself takes over. You can allow your intention to be the focal point of your awareness, while other thoughts are passing through your mind. But if these other thoughts divert your attention away from your intention, you can then bring your awareness back to the form of your affirmation to help redirect your mind back to your intention of bringing about a deeper relationship with God. As soon as the thought of your intention is reestablished, the word form of your affirmation is not necessary because you are focused on the content of your affirmation. You can begin with the first phase and progress to this second phase, or you can skip the first phase and start your practice with this second phase. The idea is to move in the direction of experiencing the divine presence and to release distracting thoughts in the least structured manner, so eventually the form of your affirmation will be less and less needed.

3. The Affirmation Leads to Faithful Awareness

In the previous phase, you let the thought of your affirmation lead you from the form of your affirmation to the content of your intention for God, which is your desire for God. In this third phase, you give your consent to His presence and His activity within you. This, of course, requires your faith that God Himself is indeed within you. By investing in your intention and your faith, you progress to this third phase, in which you have a *faithful awareness* of abiding in God's presence. In this third phase, your faith has expanded your awareness, allowing you to have an inner knowing that God is right there within you in the present moment. You are not quite resting in God's presence yet, but you can sense and experience His presence in the darkness of faith, which is your faithful awareness of Him. The previous phase was more about your desire for God and giving your permission to God to come into your awareness. This third phase is less about desire, which you have already expressed, and more about consent, which is your acceptance of God's presence that has become increasingly apparent to you through your faith.

It is hard to draw a firm line between the desire of the previous phase and your consent and faithful awareness of this third phase. After all, your awareness may certainly fluctuate back and forth between your desire for God on the one hand and your faithful acceptance of His immanent presence on the other hand. In the second phase, you desire what you apparently do not have. But in this third phase, you realize you already have what you had desired so you switch to acceptance. This third phase is a step forward, since you are becoming aware that God is responding to your intention by enabling you to recognize His presence through your consent and your faith. Your faithful awareness is God's gift to you, allowing you to become aware of Him. If your mind becomes distracted by stray thoughts and you lose your faithful awareness of the divine presence, you will need to return your awareness to one of the previous phases in order to calm your mind again.

4. The Affirmation Culminates in Contemplative Resting in God

Your maintaining of your faithful awareness of God's presence in the third phase leads quite naturally to the fourth phase, in which you rest in His presence during contemplation. This resting in God brings about an inner absorption in God that is not due to any concentrative effort on your part. In fact, this inner absorption is brought about by letting go of your own efforts and by allowing God to be God in your inmost being. Since your affirmation is an expression of your intention for union with your spiritual ideal, this resting in God is the true content of your affirmation, even though the form of the affirmation in words is not expressed at this deep level of pure awareness.

Contemplative resting in God is the destination toward which your affirmation is pointing. Although contemplation is the culmination of the inward journey toward which the affirmation is leading you, the journey to this contemplative destination needs to be repeated as an ongoing process. The process of interiorizing your affirmation will need to be repeated because initially you will only be able to rest in God for very short intervals of time before you are drawn out of this contemplative experience. Your brief intervals of contemplative rest will be interrupted by distracting thoughts, so you will have to revert back to previous phases. You may have to go back to either the first or second phase—whichever of these phases you think would best help you let go of your distracting thoughts and reestablish your awareness of your intention for divine communion.

Inner Silence Meditation consists of two parts: one meditative and the other contemplative. Meditation is the holding of one thought in the mind, which would be the maintaining of the word or words of your affirmation in your mind. Thus the meditative part of Inner Silence Meditation is your repeating of the affirmation to calm your mind and your releasing of the affirmation when your mind becomes calm. In contrast to meditation, in which you hold one thought of your affirmation as your focusing object, contemplation has no focusing object. Contemplation cannot occur until you let go of the form of the affirmation as a focusing object. Therefore, the contemplative part of Inner Silence Meditation occurs after you let go of the form of your affirmation, when your mind becomes so calm that you are drawn into a state of inner absorption that does not need a focusing object. Your awareness has left the contemplative state when you notice that your inner absorption has given way to distracting thoughts. You then let your distracting thoughts remind you to return your awareness to repeating your affirmation as a meditative practice.

Contemplation is a gift given freely by the Holy Spirit. However, to receive this gift, it is necessary to have a certain degree of receptivity. The term "unifying receptivity" may be used to describe the kind of receptivity developed by practicing Inner Silence Meditation. Unifying receptivity increases your openness to being drawn into the experience of being unified at all levels. All meditation methods develop receptivity, since all methods are an invitation for the incoming of the Holy Spirit. The Holy Spirit can transform you only to the degree of permission that you allow. Unifying receptivity opens you to all of the previously mentioned kinds of receptivity. Thus unifying receptivity is a joining together of all forms of receptivity, including physical receptivity, emotional receptivity, and mental receptivity. This in turn becomes an invitation to the Holy Spirit to transform all aspects of yourself. Your unifying receptivity expresses your openness and invitation that enables you to experience contemplation or, in other words, to enter into His World.

Your unifying receptivity is your consent to allow the Holy Spirit to be present in all aspects of your consciousness. Your primary means of consenting to the Holy Spirit is *pure faith*. The practice of Inner Silence Meditation is an exercise in faith. As you exercise your faith with this practice, you grow in faith, increasing your unifying receptivity. Since contemplation involves the incoming of the Holy Spirit based on pure faith, it may not be recorded in your conscious mind as an experience that can be felt by the senses.

However, in some cases your meditation or contemplation experience may bring about an observable feeling, which may be called a "felt experience." This felt experience of God is a mild and rather common form of increased awareness of the divine. Your increased awareness brings *inner feelings* into your consciousness. Such inner feelings may include the feelings of love, oneness, heightened awareness, light, the divine presence, peace, and/or bliss. One or more of these inner feelings may possibly occur occasionally or even regularly during your practice of meditation or during contemplation, or they may occur spontaneously in everyday life. Such inner feelings are *intuitions*. These felt experiences are signs of making progress, but they should never be considered more important than pure faith. Specific descriptions of these inner feelings or intuitions are provided in Chapter 10.

After successfully using the affirmation combined with techniques that use body awareness to calm the mind, you may want to consider using Inner Silence Meditation. However, instead of replacing body awareness techniques altogether by using Inner Silence Meditation exclusively, it is recommended to practice this technique along with body awareness methods as part of Progressive Meditation, which is described below. When first practicing Inner Silence Meditation as part of Progressive Meditation, you can set aside a few minutes at the end of your practice for this purpose. During these few minutes, just before concluding your meditation, you can simply let go of repeating the affirmation and allow yourself to "Be still, and know that I am God."[1] After you become comfortable using Inner Silence Meditation as part of Progressive Meditation, you can increase the time for this method and reduce the time for body awareness techniques. Eventually in your practice of Progressive Meditation, you may want to devote most of your sitting time to Inner Silence Meditation. Additional information about the practice of Inner Silence Meditation can be found in Chapter 7.

B. Progressive Meditation

The three body awareness techniques that have been described in the previous chapter and Inner Silence Meditation have been presented as methods that can be practiced separately. However, all four of these individual methods can be combined into one meditation practice. This practice is called *Progressive Meditation*. To practice this combination of techniques, you start with Centering Meditation, in which you hold the awareness at the navel area and mentally repeat the first half of your affirmation on the inhalation and the second half of your affirmation on the exhalation. The breathing is observed, but not manipulated in any way. You can let go of the affirmation when the mind becomes calm and is not distracted as you focus only on the navel area. If your mind becomes distracted by stray thoughts, you let your awareness of the distracting stray thoughts be a reminder for you to return to repeating your affirmation again. Each of the four techniques in this sequence of methods employs this same process of holding your affirmation and releasing it when it is not needed.

When you feel ready to move on to the second technique in this sequence, you let go of Centering Meditation and begin practicing Heart Meditation. For this practice you hold your awareness in the heart area or in the center of the chest and again repeat your affirmation in coordination with your breathing. You let go of the affirmation when your mind becomes calm and focus only in the heart or center of the chest. You decide intuitively how long to practice Heart Meditation before moving on to the next technique.

The third technique that you practice is Brow Meditation, in which you observe your breathing and repeat your affirmation while your attention remains in the brow area. Again you release your affirmation when the mind becomes calm and focus only on the brow area.

For the fourth and final technique, Inner Silence Meditation, you let go of all body awareness and focus only on your affirmation. Then when your mind becomes calm, you can let go of your affirmation and enter inner silence without any object to use as a focus for your awareness. If your mind becomes distracted by stray thoughts, you return to focusing on your affirmation. When your mind becomes calm again, you let go of the affirmation again in order to enter inner silence.

During these intervals of inner silence, your mind may at times enter a state of inner absorption that requires no object for focusing and a state in which you can let go of stray thoughts as they pass by in your mind. These experiences of inner absorption are intervals of *contemplation*, which is an overshadowing of the Holy Spirit. This contemplative experience is a gift of the Spirit, but this gift comes as a natural outcome of meeting the conditions of the gift.

There are four conditions for receiving the gift of contemplation. The first condition is a calm mind and ideally an integrated and unified mind. All of the four meditation techniques of Progressive Meditation are designed to produce this peaceful state of mind that invites the Holy Spirit to enter your consciousness and transform you. Inner Silence Meditation by itself can calm the mind to prepare you for the gift of contemplation, but the entire sequence of four techniques produces an integration and unification of all aspects of your being. This integration and unification serve as a very stable and long-lasting foundation for entering contemplation, for increasing the depth of your contemplative experience, and for allowing the experience of contemplation to become a regular part of your practice. Also, this solid foundation prepares you for handling the dynamic forces that are released by contemplation. In particular, this foundation helps you face the dark side of your nature that is brought to light by contemplation as a necessary part of your inner transformation.

The second condition of the gift of contemplation is your desire for God. The third condition is your consent to His presence. Desire and consent sound very similar, yet are different. What is the distinction between these two? Desire comes first and is about *wanting*. Consent comes after desire and is about *accepting* what is wanted. Both of these two conditions, desire and consent, involve using your will. You exercise your will through your intention to find God, which is your desire for Him. You offer your invitation to God through your will being used to desire His presence. Also, you exercise your will by consenting to the presence of the Holy Spirit in your mind. The more comprehensive and wholehearted you can make your invitation and give your consent, the more the Holy Spirit can accomplish in you to bring about an inner spiritual transformation. Your invitation and consent rests on your degree of willingness and openness.

All four methods of Progressive Meditation help you to expand your invitation and consent to the Holy Spirit by your openness to physical, emotional, mental, integrating, intuitive, and unifying receptivity. The Holy Spirit is sensitive to whatever parts of yourself that you wish to withhold from transformation and will not violate whatever limitations you place on your transformation. The sequence provided by Progressive Meditation helps you to systematically focus on every aspect of yourself so you can surrender all parts of yourself to inner transformation.

The fourth condition for receiving the gift of contemplation is your application of your faith. The amount of your faith is not nearly as significant as your implementation of whatever faith you do have. Your faith, even with your doubts remaining, needs to be directed toward your intention of drawing closer to God. Your faith tells you that God is there within you. The implementation of your faithful knowing of His presence opens you to increasing your awareness of His presence. All of the methods in the practice of Progressive Meditation represent a practical application of your faith, since you are making an investment of time and energy in these techniques as an expression of your faith. You are investing in your faith that God is present within you and that with His assistance you can expand your awareness of His presence. Your faith also opens you to allowing the Holy Spirit to bring about an inner transformation of your character and consciousness. The first three methods lead to the fourth method, Inner Silence Meditation, which helps you to increasingly rely on your faith and hopefully enter contemplation, as is explained in greater detail in Chapter 7.

Each of the four methods of Progressive Meditation can be used individually and can produce beneficial effects. But combining these four techniques in sequence is like walking up the steps of a staircase with each step leading to a higher level of awareness. What makes these four methods especially effective in raising consciousness is that this specific sequence of meditation techniques follows a natural upward progression that occurs within the body. This upward progression is related to the flow of creative energy within the body. Creative energy rises from the lower parts of the body upward and helps to raise consciousness. The four techniques of Progressive Meditation cooperate with and even facilitate this natural raising of creative energy, which in turn assists in raising consciousness.

The raising of consciousness can be symbolized by the image of a ladder. There is an analogy in a previous section that compares the affirmation to a physical ladder that leads you to the rooftop of your awareness, which is the inner silence of contemplation. The most appropriate analogy of a ladder is the symbolism of Jacob's ladder, the Old Testament ladder that Jacob experienced in a dream in which he saw angels descending and ascending from earth to Heaven. Communication with God is like this ladder, which represents the different levels of awareness, from earthly awareness of the physical realm to heavenly awareness of the spiritual realm.

The rungs on Jacob's ladder rise to progressively higher levels of consciousness. Climbing these rungs is accomplished by practicing each of the four steps of Progressive Meditation in sequence. The first level of consciousness is the physical awareness, the second level is emotional awareness, and the third level is mental awareness. The fourth level is unifying awareness. This fourth level coordinates the various levels of your awareness and brings about a certain degree of unification. This unifying awareness helps you to practice contemplation and increasingly reveals your divine oneness with God. Although there are higher rungs, higher levels of consciousness, this explanation only deals with the rungs of the ladder that lead to contemplation.

Communication with God can occur at any one of these levels. However, in order to experience your divine nature, you will need to learn to communicate on all of these levels. The lowest rung of Jacob's ladder is closest to the earth and corresponds to the physical level of your awareness. For your communication with God, this physical level is your starting point that then leads upward in a natural progression to each successive rung of the ladder that extends to Heaven.

To emphasize this point, an Eastern master gave his students a rope tied with a series of knots with no space between each knot. He asked his students to untie the rope. However, he stipulated that they must start to untie the rope in the middle and could not start at the end. The students admitted they could not untie the rope in the middle, but they could untie the rope at one end and then untie each knot in succession until all the knots would be untied. The Eastern master demonstrated to his students by this example that there is a series of steps that need to be completed in a specific sequence in order to make spiritual progress. Skipping the first step in the sequence and attempting to work on a step in the middle of the sequence is a shortcut that will not work.

Like the knot at the end of the rope and like the lowest rung of the ladder that is closest to the earth, the first level of communication with God is physical receptivity, which is learned by Centering Meditation. Then comes emotional receptivity, which is learned by Heart Meditation. This is followed by mental receptivity, which is learned by Brow Meditation.

Why is this sequence so important? It is because the rungs of the ladder and the knots of the rope are actually related to parts of your own physical body. As was well known by the Eastern master in the above story, there are different centers of consciousness in the body that need to be opened and purified in sequence from bottom to top in order to grow spiritually. Three very important centers are related to the navel area, the chest area, and the brow area. In the practice of Progressive Meditation, focusing on these three areas in succession serves as a preparation for practicing Inner Silence Meditation, which leads to contemplation.

Inner Silence Meditation can help you to open yourself to unifying receptivity, which in turn can lead to experiencing contemplation and entering His World. This form of receptivity opens you to allow the separate parts of yourself to not only become integrated so they work together in coordination, but also join together in such a way as to raise your level of awareness of the divine. Indeed, the inner absorption that occurs during contemplation is brought about by a certain degree of unification of your inner faculties produced by divine grace. Your unifying receptivity is needed to provide the invitation to the Holy Spirit to facilitate the raising of your awareness to the contemplative level. All the previously described methods help you to calm and unify the mind. Hopefully your mind will become unified enough for the Holy Spirit to take this unification process to another level, which is the contemplative level that is beyond your control, except for requiring your consent.

What if you have not done enough preparatory work of walking one step at a time up the lower rungs of the ladder of consciousness so you are able to unify to some degree the various levels of your being? In that case, it will probably be less likely for you to be drawn into contemplation. For example, if your first and only method of attempting meditation is Inner Silence Meditation, you may not be properly and fully prepared to be open to contemplation. Your task would be similar to the challenge presented by trying to untie the middle knot in the row of knots in the rope described in the previous analogy.

It's unfortunate that most forms of teaching Christian contemplation exclude any reference to the first knot that needs to be untied, namely the physical level of your being, and to the energy released at this first level. This form of Christian denial leaves out a very important element in preparing for entering contemplation. There are two ways to prepare for contemplation, one originating in the East and the other coming from the West. The one that originated in the East is the unlocking of the subtle creative energy that rises from the lower part of the body. Creative energy rises upward from the lowest end of the spine, which is the location of the "rope of knots" in your body. This rising energy unlocks seven energy centers, considered spiritual centers, in sequence within your body. This sequence of opening these centers of spiritual awareness from the bottom to the top is a natural process and natural progression. With your consent, this natural process is facilitated by the action of the Holy Spirit and can be accelerated by methods focusing on body awareness.

Yoga as a meditation practice in the East is often taught as a way of focusing on these energy centers. In this Eastern approach, meditators typically start by bringing their awareness to the lowest center first, and then progressively moving the awareness to higher energy centers. This upward succession of focusing awakens energy within the body that is purifying and prepares you to become increasingly aware of your spiritual nature. Also included in Eastern spiritual growth is the need to surrender to God, but the central focus is on practicing techniques that assist in awakening higher awareness.

In contrast to the Eastern approach of using techniques to awaken spiritual centers, the way of approaching contemplation that is usually taught in the West places the emphasis on surrendering to the Holy Spirit. Your surrender to the Holy Spirit creates a purifying effect that prepares you for contemplation, leads you into contemplation, and sustains you during contemplation. Most Christian seekers are only exposed to one approach, which in itself can succeed to draw you into deep contemplation. This surrender to the Holy Spirit is usually taught today with a focus on surrendering the mind and without any direct focusing on body awareness or the emotions as a part of this method. This approach to inward seeking, called Centering Prayer, is very similar if not identical to Inner Silence Meditation. Chapter 8 compares Inner Silence Meditation with other methods, such as Centering Prayer.

Thomas Keating has taught Centering Prayer for many years, and he states that he has met many members of contemplative communities who have never actually had the consciously felt experience of mystical graces associated with contemplation.[2] Even after practicing Centering Prayer for many years, some seekers never have the consciously felt experience of the inflowing of the divine presence into their faculties during their contemplative practice. Their persistence is a wonderful and commendable example of manifesting pure faith. Such seekers are certainly rewarded by God for their steadfast practice. The purifying action of the Holy Spirit can enter the faculties of these seekers and eventually bring about an inner transformation without a consciously felt awareness of this process occurring. Nevertheless, in my opinion, those who are seeking to have a conscious experience of contemplation would be much more successful if they started with untying the lower knots first, rather than focusing on trying to untie one of the middle knots in the rope of knots.

The Holy Spirit has the ability to unlock all your inner knots, removing all inner blockages. But the Holy Spirit can only transform you to the degree that you give your permission. If you do not give permission to the Holy Spirit to untie the lower knots of your physical and emotional faculties, then the transformation of your lower faculties will not occur in a holistic way that would prepare you for entering into contemplation. The danger of the Western approach of practicing Centering Prayer (equivalent to Inner Silence Meditation) *exclusively* is that this method of surrender to the Holy Spirit may be too much of a mental approach that only indirectly allows for the transformation of your physical and emotional faculties. Because Centering Prayer does not incorporate bringing your attention directly to important focusing areas in your body, it does not fully prepare you to surrender all of your physical and emotional faculties to the Holy Spirit. The practice of Centering Prayer by itself will to some degree positively influence your physical and emotional faculties. However, meditation methods that focus on areas of the body will have a greater impact on helping you surrender the physical and emotional levels of your being.

Just as there is a danger with the Western approach, there is a danger with the Eastern approach, especially when meditation is not practiced in moderation. The Eastern method of consciously focusing on the centers of awareness in the body from the lowest to the highest has the danger of the seeker allowing his ego to be too much in control. Placing your ego in control of your spiritual growth is like letting the fox guard the chicken coop. There are ways of forcing the creative energy upward that can be caused by self-will, and doing so does not produce the natural purification and integration that is a preparation for contemplation. In fact, some extreme Eastern practices can at times be harmful for your physical, emotional, and mental well-being.

However, this manual emphasizes that both the Eastern approach and the Western approach to contemplation are more effective when combined, and indeed they probably occur together for anyone who is successful at entering the contemplative state of awareness. The Eastern meditator who is successful at raising his creative energy is most certainly assisted by the Spirit within in his process, even if he is not consciously aware of this assistance. Likewise, the successful Western seeker who regularly experiences contemplation through consciously and consistently surrendering to the transforming action of the Holy Spirit will probably not be consciously aware of what is happening at an energy level within his body. Through his surrender he allows the Holy Spirit to bring about the same raising of the creative energy and the same purifying effect that occurs for the Eastern meditator, but perhaps without the conscious awareness of these energy changes.

The advantage of using Progressive Meditation is that this approach combines the best of what the East and the West have to offer. The result is a *synergy*, meaning that the combined effect is greater than the sum of the parts. Just meditating to consciously raise the creative energy or just surrendering to the Holy Spirit are not nearly as effective when practiced alone as they are when practiced together. By combining four techniques, Progressive Meditation produces a holistic effect that joins all the levels of your being and is your best preparation for entering contemplation.

The experience of contemplation itself may be considered as a state of spiritual unification brought about by the overshadowing of the Holy Spirit. Before being ready to enter this spiritual unification, you will need to make a certain degree of progress toward unifying yourself at all the levels below the spiritual level. Your request of the Holy Spirit to transform you by bringing you into the contemplative state of unification cannot be merely a mental request. Making a mental decision of the intellect alone, no matter how firm or sincere, can only carry the weight of the mental level of your being. To increase the effectiveness of your invitation to the Holy Spirit, your request will require a certain degree of experiential wholeheartedness. Since a house divided cannot stand, all the levels of your being need to be speaking with one voice, requesting the incoming of the Holy Spirit. There needs to be a certain degree of integration between the physical, emotional, and mental levels of your being in order to make a wholehearted invitation for the Holy Spirit to open you to higher consciousness.

Progressive Meditation is recommended as a way to invite the Holy Spirit into the physical, emotional, mental, and unifying levels of your being. When the first three techniques of this sequence of methods are combined, a creative energy rises within the body, bringing about a purifying effect, an integration, and a sense of oneness. The integration and unification of the various levels of your being serve as a solid foundation necessary for entering into the higher consciousness of contemplation. Such a foundation of stability will be necessary before proceeding into the uncertainty of the unknown, relying only on pure faith during the experience of contemplation.

Having acquired this solid foundation then prepares you to be open to revealing your true spiritual nature. The fourth method, Inner Silence Meditation, can be practiced without this foundation, but is much more effective with it. For that reason the combination of four techniques in Progressive Meditation is recommended as a method that would benefit anyone seeking to enter into contemplation.

The process of learning to go into inner silence during Inner Silence Meditation may not be easy to learn. Therefore, it is recommended that initially you only set aside a few minutes at the end of Progressive Meditation in order to gradually expose yourself to experiencing the inner silence for brief periods of time. After being successful at this, you may choose to increase the amount of time for inner silence. Eventually most of your Progressive Meditation practice may consist of this inner silence in which contemplation takes place.

This experience of dwelling in inner silence during contemplation opens your subconscious mind, which allows unresolved thoughts and feelings that were previously hidden to be revealed so you can release them. You will also have to deal with the ordinary ego-based thoughts and feelings that accumulate every day. The long-standing thoughts and feelings that surface from the past as well as the daily parade of thoughts need to be processed in contemplation in the same way: You need to let them pass by in your mind through practicing nonattachment—having no desire to keep these thoughts and having no desire to ward off these thoughts.

Likewise, you may experience various unusual experiences during your opening to contemplation, in which you are overshadowed by the Holy Spirit. These unusual experiences may be sensations, emotions, or other by-products of meditation and contemplation. These experiences are to be released just as any other stray thoughts are released. It is recommended that you neither invite unusual experiences by attraction nor push them away by aversion. The best way to respond is to let go of these experiences in the same way that you let go of any thoughts that float by in the mind without paying any particular attention to them.

During the practice of Progressive Meditation, an arbitrary decision cannot be made on how long each of the four techniques should be employed. The timing of when to switch from one technique to the next technique is an individual matter to be decided intuitively. As your experience with Progressive Meditation increases, you may find that one particular technique is especially helpful and effective, so you can increase the amount of time for that technique and reduce the time for the other techniques. If Progressive Meditation becomes your regular form of meditation, your meditation experience will deepen. Then you might feel comfortable increasing the time for Inner Silence Meditation, which will lead you into contemplation.

However, Inner Silence Meditation is not the only technique during which contemplation can occur. In fact, contemplation may happen spontaneously during any meditation practice if there is an openness for this to happen. The spontaneous occurrence of contemplation that sometimes occurs during the practice of body awareness techniques is described in Chapters 7 and 10.

---

1. Psalm 46:10.
2. Thomas Keating, *Open Heart, Open Mind: The Contemplative Dimension of the Gospel* (New York, NY: The Continuum International Publishing Group, 2001), Copyright 1986, 1992 by St. Benedict's Monastery, reprinted by permission of The Continuum International Publishing Group, p. 11.

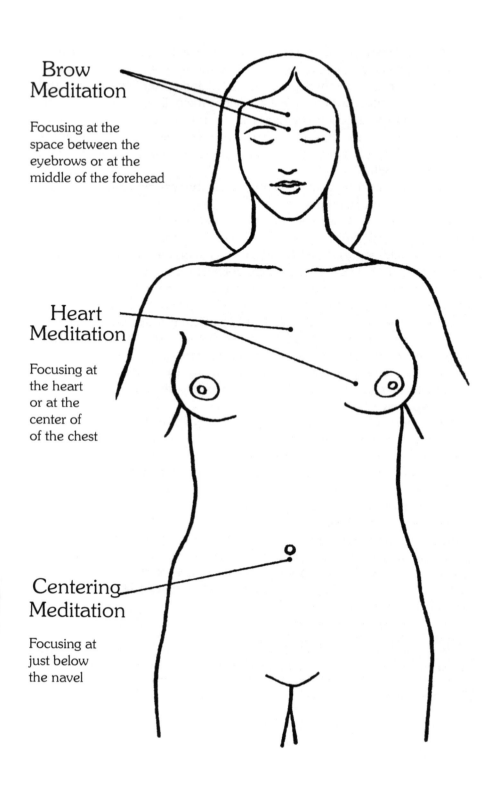

Brow Meditation

Focusing at the space between the eyebrows or at the middle of the forehead

Heart Meditation

Focusing at the heart or at the center of of the chest

Centering Meditation

Focusing at just below the navel

6

THE TWENTY-EIGHT DAY DEMONSTRATION

~ o ~

A. The First Three Days

The Twenty-eight Day Demonstration is recommended as a means of demonstrating your intention to increase your awareness of the divine presence within. The previous two chapters provided descriptions of four meditation techniques and how to combine these in the practice of Progressive Meditation. The following sections in this chapter provide an outline of how to proceed in a systematic way that will allow you to experience these meditation techniques.

For the first three days of the Twenty-eight Day Demonstration, you practice only Centering Meditation. For this meditation method, you hold the awareness at the area just below the navel. You repeat the first half of your chosen affirmation on the inhalation and repeat the second half on the exhalation. You allow the breathing to be normal and relaxed. When the mind becomes calm, you can let go of focusing on your affirmation and breathing and just focus on the navel area. If the mind wanders because of stray thoughts, you can gently return to focusing on your affirmation in coordination with your breathing while also holding your focus on the navel area.

B. The Fourth, Fifth, and Sixth Days

For the fourth, fifth, and sixth days, you employ only Heart Meditation, in which the awareness is focused in the heart or in the center of the chest. You coordinate the affirmation with the breathing as previously described. You can let go of focusing on the affirmation and breathing if the mind becomes calm and only focus on the heart or center of the chest. If you become distracted by stray thoughts, you can return to your affirmation and breathing along with your focus in the heart or the center of the chest.

C. The Seventh, Eighth, and Ninth Days

For the seventh, eighth, and ninth days, you practice only Brow Meditation, in which the focus of awareness is in the brow area and the affirmation and breathing are coordinated in the same way as the previous methods. When your mind becomes calm, you let go of focusing on the affirmation and breathing and only focus on the brow area. If your mind becomes distracted by stray thoughts, you can return to focusing on your affirmation and breathing while continuing to focus on the brow area.

D. The Tenth, Eleventh, and Twelfth Days

For the tenth, eleventh, and twelfth days, you employ a short version of Progressive Meditation, which includes only the first three methods used in the following sequence: Centering Meditation, Heart Meditation, and Brow Meditation. For these three days, you do not use Inner Silence Meditation, the fourth method of Progressive Meditation. While practicing this short version of Progressive Meditation, you decide intuitively when to make the switch from one method to the next.

E. The Thirteenth and Thereafter

The first thirteen days are designed to familiarize you with the first three basic methods of Progressive Meditation that use body awareness. For the remainder of the Twenty-eight Day Demonstration you practice the complete version of Progressive Meditation, which is the combination of all four of the techniques, including Inner Silence Meditation. You incorporate body awareness while using the first three techniques in the following sequence: Centering Meditation, Heart Meditation, and Brow Meditation. Then for your fourth and final method, you let go of body awareness to practice Inner Silence Meditation. All four techniques of Progressive Meditation involve the use of an affirmation. While using Progressive Meditation, you decide intuitively when to make the switch from one method to the next.

A method that may initially be difficult for you to practice is Inner Silence Meditation, which is more advanced than methods that use body awareness. It may take time to learn how to practice letting go of the affirmation and entering into inner silence. Initially when you practice Progressive Meditation, you may want to limit the amount of time you use Inner Silence Meditation. As you feel more comfortable using Inner Silence Meditation, you may increase the time for its usage and reduce the time for using the three techniques that use body awareness.

The detailed structure provided previously for the Twenty-eight Day Demonstration is designed only as a guideline. Please feel that you have the freedom to make any adjustments that will meet your individual needs. Whether you are a beginner or an experienced meditator, you need to be sensitive to the inner prompting of the Holy Spirit in how you apply what is presented here. For example, in the procedures for meditation outlined in Chapter 2, there are many optional choices to be considered, so you need to decide inwardly what feels right for you based on your guidance. Even the procedures and structures in this book that are not specifically identified as "optional" are in fact optional in the sense that you will need to exercise your free will option to use or not use any procedure or structure based on your being guided primarily by the Holy Spirit.

If you discover that a certain method or aspect of meditation is quite difficult for you, that difficulty may be a blessing in disguise. Since you are venturing into His World, where the self is losing control, the self may try to convince you to avoid areas of growth that would be difficult but very beneficial. During the Twenty-eight Day Demonstration, you will need to discern when you have a true spiritual prompting, which needs to be followed, even if it is perhaps a deviation from the precise structure provided here. You will also need to discern when the self is seeking to express some resistance to change or fear, or a desire to avoid aspects of the demonstration that are difficult challenges, but are areas where you really need to grow.

F. The Beginner's Challenge

If you are a beginner, your primary challenge will be to develop the ability to focus the mind, which at first will be like a wild horse that has not been tamed. Every time the mind wanders, and it will countless times, you will need to gently bring it back to your chosen affirmation. You can let your wandering mind be just a reminder to return to the affirmation. If you refocus your mind every time you notice it has wandered, then your meditation will deepen. But sometimes you may notice that the mind has wandered and instead of refocusing immediately, you will judge yourself for having allowed your mind to wander. The wandering mind itself is a problem for every meditator, yet it becomes a much greater problem if you focus on it as a problem rather than refocusing on the affirmation.

You are accustomed to solving problems by evaluating them, but in this case *the evaluating itself is the problem*. Of course, very little meditation can be occurring if you let yourself evaluate how well you are meditating by judging yourself in the process. Regardless of whether you are evaluating yourself positively or negatively, self-evaluating thoughts are the self's way of remaining in control. Self-evaluating thoughts that attempt to judge your meditation experience, just like any other distracting thoughts, need to simply be a reminder to return to your affirmation. It takes an effort of the will to control the mind, but it needs to be an unstrained effort that relies on the affirmation and God's grace.

During your meditation practice, thoughts cannot be considered as good or bad for that gives them power to affect you. If you think some thoughts are good, such as special insights, even spiritual insights, then you will encourage and entertain them in your mind and leave your purpose of seeking God alone. If you think some thoughts are bad, such as memories of past mistakes, you will judge yourself for having such thoughts and leave your purpose of seeking God. You need to be neutral toward your thoughts so you do not encourage them by attraction and you do not attempt to push them away by aversion. Both attraction and aversion create inner tension that prevents the mind from becoming calm.

Every mind is filled with thoughts. Normally these thoughts follow a progression so that one thought leads to another. The goal of the beginner cannot be to stop this sequence of thoughts from occurring. As thoughts float by in your mind one after another in sequence, the passing thoughts themselves do not have the power to interfere with your meditation practice. It is possible for you to be in deep meditation or contemplation and be undisturbed by this parade of thoughts.

To explain how thoughts can be passing through your mind without disturbing your practice, think of professional athletes who say that they are in a "zone" when they are at the top of their game. When in this zone, they can tune everything out, except their role in the game. For example, a good hitter in professional baseball will stand at home plate with his bat cocked as he waits for the baseball to come his way. Thousands of screaming fans may be in the stands, yet because he is not paying attention to these fans, their sounds recede from his awareness. These sounds register in his consciousness as background noise, but do not entirely disappear from his awareness. The hitter does not pay attention to this background noise because his mind is locked in only to the flight of the ball as it heads toward home plate. Just as the good hitter can place his whole attention on the ball and allow the sounds of the fans to recede in his mind, you can learn to place your whole attention in faith on your divine intention. As you focus on your divine intention only, you can allow the passing thoughts to recede from your conscious awareness by not paying attention to them.

Becoming a good hitter takes time, patience, and practice. Similarly, learning to have a single-minded focus in meditation takes time, patience, and practice. Therefore, if you are a beginner in meditation, you will not be able to completely tune out the passing thoughts of the mind. You will find yourself noticing a particular thought, and instead of letting it pass by, you will have *a thought about that thought*, which means you have become distracted. Then you may even judge yourself for being distracted, which causes more distraction. When you become aware of your distracting thoughts, you will need to learn to have a single response. Your single response to distracting thoughts will need to be reminding yourself to gently return to your affirmation.

If you are a beginner, you will need to accept distraction as an ongoing and necessary part of your learning experience. In fact, your meditation will invariably be a process of repeating your affirmation followed by distracting thoughts. It would be unrealistic for you as a beginner to expect any more than this repeated thought pattern of your affirmation followed by distracting thoughts. When you make progress at practicing Inner Silence Meditation, your repeated pattern will hopefully have three distinct parts in the following sequence: Part one would be your affirmation. Part two would be inner silence. Part three would be distracting thoughts. Your distracting thoughts would simply remind you to return to the affirmation to start the whole pattern over again.

Consequently, even as you make progress you will still find yourself in the process of refocusing the mind. Much of the benefit of this refocusing is not in what you are refocusing to, which is your affirmation, but in the act of patiently refocusing itself. If this refocusing is done properly with a light touch, it is a continuous exercise in nonattachment. You are learning to let go. Ultimately your desire for God is a desire to let go of the false self. Your refocusing is a process of letting go of the false self by letting go of your thoughts one at a time. The cumulative effect is that you are no longer held fast in the grip of the false self, which itself is simply a collection of false thoughts about who you are. While you cannot let go of all thoughts, you can let go of your attachment to them. As you develop detachment from your inner thoughts, you may discover this detachment carrying over into your daily life, so you develop *equanimity* in which you are not disturbed by the highs and lows of everyday life.

Even though dealing with the wandering mind is the major challenge for the beginner, you need to remember that your meditation is not a demonstration of how well you can control the mind. It is a demonstration of your intention and commitment to seek God. Even if you can make only limited progress in controlling the mind, you have still set your heart's desire on God, and in doing so have reached beyond your world and into His World. It is the self that wants magnificent results. As you apply your will to focus the mind, you can safely place your trust in God and leave the results to Him.

If you choose to make a firm commitment to daily meditation for twenty-eight days, then your commitment needs to be based on pure faith without expectations. Your pure faith tells you He will respond to your desire to deepen your relationship with Him. Indeed, your pure faith during meditation aids you in being open to receiving His response of love. But your expectancy for His response can only remain pure if you have no expectations for Him to respond in any specific way you have chosen. The effects of meditation are often subtle and not immediately noticeable to the beginner. Thus you need to trust that He is responding to you, even when there is no apparent outward manifestation of His response.

G. Commitment

The Twenty-eight Day Demonstration is your opportunity to make a commitment to deepening your relationship with God and to put your commitment into practical application through the practice of daily meditation. For this commitment you will need to set aside a minimum of one twenty-five-minute period each day. But it would be preferable to set aside two such periods, perhaps one in the morning before breakfast and another one at some time before dinner. Another option is to meditate before bedtime, if tiredness is not a problem for you in the evening.

Your world may be very busy and finding time, or rather making time, to enter into His World may seem difficult, but it is necessary if you truly want to deepen your relationship with God. You may think of it in terms of the way a relationship develops between a man and a woman. If you feel the relationship is important, you adjust your world to accommodate the needed time. At first, you only need a little time to get to know one another. Then you expand this time if you really want to know each other at a deeper, more intimate level.

As you deepen your human relationship with another person, you notice your world overlaps into the other person's world and the other person's world overlaps into your world. Your relationship with God is different, but also has some overlapping. When you enter His World, you must leave your world, because your world cannot overlap His World. As you go deeper into His World in meditation and then return to your world, you discover a curious thing—that His World completely overlaps and interpenetrates your world. Also, you realize that He, the silent One, has been quietly in your world all along, yet you had been blind to His presence. Consequently, you learn to see two realities— the everyday reality you live in, which is a "physical, emotional, and mental world," and His Reality, which is a "spiritual world" that is the source and substance of your world.

This is more than merely a new intellectual viewpoint, because it has a practical application to your life. After entering His World, you come back to your world with a new awareness that allows you to bring forth His hidden presence into your world. The result is that you allow Him to be the master of your life in your world. There are many benefits to practicing meditation, both those that may come to your conscious awareness and those that you may not consciously realize. But the most significant result of your inner practice is the effect that it produces in your everyday life. Deepening your contact with the divine within allows His loving presence to flow through you into your everyday world and relationships expressed through a life of service.

H. Application

A wise old gentleman who had meditated for many years told me that there are three rules for meditation, which are as follows:

> The first rule is "sit."
> The second rule is "sit."
> The third rule is "sit."

There is a vast difference between *intellectual understanding* and *wisdom*. If you acquire intellectual understanding, but do not apply that understanding to your daily life, then your understanding is useless intellectual theory. On the other hand, if you put the understanding you receive into practical application in your life, then the result is wisdom. This is true especially about the understanding of meditation, since meditation itself is not a theory—it is a practical experience.

The purpose of this book is to supply you with understanding, yet it is up to you to decide if you want to apply that understanding and transform it into wisdom. The most important kind of wisdom worth having is the awareness of God's presence felt inwardly and expressed outwardly. The Twenty-eight Day Demonstration will enable you to put the understanding you have received into practical application.

Some of what has been expressed here has only been explained partially and will be elaborated upon later. Thus, in order to expand your understanding of meditation, it would be helpful for you to read this entire manual. But right now you already have acquired in these first six chapters all of the understanding that you need to begin the Twenty-eight Day Demonstration. In particular, if you are a beginner, this will be your opportunity to conduct this demonstration of your desire and commitment to open yourself to God's presence within.

Likewise, if you already have experience with meditation, the practical experience gained through using the techniques in this demonstration will serve as a solid foundation for growing toward contemplation.

If you are considering whether or not to make a commitment to conducting the Twenty-eight Day Demonstration, you are encouraged to turn to God in prayer and ask Him if conducting this demonstration would be helpful for you. If you do decide to conduct the Twenty-eight Day Demonstration, this demonstration of your commitment to spiritual growth will help you to become more aware of God's presence in whatever way He might choose to increase your awareness.

I. Preparations for the Twenty-eight Day Demonstration

1. COMMITMENT— Before beginning, you will need to decide if you are willing to make a commitment to meditate every day for twenty-eight days.

2. TIMING — You will need to decide the exact time when you want to meditate for a minimum commitment of one twenty-five-minute period at the same time each day. If you decide to make a deeper commitment, you can choose two twenty-five-minute periods each day—for example, one in the morning before breakfast and one sometime before dinner.

3. PLACE — It is important to choose a quiet place to sit and to use the same place each day.

4. POSTURE — You may decide to sit in a chair. You may prefer to sit on a folded blanket or a pillow in a cross-legged position on the floor. You can choose whatever sitting posture and whatever hand position is most comfortable for you. Before beginning to meditate, you will need to check your posture to make sure that your spine is in proper alignment.

5. SETTING THE IDEAL AND THE MENTAL ATTITUDE — You will need to choose your spiritual ideal, and then choose a mental attitude that will help you grow toward your ideal. You may want to write both of these down on paper for the sake of clarity. You will need to select an affirmation, which may be a word or a brief combination of words, such as a form of the Divine Name, that will represent your spiritual ideal or remind you of your ideal.

6. SCHEDULE — Before following this schedule, make sure you have reviewed and clearly understood the detailed directions given for how to practice these techniques that are described in the previous two chapters.

a. The First Three Days —

- Centering Meditation exclusively

b. The Fourth, Fifth, and Sixth Days —

- Heart Meditation exclusively

c. The Seventh, Eighth, and Ninth Days —

- Brow Meditation exclusively

d. The Tenth, Eleventh, and Twelfth Days —
You employ a short version of Progressive Meditation, which includes only the first three methods in the following sequence:

- Centering Meditation
- Heart Meditation
- Brow Meditation

e. The Thirteenth and Thereafter —
You employ the complete version of Progressive Meditation, consisting of the following sequence of all four techniques:

- Centering Meditation
- Heart Meditation
- Brow Meditation
- Inner Silence Meditation

7. STARTING DATE — You will need to decide when you are going to begin the first day of the Twenty-eight Day Demonstration.

J. Daily Procedures for Each Meditation Period

1. CLEANSING (optional) — You will need to approach meditation with the understanding that this is a purification process in which the self is being emptied so there may be greater receptivity to the Spirit. Although it is not necessary, some meditators choose to perform an outward form of cleansing, such as drinking a small amount of water or taking a shower, as a symbol of this cleansing process.

2. RELAXATION (optional) — Before starting your meditation, you may want to employ a relaxation method of your choosing. Some examples are relaxing the body with mental suggestions, doing head and neck exercises, practicing yoga postures, or using yoga breathing practices.

3. DEDICATION (optional) — You may want to dedicate your meditation by inwardly stating your spiritual ideal and the mental attitude that will help you grow toward your ideal.

4. PREPARATORY PRAYER (optional) — You may offer a spontaneous or formal prayer to help turn the mind and heart in the direction of becoming quiet and to invite the incoming of the Holy Spirit. If desired, you can imagine the body to be surrounded and filled with white light.

5. MEDITATION — For the Twenty-eight Day Demonstration, you will use the method or methods of meditation appropriate for the day on which you are meditating. In general, for all meditation techniques, you will close the eyes and mentally repeat the affirmation of your choice. You will want to be sure that the breathing is normal and relaxed. You allow thoughts to pass by in the mind without paying any attention to them. You can let go of your affirmation when your mind becomes calm. If your mind becomes distracted by stray thoughts, you allow the distraction to be a gentle reminder to return to repeating your affirmation.

6. COMPLETION OF MEDITATION (optional) — After your meditation ends, you may want to restate your spiritual ideal and mental purpose and/or offer any spontaneous prayers for yourself or others. To complete your meditation, you may want to use a bowing forward gesture. It is best to remain seated for a minute or so, and then get up slowly and gently without disturbing your peace.

7. WITHHOLD JUDGMENT — It is very important to set aside any judgments about the depth of your meditation experience and also to release any expectations of specific results you want to see happen. You need to be willing to patiently wait the full twenty-eight days before evaluating your meditation practice and trust that, whatever happens, God is guiding you and will meet your deepest, truest needs in the way that is most appropriate for you.

PART TWO

~ . ~

GUIDELINES FOR DEEPENING MEDITATION

7

AFTER THE
TWENTY-EIGHT DAY
DEMONSTRATION

≈ ● ≈

A. Evaluating with Faith

The Twenty-eight Day Demonstration is a way to express your intention to become increasingly aware of God as a living reality within your being. However, once you have completed the demonstration, how can you be sure that you have contacted God's presence within you? There are many rational arguments to prove the existence of God's presence within you. Nevertheless, none of these intellectual proofs will convince you fully, since the mind can only have concepts about God. The rational mind cannot experience God.

I ask you to evaluate your twenty-eight days of meditation by faith. Even your rational mind will have to acknowledge that something was happening in meditation beyond the thinking mind's ability to grasp. Although you may be like most people who have difficulty controlling the wandering thoughts of the mind, your meditation experience will tell you there is still something occurring deep within that can only be experienced by faith. Your faith encourages you to start meditating, helps you to recognize the value of meditation, and inspires you to continue meditating on a daily basis.

What is faith? Faith is an inner knowing without intellectual proof of the rational mind. When you have an inner feeling and an inner knowing about something that proves to be true, you call this an "intuition." How then is intuition different than faith? They are not different except to say that faith is the highest form of intuition. Intuitions can be described as inner feelings. But faith is too exalted of an intuition to be called an inner feeling. A certain kind of intuition may tell you spontaneously to visit a friend one day, and you may discover that your friend very much needed your help at that particular time. Faith differs from this sort of inner knowing in that it is directed toward the source itself of all intuition. In other words, when your intuition is focused on God Himself, you can call that faith. The very fact of turning toward God is faith. Why would you turn to God unless somewhere inside of yourself you know that He is there? Faith is simply this inner knowing that says, "He is there." Your inner knowing of the divine presence may be called your *faithful awareness*. This awareness is elaborated upon later in this chapter in Section D titled "Inner Silence Meditation."

However, faith is not a matter of just saying, "I believe God is in me." Mental belief is only the result of faith. Faith is a matter of inner trusting. If you have ever trusted another person, you know that this is a matter of the heart and not the head. Yet what if you feel that you have only a little faith? Perhaps your faith is only a mental belief, which may contain some doubts about God's presence. You do not need to be discouraged or allow this to be a stumbling block for your meditation. The only way to increase your faith is to express what little faith you do have, along with your doubts, and know that God accepts you right where you are in this moment. You can follow the example of the man who was asked by Jesus about his faith, and he responded, "I believe; help my unbelief!"[1]

Faith is trusting in what is not seen. If it is not seen, it is in doubt. In most cases, for faith to be present so must doubt also be present. Thus there cannot be faith without doubt by which faith is tested. It is true that some individuals overcome their doubts and are blessed by God with a faith that is an inner knowing without doubt. But for most individuals, the development of faith is a gradual learning experience that includes doubts. Consequently, God does not require you to have a faith without doubts. He only asks you to express whatever faith you have already been given as a foundation to build upon in order to increase your faith.

Practicing meditation is a practical way of expressing your faithful awareness that God is present within you. An important characteristic of your faith that enables you to reach into His World during meditation is that it requires no experience on your part to confirm His presence. Not seeking an experience, but rather allowing God Himself to remain the object of your faith is expressed by waiting for Him in meditation and emptying yourself of any expectations of how He might respond to produce an experience in you. But there is hardly a beginning meditator who does not carry within himself a hidden fantasy of being filled with some great light and raised up to God's presence in a wave of bliss.

However, in the everyday practice of meditation, you may experience nothing happening, boredom, passing disharmonious feelings, scattered thoughts throughout, and a whole range of ordinary responses. Precisely because you seek God's presence in faith, knowing that He is there, these impressions and responses test your faith. You have to accept the fact that you still have the mask of self to deal with and its diversions that would carry you away from expressing your faith. Yet it is your faith that tells you by inner knowing that, in spite of appearances, you are reaching beyond your momentary responses and diversions in meditation to the place where you are truly one with God.

It is true that some meditators do at times feel the divine presence as a conscious experience of heightened awareness, but not the awareness of intellectual thinking. This conscious experience may come to your awareness as inner feelings, which are described in detail in Chapter 10, along with a description of ways of opening to these inner feelings. Nevertheless, whether you have a conscious experience or not, your meditation practice fosters within you an inner receptivity to the divine presence. Your meditation itself is not merely a technique of affirmation. More importantly, it is also an *invitation* for God to fully permeate your subconscious mind and allow His Will of love to be done in you and through you. Even though your meditation practice may seem to be scattered to your conscious awareness, your faith confirms that your loving Father cannot refuse to accept your invitation. At first you may have only a provisional faith, which is merely an openness to God's presence. However, through the repeated practice of meditation, your faith will gradually grow as you learn to trust in His unseen presence.

Your faith may not be great, but if it is pure, it is pleasing to God. I know a woman who is a good example of faithfully seeking God with a pure intention. While meditating, she can hardly go for a few minutes without her mind wandering. Therefore, she always feels she is miles away from God. I asked how long she had been meditating, and she said she had been practicing daily meditation for over five years. Many people get discouraged when they cannot control the mind and, lacking perseverance, they stop meditating. I asked her why she has steadfastly continued when she feels so blocked in her meditation experience. She had a very simple response: "Because it's the only thing that matters!" Then she paused and added, "If I have God, I have everything."

When I told her what a wonderful example of faith she presented by persevering all these years, she responded that she didn't feel she had a deep faith. She said she lacked that inner sense of feeling God's presence, and what little faith she had was based mostly on a mental belief in God. Nonetheless, it seems to me that the depth of your faith is proven by your willingness to act on whatever amount of faith God has given to you. What greater faith or love can you express than waiting for your Beloved year after year as this woman has done? Your faith tells you He is there and that He will come, and your love is your desire for Him to come.

It is your faith that says, "Yes, You are in me and I am in You," when everything in your world says, "No." Through your faith you are able to give up expectations of what you can get out of your meditation so you can have purity of heart and seek Him alone beyond appearances.

Faith is the best way to evaluate your meditation experience, but there is another significant means of evaluating your practice. You can look at the effects that your practice produces in your daily life. You may find that you are more peaceful and your thinking is clearer. But the most important outer sign of progress is an increased ability to cooperate with others and extend love to others. A dramatic change in your expression of love may not be noticeable after the Twenty-eight Day Demonstration. Nonetheless, learning to be more loving will be the long-term effect of ongoing daily meditation practice. By focusing on improving your relationship with God in meditation, you will naturally find that your personal relationships with others will also improve. Meditation itself may appear to be a solitary experience between yourself and God alone, yet it is actually a way of joining with others, who have the same center in God as you do. Thus learning to love God automatically means learning to love your brothers and sisters in whom God is equally present. Your relationships therefore become your means of determining how much progress you are making in regard to your seeking of God.

B. Continuing to Practice Meditation

When the Twenty-eight Day Demonstration is completed, your faith will guide you in being able to judge for yourself if you want to continue to practice meditation. If you decide to continue to meditate, you will become either an intermittent meditator or a daily meditator. Those who meditate intermittently usually find it difficult to increase the depth of their meditation experience. In fact, they are often not able to maintain the stillness of mind that they achieved through daily meditation during the demonstration. An intermittent meditator is like a person who is trying to drill a well by continually moving around and drilling many holes, without ever drilling deep enough to find water. But if that person would spend the time necessary to stay in one place and drill deep enough, he would succeed.

Likewise, if you want to go deep within to reach the "living water" of your spiritual depths, it is necessary to make a commitment to meditation as a daily experience. It's like brushing your teeth. You don't debate with yourself every day over whether you should or should not brush your teeth. You just do it. It's a habit. It's part of your daily routine since you feel it's necessary, and you have made a commitment to yourself to do it.

A world-famous musician was asked if he still had to practice on a daily basis after becoming so accomplished in his art. The musician answered that when he missed even one day of practice, he noticed the difference. When he missed two days, the critics noticed the difference. When he missed three days, the audience noticed the difference.

To be really effective, growth in meditation must be a continuous process, because the effects of meditation are cumulative and produce a gradual deepening of meditation. A meditation practice of twenty-five minutes twice a day is recommended. Yet if twice a day is too much of a commitment, then one twenty-five-minute meditation period per day is the minimum commitment needed to make continuous progress in deepening your meditation. Another option is to meditate twice a day on weekdays when there is more tension due to the stress of work, and meditate one time per day on the weekends. The best time to start your commitment to daily meditation is immediately after the end of the Twenty-eight Day Demonstration. This is because you already are experiencing the benefits, and you have the habit and conditioning going for you, so it's easy to just keep right on going.

After making this commitment, then you have to decide what you would like to use as your own regular form of meditation. If you want to use one consistent practice as your continuous approach to meditation, Progressive Meditation is recommended. This combination of three body awareness techniques followed by Inner Silence Meditation has been described already, but a more detailed explanation of these techniques is provided below in case you would like to continue with Progressive Meditation as your ongoing practice.

For Christian seekers the goal of all meditation techniques is to go beyond techniques in order to enter into contemplation in which you are overshadowed by the Holy Spirit. With this in mind, you need to consider what techniques will prepare you for contemplation. Since Inner Silence Meditation is the most effective means of leading you to contemplation, it is best to grow in the direction of using this technique increasingly over time. But other methods can be used to prepare you to make Inner Silence Meditation more effective. Progressive Meditation is recommended as your ongoing meditation practice because the three body awareness techniques combined with Inner Silence Meditation in this method lead you to proceed one step at a time up the ladder of your awareness toward contemplation. This internal ladder of awareness is symbolized by the image of Jacob's ladder that stretches from earth to Heaven. As your meditation deepens, you may find yourself reducing the time for the first three methods and expanding the time for Inner Silence Meditation, which will lead to contemplation.

However, instead of practicing Progressive Meditation as an ongoing practice, you can climb the ladder of your awareness in a slightly different way. Rather than using all of these techniques together in one practice, you can use these same techniques separately for a month at a time in order to go to a deeper level with each individual method. After first going to a deeper level with individual techniques by using them exclusively for a month at a time, you can then combine them in the practice of Progressive Meditation and find that your overall meditation deepens.

When using individual techniques exclusively for one month at a time and then combining them, it is important to follow a particular sequence that would best help you climb the ladder of your awareness, leading to contemplation. This particular sequence is:

- Centering Meditation for the first month
- Heart Meditation for the second month
- Brow Meditation for the third month
- Inner Silence Meditation for the fourth month
- Progressive Meditation for the fifth month
- Decide what method to use thereafter

After having practiced Centering Meditation for the first month, Heart Meditation for the second month, Brow Meditation for the third month, and Inner Silence Meditation for the fourth month, your practice of Progressive Meditation for the fifth month will be enhanced. This will be the beneficial result of the previous four months of using each of the four techniques of Progressive Meditation separately. Then you can make an informed decision on what meditation practice you would like to use on an ongoing basis.

After completing your Twenty-eight Day Demonstration, you may want to continue with Progressive Meditation as your daily practice, or you may decide to experiment for a while with different methods. For example, you may want to practice Inner Listening Meditation, which is described later in this chapter. There are additional methods described later in this manual for your consideration. For instance, Chapter 11 explains how to practice Inner Light Meditation, Expanded Progressive Meditation, and Inner Love Meditation, which are methods that help you to open to the inner feelings of light and love. Once you have found what technique feels right for you, then stay with your choice for as long as you feel guided to do so.

There are many possible ways in which you may be prompted to practice meditation. Once you have firmly established your spiritual ideal, preferably in Christ, and your mental attitude, such as doing God's Will, then the application of your ideal will become apparent. The Spirit within you knows your individual needs and will show you what methods would be most helpful for you and how to use them and when to let go of them. Each technique that you use may be seen as a bridge that leads from one area of development to another. Because the bridge is used only for crossing, it is just a means to an end and must be left behind in order to make progress. You need to be careful not to allow techniques to become ends in themselves. The single most important thing to remember about techniques is that their main purpose is to help you to be receptive to a greater awareness of the Holy Spirit and the love that the Spirit would enkindle in you. In your future growth, allow your inner guidance to draw you in the direction that would be best for your development.

C. Body Awareness Methods for Receptivity

The first three methods of Progressive Meditation are body awareness methods, which work together to create inner harmony and increase your receptivity to the Spirit. You are truly a spiritual being. Your true Self is the core of your being where you are one with God, Who is the source of your existence. The nature of your true Self is love, just as God Himself is love. But your true Self, which may be called your Christ Self, is clouded over by the doing self that is identified with the body and mind, though not with your spiritual source in God. Your spiritual growth is dependent on your willingness to give over the functions of the self to the Spirit so that the self may be a servant of God's Will of love. The self has three basic aspects that need to be surrendered to the Spirit. These are the physical aspect, the emotional aspect, and the mental aspect. The self has selfish desires for using each of these aspects. You need to train the self to release these selfish desires and become receptive to allowing the Spirit to control these functions so your desires originate from your true nature of love. Even though you may consciously want to surrender the physical, emotional, and mental desires of the self to the Spirit, you may have difficulty in letting go of the inner tension that selfish desires have created within you.

The Spirit always acts on you to create integration and wholeness by filling you with God's Love and helping you to be aware of your own love nature. However, inner blocks reduce your receptivity, which limits the amount of love you can accept into your conscious awareness. Your receptivity to the Spirit is blocked by inner tension originating from selfish desires. Meditation may be considered as a method of helping you to become inwardly relaxed so you can let go of physical, emotional, and mental tension, yet the process of relaxing to let go of tension is not as easy as it may sound. As a beginner, you may be aware of only the relaxing and calming effects of meditation in your initial experiences with meditation. Later in your development, you may deepen your meditation and become more sensitive to inner tension and the process of its removal.

In your everyday life when you make unloving choices, you create disharmony within yourself. What's the result? Tension is produced within the body, emotions, and thoughts. This is where the term "disease" comes from, because it is a combination of "dis" and "ease," meaning not being at ease. Long after you may have forgotten specific unloving choices, the resulting tension remains at an inner level of which you are normally not aware. Some of this tension comes from childhood experiences that remain in the subconscious mind. Meditation increases your awareness and allows you to become aware of the inner tension you have created. To correct the effect of past unloving responses that created this inner tension, meditation lets you to experience this tension with a loving awareness produced by your receptivity to the Spirit.

In practical terms this means that as your meditation experience deepens, it is not always peaceful. Rather, it is a dynamic process that allows tension to surface so it can be faced and then released. Tension may appear to the conscious mind at the physical level as unusual body sensations, at the emotional level as unexpected emotions, or at the mental level as uncommon thought impressions. When such symptoms of tension reach your conscious awareness as meditation deepens, you learn to let go of this tension and continue with your meditation practice that allows the Spirit to penetrate, heal, and control the physical, the emotional, and the mental aspects of yourself.

Tension and selfish desires that cause tension are associated with various parts of the body. Physical desires that cause physical tension are primarily, though certainly not exclusively, related to the generative functions and to the lower part of the body. Emotional desires that cause emotional tension are generally related to feelings associated with personal relationships and to the heart area. Mental desires that cause mental tension are usually related to the rational thinking process and the head.

The first three techniques of Progressive Meditation, which are Centering Meditation, Heart Meditation, and Brow Meditation, are designed to systematically focus on each of these parts of the body. The purpose is to focus on the lower part to develop *physical receptivity*, to focus on the heart area to develop *emotional receptivity*, and to focus on the head to develop *mental receptivity* to the Spirit.

In order to do this in a step-by-step fashion, these first three methods of Progressive Meditation include three specific focusing areas, which are the navel area (actually just below the navel), the heart area (in the heart or in the center of the chest), and the brow area (the space between the eyebrows or forehead area). Meditating at each of these focusing areas helps to produce receptivity to the action of the Holy Spirit.

Meditating with a focus on the navel area helps in particular to let go of inner physical tension and allows physical receptivity to calm and to beneficially affect the physical body. Through this openness the physical functioning of the body is given over to the action of the Spirit and results in a strengthening of the body to make it a better vehicle for expressing God's Will.

Focusing at the heart area fosters emotional receptivity. This kind of receptivity removes emotional tension and promotes balanced emotional responses that express God's Will. Emotional receptivity encourages and intensifies the development of devotional qualities.

Meditating at the brow area in particular alleviates mental tension and induces mental receptivity that enables the mind to be guided by the divine influence. The result is that the mind can become a loving instrument of the Spirit.

Ideally meditating on these three focusing areas of the body would not be necessary if you could wholeheartedly say, "Here I am, Lord. I am Yours to do as You will," and fully mean it from the bottom of your being. However, even though you may want to surrender yourself completely to God now, you may find that you are not able to do so. To give something to someone, you must first possess it as your own, and then you can give what is yours to another. You may think you possess your physical, emotional, and mental responses, but often it is truer to say that these *possess you*. You are frequently driven by your desires at each of these levels. Even if you gain control of these desires consciously, they are not cut off at the root. Therefore, they remain deeply imbedded in the subconscious mind and so motivate much of your life. Your physical, emotional, and mental drives are often on automatic pilot, so even if you say you give these to God's Will, you will most likely not be able to bring these under your control to truly give them to God. As you make the attempt to give these over to God, you will be holding back much of yourself from Him.

Generally speaking, the aspect you will hold back most frequently will be your physical functioning if you may consider this either unimportant or unspiritual. In this case, you will simply avoid that part of yourself and imagine that you can transcend the body by ignoring it. When the physical vitality of the body is not handed over to the Spirit, then your devotion may lack strength and intensity, and your ability to focus the mind may be weakened. It is important to realize the body is a spiritual vehicle, and all of its functions can be used to the honor and glory of God.

When you hold back the emotional aspect, you may know mentally all about spirituality, but never quite get the feel of it. After all, you are seeking here to deepen your relationship with God and in turn allow that inner relationship to affect all of your outer relationships. Relationships, whether inner or outer ones, are a matter of feeling in the heart and so the heart must be given over to the Holy Spirit.

If you hold back the mental aspect, you may be open hearted, yet scattered and unable to focus the mind. You won't have the mental clarity to discern how to manifest your inner feelings. If the Spirit is not allowed to guide the mind, then you cannot do God's Will effectively because the mental ability to understand and discern God's Will is lacking.

Initially in your meditation experience, if you do not focus on all three of these areas, it is quite likely you will develop one area of strength and avoid the other areas. Whatever you hold back from God will remain in control of the self and will prevent the self from being a servant of God's Will. Since the self is so much in control of your life already, it will not totally give over any of these functions without resistance. Allowing the Spirit to take control of your life at the physical, emotional, and mental levels is not a quick or easy process. It is a gradual letting go of the self, which is all the more reason for repeating the affirmation of your spiritual ideal at each focusing area to make a deep inner impression of your desire and willingness to be receptive to the Spirit.

It is important for you to allow the Holy Spirit to control the physical, emotional, and mental aspects of yourself. Allowing the Holy Spirit to control each of these different aspects involves being open to an integration and coordination of all these aspects producing inner harmony.

Progressive Meditation allows you to decide how long to use each of these three individual methods while progressing from one focusing area of the body to another. Therefore, if you feel you need one method more than the others, you can choose to employ that technique for more time while allowing less time for each of the other techniques. These three methods that use body awareness lead to the fourth method, Inner Silence Meditation, which does not use body awareness.

D. Inner Silence Meditation

For Inner Silence Meditation, you use an affirmation and then let go of it when the mind becomes calm. With the other three methods of Progressive Meditation, you retain your awareness on some form of body awareness, but for this method you let go of body awareness altogether. You enter inner silence by allowing the mind to switch from the thought of your spiritual ideal in the words of the affirmation to an inner awareness of the spiritual ideal in silence. Even without repeating the affirmation consciously, you are still aided by the affirmation when you go into silence. This is because, besides serving as a tool to reduce stray thoughts, the thought of the affirmation remains in your subconscious mind as a dominant thought pattern that can serve to counteract the ego-based thought patterns of the mind. If your mind is dominated by ego-based thought patterns, it will be difficult to go into inner silence without being distracted by stray thoughts. However, by having built a dominant thought pattern in your subconscious mind of your spiritual ideal, you are better prepared to remain in inner silence without being distracted.

Although you do not take the repetition of the affirmation into inner silence, the thought pattern of your spiritual ideal remains in your mind. Of course, your affirmation in word form is only a symbol of your spiritual ideal. However, having built this symbol into your mind, it remains there as a mental representation of the reality of your spiritual ideal. Besides representing your spiritual ideal, it more importantly symbolizes your desire for God, which welcomes the Holy Spirit to come into you in order to transform your awareness. Before learning to meditate, your mind is most likely dominated by ego-based desires, to which you have previously given your invitation, but which are now running on automatic pilot. This is why you may at times have emotional reactions, which you seem to be unable to control. Many of these reaction patterns are locked away in your subconscious mind and are still affecting you without your conscious awareness. Your affirmation builds within you a thought pattern that is in direct opposition to your ego-based desires and reaction patterns.

When you go into inner silence, you will find that you can remain there only briefly, and then you will be assailed by stray thoughts of the self. You can let go of these stray thoughts by not reacting to them, expressing neither attraction nor aversion. For intervals of calmness, you can let these thoughts pass by in your mind without allowing them to distract you from resting in inner silence. But then you will find yourself reacting in some way to passing thoughts by holding on to thoughts. You may realize you are monitoring or analyzing your thoughts instead of letting go of them. You let your awareness that your mind has wandered be a gentle reminder for you to pick up your affirmation and use it as a way of calming the mind.

Each time you calm your mind with your affirmation and then let go of your affirmation, you will have an opportunity to enter inner silence. This inner silence will not be simply an empty void, but rather an opportunity to consent to the presence of your spiritual ideal at an even deeper level, the level beyond words. It is that consenting to a closer union with the presence of your spiritual ideal that then allows you to rest in inner silence during Inner Silence Meditation. Your previous experience with meditation in which you have built your affirmation within as a dominant thought pattern in your mind can serve as a foundation for being able to enter inner silence.

Assuming that your spiritual ideal is a name for God or a reminder of God, you will be consenting to the divine presence when you practice Inner Silence Meditation. As you rest in inner silence, you will only be able to rely on your pure faith to sustain you. Your pure faith will tell you that the divine presence is there with you in the inner silence. As you enter inner silence, you move away from meditation, which focuses on the thought of your affirmation. Through the letting go of concepts, you experience contemplation, which is both a restful and dynamic state of inner absorption.

Unlike meditation, which requires concentration, contemplation is not the result of focusing the mind. It is a state of openness into which you are drawn by meeting the conditions that would produce this state. There are four conditions that need to be met in order for you to be drawn into contemplation. The contemplative state of resting in God cannot occur if your mind is preoccupied with distracting ego-based thoughts, so the first condition to be met is to have a calm mind, undisturbed by passing thoughts. Contemplation cannot come to you if it is not wanted, thus the second condition is your desire for the divine presence. Another word for your desire is your *intention*, which is expressed by your affirmation. Your intention is related to your wanting of contemplative communion. But when that wanting manifests as the actual experience of the divine presence, you will need to give your consent to this presence. Consequently, your consent to the divine presence is the third condition of contemplation. Although the experience of contemplation is a very receptive state, you do assert your will to draw this divine communion to yourself. You exert your will to desire God, and you exert your will to consent to both the divine presence and the divine activity within you.

Contemplation cannot happen if you are investing in faithlessness, so the fourth condition for resting in God to occur is investing in your faith in God. If you are like most people, you are not black or white in regard to faith. You are not entirely faithless, and you are not entirely full of faith. Everyone has doubts, and the root source of doubts is fear. Everyone is aware of some degree of faith, and the root source of faith is your true nature of love, given to you by God. You do not have to determine how many doubts you have based on fear, and you do not have to evaluate how much faith you have based on love. The relevant concern you need to address is, "Where am I making my investment— in which direction am I turning my awareness?"

You can turn the awareness of your mind toward faithlessness or toward faith, similar to the way you can drive your car north or south. You cannot drive your car north and south simultaneously, so you need to choose one direction for your car and likewise you need to choose one direction for your mind. Once you choose your direction, you may go off course at times, but at least you have set your purpose on investing in one direction. You cannot invest in faithlessness and in faith simultaneously because these two are mutually exclusive, just like fear and love are mutually exclusive. Investing in the direction of faithlessness leads to fear, which is its source. Investing in the direction of faith leads to love, which is its source. If you choose to turn your awareness in the direction of faithlessness, you close the door to the contemplative experience. Even though you are not free of doubts, if you turn your awareness in the direction of your faith, you are seeking to be led by the Holy Spirit.

It is not enough to say you believe in God as an idea. You will need to implement your faith by applying whatever amount of faith you already have. Applying your faith is certainly learning to see God as your final goal, but in practical terms, applying your faith is also learning to rely on God as the means to that final goal. Through relying on God to supply the means, your trust allows God to guide you to the awareness of His presence. Your implementation of your faith in God is the condition needed to allow yourself to become aware of His loving presence in contemplation and become embraced by His rest, like a child sleeping in the safe arms of his mother.

In summary, the conditions that need to be met for contemplation to occur are:

The Four Conditions of Contemplation

1. Calmness of the mind
2. Desire for God
3. Consent to the divine presence
4. Faith invested in God

Consequently, to prepare yourself to receive the gift of contemplation, it will be necessary to have a calm mind, a desire for a closer union with Spirit along with your consent to the divine presence, and the application of your faith in the direction of God. When you meet these four conditions, contemplation is a natural result.

The Spirit is always ready to enter your consciousness and draw you into the contemplative state with your consent. The contemplative state is both restful and dynamic. During contemplation a natural inner absorption takes place in which stray thoughts may come and go, without causing you to let go of this inner absorption. However, if stray thoughts cause your mind to wander, you can then practice meditation again by picking up the affirmation. When repeating the affirmation has stilled the mind sufficiently, you can let go of the affirmation again and return to the inner silence and rely on your pure faith in the divine presence.

Four phases of using your affirmation in Inner Silence Meditation, as a way of leading you in the direction of contemplation, have already been described in Chapter 5. The first, second, and third phases meet the four conditions for contemplation to happen. Therefore, these phases are a preparation for the experience of contemplation itself, which happens in the fourth phase of using the affirmation. The list below summarizes the phases of using your affirmation and how these phases meet the four conditions in order for contemplation to be the natural outcome:

Four Phases of Using the Affirmation in Inner Silence Meditation

1. Mentally Pronouncing the Affirmation
• the structured and form-related phase
• meets the first condition of a calm mind

2. Allowing the Affirmation to Be as It Presents Itself
• the intention phase
• meets the second condition of desire for God

3. The Affirmation Leads to Faithful Awareness
• the acceptance phase
• meets the third condition of consent to the divine presence
• meets the fourth condition of investment in faith in God

4. The Affirmation Culminates in Resting in God
• the contemplation phase
• the four conditions have been met and contemplation occurs
• pure faith is essential to maintain this state
• inner feelings may or may not be experienced

The first phase, which relies on the structure and form of repeating the word or words of the affirmation, is recommended to help produce a calm mind, but this phase is optional. If you are a beginner, you will probably find it very helpful to repeat the sound of your affirmation as a means of letting go of distracting stray thoughts and affirming your intention of deepening your relationship with God. If you become very distracted by unwanted thoughts, you may want to temporarily coordinate the repeating of your affirmation with your breathing in order to overcome this difficulty.

But generally you can release distracting thoughts by redirecting your mind to your affirmation without coordinating the affirmation with the breathing. Also, the affirmation does not have to be distinctly repeated as with earlier described techniques in which each syllable is repeated and extended so the sound is mentally pronounced. You may initially choose to repeat the affirmation in word form in the first phase. However, then you may choose to move on to the second phase, in which you set aside the sounding out of the word form mentally and instead allow the thought of the affirmation to come to your mind in whatever way it presents itself.

Having this thought of the affirmation come to your mind, of course, does not mean to "think about" the affirmation and what it signifies intellectually. It means to let the affirmation come to your awareness without predetermining the specific form this will take. The affirmation may come to your mind as the words of the affirmation with or without the sound of those words. In addition, the affirmation may appear as a clear thought or a vague thought, a movement of the will, or as an inner feeling. Because the second phase is less structured and less form-related than the first phase, this second phase has a greater emphasis on the desire that your affirmation symbolizes. The affirmation, however it comes to your awareness, is simply a reminder of your desire for your spiritual ideal of God.

The first phase includes your desire for God, similar to the second phase, but the first phase is primarily designed to meet the condition of having a calm mind in order to enter contemplation. The structure and form of repeating the affirmation in the first phase can calm the mind. However, this first phase is optional because you may at some point, sooner or later, be able to calm the mind without needing to repeat the affirmation in such a structured manner. If you can meet the condition of a calm mind by implementing the less structured approach of using your affirmation in the second phase, you can skip the first phase. An affirmation of one word, perhaps a word having only one syllable, such as "Christ," may be the most effective affirmation for the second phase, which leads to the next phase of setting aside the affirmation altogether.

After the affirmation is released, you shift your focus of awareness from the thought of the word form to a *faithful awareness* of the reality of the divine presence, for which the word form is only a symbol. The desiring of the divine presence expressed in the second phase allows you to make a natural progression to the accepting of the divine presence in the third phase. Your acceptance of the divine presence is the giving of your consent, which allows the Holy Spirit to bring about an inner transformation. Of course, God is always present within you. However, in this third phase, you learn to increasingly accept His presence and His activity within you. Your acceptance of His presence requires your faith—an inner knowing, which is not based on the normal mental process of rational thinking. Your faith in the divine presence implies a faithful awareness of an inner reality, and in addition an awareness of a reality that loves you. Naturally your faith in God's presence is important for all the phases of using the affirmation during Inner Silence Meditation, but in this third phase, you can let go of your affirmation and rely on your faithful awareness alone. Although the first phase and second phase also include a certain degree of investing in your faith, this third phase represents a much deeper investment. This deeper investment involves both the third condition and fourth condition of contemplation. In this third phase of using the affirmation, you give your consent to the divine presence, which is the third condition of contemplation. In addition, the third phase of using the affirmation represents a greater faithful trust in God, which is the fourth condition of contemplation. Because you are increasingly letting go of other investments and making a single-minded investment in faith above all else, you are fulfilling the final condition for contemplation to occur during Inner Silence Meditation.

To illustrate the faithful awareness expressed during Inner Silence Meditation, you can imagine that you are in a completely dark room, and you are only aware of yourself in this silent room. At some point you sense that there is—and has been all along—someone else in this room with you. You cannot see or hear this other one, but you somehow feel this one is there, even though you cannot confirm his presence by your normal senses. Although his outer appearance is hidden from you, you inwardly know that this one is of one mind and of one heart with you. Most of all, you sense this one to be a loving presence. Your faithful awareness of his loving presence creates in you a different consciousness than when you were only aware of yourself alone. You want a closer union with this loving presence, so you are open and receptive, waiting for this one to reveal himself. On the other hand, you are grateful just to know that this one is there as a loving presence. You know that it is up to this one's initiative to reveal himself or not, and so you must wait patiently.

As this analogy illustrates, your meditation experience often begins by you only being aware of yourself as alone and separate. Yet as you become quiet within, you may have a faithful awareness that you are not alone. This faithful awareness is a recognition that is not confirmed by the senses or the rational thinking of the mind, but relies on a faithful inner knowing that the divine presence is there. You cannot force the divine presence to be revealed to you at a deeper level. All you can do is to be open to whatever way this presence might be revealed to you and to be content even if this presence is not revealed to you. This requires waiting patiently.

Your faithful awareness may lead you into the fourth phase, the resting in God of contemplation. In this restful state, there is an inner absorption that allows you to disregard stray thoughts as they float by in your mind. However, after your meditation practice, you may not be able to pinpoint or describe what has occurred during your contemplative experience. Some meditators do not have a "felt" experience during their times of inner silence, and your pure faith does not require such experiences to confirm that you have encountered the divine presence.

Yet some meditators do experience inner feelings of a positive nature, such as feelings of love or peace. Having these inner feelings are signs of progress. Nonetheless, equivalent progress can be made without such experiences. Inner feelings point in the direction of God, but are not God Himself. If you are being guided to be open to experiencing these inner feelings, then accept what you are being given without attachment or aversion. But these inner feelings are not your goal. God is your goal. Thus your inner feelings can be helpful as long as they inspire you to continue to be open to God Himself. These inner feelings are discussed in Chapter 10, which also describes ways of increasing your openness to these inner feelings in your journey of awakening to God.

There are different ways in which you may encounter the divine presence. Usually, however, your awareness of the divine presence cannot be pinned down and categorized any more than God Himself can be clearly defined. A young monk said to an old monk, "I want to find God and hold on to Him. How can I do that?"

The old monk replied, "Go outside and catch the wind and bring it inside."

When the young monk returned, he said, "I grabbed at the wind, but I could not catch it."

The old monk replied, "If you can't catch the wind, what makes you think you can catch hold of God? But if you simply stand still outside, the wind will encompass you. In the same way if you allow your mind to stand still, God will encompass and possess you."

Although Inner Silence Meditation is a technique that leads beyond techniques to contemplation, the inner absorption of contemplation may occur spontaneously during any meditation method. You may be using any of the first three techniques of Progressive Meditation when you may be overshadowed by the Holy Spirit. You may first calm your mind sufficiently using your affirmation and then let go of your affirmation so you are holding your awareness only on the focusing area appropriate to the particular method you are using. While placing your awareness on a specific focusing area of the body, you may experience the contemplative state of inner absorption. If this happens, you may let go of holding your attention on a focusing area of the body and rest in the contemplative state as long as it lasts. If your mind is attracted to stray thoughts, you can then return to your affirmation and the focusing area of the body.

Though the experience of contemplation may occur while practicing any of the methods of Progressive Meditation, it is most likely to occur during Inner Silence Meditation. It is natural for contemplation to occur during this fourth method of Progressive Meditation since the sequence of techniques used prior to Inner Silence Meditation helps to open the spiritual centers from the bottom to the top. When you are practicing Inner Silence Meditation and when contemplation occurs, the Holy Spirit acts to open you to the universal consciousness and to produce a dynamic inner absorption typical of the contemplative state.

The first three techniques of Progressive Meditation cooperate with the Holy Spirit in a purification process that includes raising the creative energy in the body. Also, the experience of contemplation during Inner Silence Meditation cooperates in this purification process. The Holy Spirit with your invitation regulates the raising of the creative energy in a way that is most beneficial for you. In the first three techniques of Progressive Meditation, you play a somewhat more active role in cooperating with the Holy Spirit in purifying and raising the creative energy. As you reach Inner Silence Meditation in Progressive Meditation, you play a much less active role because you do not focus on any particular center of awareness in the body. When you experience contemplation, you play the least active role of all because you are releasing all your thoughts, and you are even letting go of holding onto your affirmation. During contemplation you are relying on pure faith, so you are surrendering yourself most fully to the Spirit. At this time the Holy Spirit raises the creative energy in the way that would be most helpful for you.

Contemplation has been described as an overshadowing of the Holy Spirit. The function of the Holy Spirit is to be a guide and communication link between your physical world, where your ego is at home, and His World, which is your true Home. The Holy Spirit coordinates and integrates all the centers of awareness. By giving your consent to the Holy Spirit during contemplation, you prepare yourself to enter His World. During the practice of Inner Silence Meditation, you are not focused on body awareness, so contemplation allows you to transcend the three-dimensional world of form, space, and time. When you enter His World during contemplation, you can think of this as experiencing another dimension that encompasses, interpenetrates, and transcends your three-dimensional world. The effect of the universal consciousness that manifests in contemplation is a two-edged sword. One effect is a unifying energy. The other effect is a disintegrating influence on barriers to unifying. The disintegrating effect dissolves ego-based emotions and thoughts. The positive unifying effect of contemplation has already been described and emphasized.

E. Inner Listening Meditation

Another method of meditation, called *Inner Listening Meditation*, may be practiced in conjunction with Inner Silence Meditation. If a continuous humming tone presents itself while you are practicing Inner Silence Meditation, you may ignore this steady inner sound and simply continue your practice or you may want to practice Inner Listening Meditation. If you are repeating your affirmation when you hear the humming sound, you can practice Inner Listening Meditation by releasing the affirmation and listening to this humming sound as long as it lasts. When the humming cannot be heard after a while, you can return to practicing Inner Silence Meditation. If stray thoughts have distracted you, you can return to using your affirmation. If your mind is not distracted by stray thoughts, you may let go of your affirmation in order to return to inner silence.

Let's imagine that you are practicing Inner Silence Meditation and that you have already let go of your affirmation and are experiencing the inner silence and rest of contemplation. While you are in this contemplative state, how would you respond if you heard the inner sound? You can listen to the humming sound if you are guided to do so. However, generally speaking, it is best to ignore the humming sound in this case because your contemplation experience is a deeper level of awareness than the humming sound. Nevertheless, if the inner sound grabs your attention, drawing you out of your contemplative rest in God, you can just focus directly on listening to the humming sound. When the humming sound disappears, you can then return to your affirmation if you are distracted by stray thoughts or return to the silence of contemplation if you are not distracted by stray thoughts.

Actually the humming sound may occur during any of your meditation practices that use an affirmation or that use some other way of focusing. Regardless of the method you are using, you can switch to Inner Listening Meditation, if you feel guided to do so. Without exerting an effort to try to hear the humming sound, you can just allow this sound to come of itself as a result of repeating your affirmation. If you hear the humming, you can let go of the affirmation and allow the sound to be your focus of awareness as you remain relaxed. Some meditators hear this humming and become concerned with clinging to it, rather than listening to it in a relaxed manner. Being concerned about clinging to the sound produces a tension, which makes the humming leave the awareness of the mind. As you listen without attachment, the humming sound will continue naturally, without any effort on your part to hold on to it. Through this effortless inner listening to the humming vibration, it becomes a positive spiritual force that expresses itself naturally, and occasionally may even come into your conscious mind at times outside of your meditation practice.

The word "humming" is used to describe this steady tone for lack of a better term to identify the inner sound. Actually it would be more accurate to say that the inner sound is a very clear and continuous tone that does not fluctuate. In meditation you may hear a steady tone in one ear or in the other ear, but this is not the inner sound. The inner tone is heard emanating from within the center of the head. If you want to try a simple test on yourself, you can put your thumbs in your ears. Listen within yourself to any interior sounds. What do you hear? If there is perfect silence, then either you are a soul at deep peace or you weren't listening very carefully. If you hear the continuous and steady inner tone, then you are at peace, yet not quite as peaceful as the one who is in the silent state. If you are like most people, you will hear some other sound or combination of sounds. Examples of sounds that may be heard are the roar of the ocean, the sound of running water, bells, wind blowing, the sound of a lute, a buzzing sound, or other sounds that may be less distinct. These sounds are quite normal, yet they indicate the lack of a more peaceful harmony.

The hearing of the inner sound indicates that meditation is bringing about increased harmony and peace. When the creative energy in the spine is gradually rising during meditation, this increases the ability to hear the inner sound. In yoga philosophy the inner sound is called the "nada" and can be considered the uncaused sound. This inner sound is the OM. This inner tone should not be thought of as something caused by the mind because it has a spiritual origin. When the various other interior sounds that are created by the mind are silenced through the use of an affirmation, the inner sound that is not created by the mind can then be heard.

While holding the awareness within the center of the head, some meditators feel themselves becoming one with the inner sound. Even though the inner sound emanates from the center of the head, it may feel like it is penetrating into every cell in the body. This feeling of becoming in tune with a single steady tone may seem dull compared to your usual preference for sounds that have musical variations in tone. But the actual experience of listening within to this one unifying tone can be quite pleasant.

Clarity, purity, and love are at the center of your true nature in God. Because the inner sound emanates from your spiritual core, its tone carries some of these inner qualities. Consequently, the inner sound is transformative since it helps you to become in tune with your spiritual nature. This transformation produced by listening to the inner sound is so subtle and gentle that you may fail to understand or appreciate its effectiveness. Methods that use affirmations are important for building within your mind a deep impression of your commitment to your spiritual ideal. However, after your dedication to your spiritual ideal is firmly established, you may hear the inner sound and find Inner Listening Meditation to be more effective than using an affirmation.

Although the inner sound comes from a spiritual source, it should be understood that listening to this sound is not the ideal meditative state. By God's grace you may come to know the silence of the Father from which all sound originates. Listening to the inner sound in Inner Listening Meditation can lead you in the direction of that silence. Using Inner Listening Meditation in conjunction with Inner Silence Meditation is a good combination because you can alternate between the steady spiritual tone and the inner silence that leads to contemplation. But keep in mind that the silent contemplative state leads to a deeper level of consciousness than the steady humming tone. Regardless of whatever technique of meditation you have chosen for your regular practice, if the humming sound presents itself, you may practice Inner Listening Meditation if you are prompted to do so by the Holy Spirit.

F. Healing Meditation Using External Aids

Edgar Cayce, the "Sleeping Prophet," recommended a device called the "radial device" or "radial appliance" as a means of healing the body. He said using this device would be helpful for everyone. The energy centers within the body are called "chakras." The energy around the body is called the "aura." The chakras and the aura have many layers, producing an energy field that can gradually accumulate blockages caused by fearful responses to stress. The radial device takes your own energy and redistributes it in a harmonious way. This redistribution of your energy creates inner balance and repairs the effects of stress. At first the device primarily heals the outer aura. Each time the device is used, its harmonizing effects penetrate deeper into the body's various energy systems. After you continue to use the radial device for years, the beneficial effects can produce all sorts of healing within the body, just as rest during sleep can aid the natural healing process. To help facilitate inner healing, the radial device is recommended for use while your mind is focused in a positive way. One way to focus the mind positively while using the radial device is to practice sitting meditation.

Another way to use the device is to rest horizontally while listening to relaxing or uplifting instrumental music without necessarily meditating. Using the device while watching television is not recommended.

However, it is beyond the scope of this book to go into detail about how to use the device itself. For more information, you can contact either Phil Thomas about his "Radial Device"[2] or James Knochel[3] about his "Radial Appliance." You can also contact Tom Hildebrand about his "Copper Ice Appliance," although his "Economical Ice Appliance" is not recommended because it is not made according to the specifications of the Edgar Cayce readings. Other manufacturers do not correctly follow Edgar Cayce's instructions for making the radial device.[4]

Physical symptoms of sickness in the body are caused by the mind and always involve fear. In addition to fear, sickness invariably includes subconscious guilt and the misguided idea of deserving punishment for wrongdoing. Self-imposed guilt and fear associated with it produce in the body a constricting effect, which restricts circulation. To counteract the constricting effect of fear and guilt, the body attempts to heal by producing inflammation to increase circulation. The most effective way to remove the symptoms of inflammation is to let go of the fear and release any guilt that caused the original restriction of circulation.

During sitting meditation, you can use Centering Meditation to raise energy from the base of the spine. You can focus on love in the physical heart during Heart Meditation and focus on the brow area during Brow Meditation. You can learn to simultaneously raise energy from the base of the spine, extend love in the heart to the part of the body you want healed, and still focus on the brow area. Just as light dispels darkness, love dispels fear and guilt. This healing meditation uses the energy of focused love to replace the fear and guilt that caused the health problem. To enhance the healing effect, you can tape an azurite crystal over the physical heart to bring more love. Edgar Cayce recommended using the best quality of translucent azurite crystal as an aid to meditation and psychic development. Also, to increase the healing effect, you can use the radial device for sitting meditation. But the radial device is most often used with the body lying horizontally because the experience is so relaxing. In fact, this device has been used quite successfully to cure insomnia. The radial device and azurite stone are rather unusual aids to meditation, so they will not appeal to most meditators. However, these options can assist the Holy Spirit in your attunement and healing.

---

1. Mark 9:24.
2. http://iodinesource.com/Products.php#RadialDevice/.
3. http://radialappliance.teslabox.com/.
4. http://www.radialappliance.org/acceptable-suppliers/.

8

DIFFERENT
APPROACHES TO
CONTEMPLATION

~ • ~

A. Christian Meditation Advocated by John Main

This meditation manual offers a new approach to the divine embrace of contemplation. To address why a new approach is needed, it will be helpful to first identify two alternative approaches to inward seeking that are in some ways similar to the techniques offered in this book. These two approaches are contemporary movements that represent a renewal of traditional Christian contemplative practices. One of these movements is *Centering Prayer*, which is described in the next section. The other is called *Christian Meditation*. While John Main was a British diplomat in Malaysia, he learned how to meditate from a Hindu guru. He returned to England and became a Benedictine monk and taught the practice of Christian Meditation. In 1972 John Main came to Canada and began teaching Christian Meditation at a house of prayer, which he founded in Montreal. When John Main died in the early 1980s, his work was carried on by another Benedictine monk, Laurence Freeman, who promoted The World Community of Christian Meditation as the organization through which Christian Meditation has become known worldwide.[1]

Since John Main learned his method from a Hindu guru, it is not surprising that Christian Meditation relies on the repeating of a mantra, which may likewise be called a sacred word or affirmation. The outstanding distinctive feature of this method is that the mantra is repeated continuously throughout the entire meditation, which is the traditional way the mantra is used in many Hindu meditation practices. The idea is to choose just one mantra that through repetition can dominate all the other thoughts of the mind and become a spiritual anchor for one's consciousness.

An example of one widely used word advocated by John Main and in turn by his disciple, Laurence Freeman, is "Maranatha." This is an ancient Aramaic word meaning "Come, Lord." Maranatha, being an uncommon word, does not lend itself to creating mental images or mental associations that would be distracting to the meditation process. This word is pronounced "Ma-ra-na-tha" so that each syllable is mentally repeated with an equal emphasis.[2]

Once the meditator chooses a sacred word (or words), this choice is not generally changed, unless there is clear inner guidance to make a change. The whole purpose of the mantra is to interpenetrate the mind and to free the mind from being attached to self-centered thinking. The repetition of the mantra continuously from the beginning to the end of each meditation period and the consistency of this practice over many years help to transform the mind.

There are two premises that support the use of Christian Meditation. The first premise is that choosing a sacred word directs the mind toward the presence of God and away from your self-centered thinking, which revolves around your image of yourself as a separate being. The second basic premise is that the nature of the mind is to be active and to produce a multiplication of thoughts. You cannot expect the mind to become perfectly silent because that is not the nature of the mind. The active nature of the mind creates a steady stream of unending thoughts. This ongoing stream of thoughts will be constantly fluctuating and producing instability, but by giving the mind one thought, one sacred word, the mind becomes stabilized and directed toward God.

Christian Meditation is correctly identified as an example of meditation, since by definition meditation is the holding of one thought in the mind continuously. But is Christian Meditation a form of contemplation? The answer depends on how you define contemplation. If contemplation is defined loosely as any form of inward receptivity to the divine, then Christian Meditation can be called "active contemplation" or "acquired contemplation." The activity of using concentration and continuous effort on the part of the seeker is the reason why Christian Meditation is an example of active contemplation. Acquired contemplation, synonymous with active contemplation, conveys the meaning that the seeker is exerting his own efforts to bring about an inner transformation. But Christian Meditation is not entirely active since there are many receptive elements present. For example, the repeating of the sacred word allows for a certain degree of divine receptivity because distracting thoughts, including self-analysis, the imagination, and the memory, are all set aside. It is these receptive elements that give meditation a contemplative aspect and bring about an openness to the divine influence.

Sometimes contemplation is defined as inward seeking that produces mystical awareness in which God's grace manifests in the form of a felt experience or occurs without the seeker having any conscious experience that would confirm the divine presence. Using this definition Christian Meditation can also be considered a contemplative experience in which God's work of transformation takes place in overt or less obvious ways. Christian Meditation does invite divine grace and succeeds in producing inner transformation because of the intent of the seeker for this to happen, which gives the Holy Spirit permission to bring about inner changes.

There is no question here of the effectiveness of Christian Meditation as a beneficial means of spiritual transformation, but there is a semantic question regarding how to define contemplation. This meditation manual offers a very precise definition of contemplation in order to make a clear distinction between meditation and contemplation. In contrast to the broad definition of contemplation as any form of inward receptivity or mystical experience, this meditation manual defines contemplation more specifically as simply resting silently in the divine presence without words being used. Contemplation involves a giving up of concepts. Meditation involves a giving up of many concepts by holding on to one concept as a focusing object, which is usually in the form of a word or words. Unlike meditation, contemplation involves letting go of concepts without having one thought as a focusing object. Thus contemplation is a state of objectless awareness.

Using this definition, contemplation is not active at all, but only passive. Being passive means placing no distracting self-created thoughts between yourself and God. It is possible at times to be in a temporary state of deep contemplation without any thoughts. However, you can be in a contemplative state even if thoughts are present in the mind as long as the thoughts do not become distracting by drawing your attention to them. Contemplation produces an inner absorption in which thoughts come and go without your paying attention to them as they pass by in your mind. Avoiding distracting thoughts creates an empty space, which allows God to be Himself in you. Resting passively in God is a time of not doing—meaning not even doing the holding of a sacred word. Resting in God is a time of *being* only. It is a letting go that creates a nonverbal invitation for the divine to take over within to produce an inner transformation. Contemplation occurs due to an overshadowing of the Holy Spirit in which the divine within becomes the active principle precisely because the seeker withdraws all self-initiated activity.

Using the definition of contemplation as resting silently in the divine without words being used, contemplation would not be associated with concentration or active practices. From the frame of reference of perceiving contemplation as resting in God, the term "active contemplation" would be a meaningless contradiction in terms. Christian Meditation or any other kind of meditation that uses active concentration could not be called contemplation, which is entirely receptive in nature. But saying that Christian Meditation is not contemplation, as it is defined in this manual, is not intended to imply that this method is not a valuable means of spiritual transformation as a meditation method.

The strength of Christian Meditation is the positive effect produced by the continuous repetition of a single mantra used unchangingly in daily meditation. The self-centered nature of modern society creeps into every aspect of daily life, including into spiritual endeavors. Focusing the mind consistently on a sacred word can free you from this self-centeredness and redirect your mind toward being God-centered. During meditation your mind will at times become distracted by stray thoughts. However, when you notice you have inadvertently forgotten your sacred word, you simply return to repeating your mantra again. This process of holding on to your sacred word allows you to disconnect from the habitual self-concern and self-consciousness that promotes anxiety and to become receptive to the peace that comes from trusting in God.

Christian Meditation can take you very far along on the spiritual path and produce many positive changes in consciousness. Many seekers are drawn to use this method exclusively as their lifelong means of divine attunement. Although the use of Christian Meditation is a very beneficial practice, the use of this method as one's sole way of inward seeking is not recommended in this book *as a lifelong practice* because the main purpose of this manual is to lead you to the experience of contemplation. The strength of Christian Meditation lies in its ability to help stabilize and calm the mind. This strength is very helpful especially for the beginning meditator, who may find it challenging initially to focus the mind because of numerous distracting thoughts.

On the other hand, the limitation that Christian Meditation presents is an inherent result of its strength. The strength of continuously holding the sacred word means that Christian Meditation is not contemplation and cannot lead directly to contemplation because this method does not allow you to completely rest in the objectless awareness of God. It is very true that repeating the sacred word will help to bring about a certain degree and perhaps a high degree of divine peacefulness by calming the mind. But Christian Meditation will not allow the complete emptiness of thought—empty even of repeating the sacred word—which would allow the deep resting in God that occurs in contemplation, as defined in this manual. This limitation is not really a problem for beginners because most beginning meditators are very easily distracted by stray thoughts and would find it very difficult to let go of all thoughts and enter contemplation. Consequently, most beginners would benefit by practicing Christian Meditation or a similar meditation practice using continuous concentration on one word or one focusing object.

In spite of the benefits of repeating a sacred word continuously, the time may come when the practice of Christian Meditation can be replaced by other methods that lead toward wordless contemplation, if that is your goal. Using Christian Meditation cannot produce contemplation, but it can help you make progress in calming the mind and thus increase your potential for being able to let go of thoughts. When you reach the point where you feel you have a greater potential for silencing the mind and resting in God during contemplation, it would be helpful for you to ask in prayer for inner guidance. You might want to ask a question such as, "Lord, would you want me to let go of repeating my sacred word continuously during my attunement in order to learn how to reach a deeper level of being aware of Your presence in the objectless awareness of contemplation?" If the answer is "No," then you can simply continue with your current practice of holding on to your sacred word continuously as the advocates of Christian Meditation recommend. If the answer is "Yes," then you can consider options for practicing contemplation.

If you are currently using a method of meditation, such as Christian Meditation, that uses the sacred word continuously, and if you decide to move in the direction of experiencing contemplation, you will not have to give up the use of the sacred word entirely. The techniques that have been presented previously in this manual describe how to hold on to an affirmation of a sacred word or words, similar to the practice of Christian Meditation. But these techniques also indicate how to exercise the option of letting go of the affirmation in order to experience contemplation. When using the techniques in this manual, if you are a beginner, you may find it necessary initially to hold on to the affirmation for all or most of your meditation period. However, the purpose of the meditation techniques presented in this manual is to serve as a stepping stone that hopefully will lead you to the letting go of your affirmation in order to experience the silence and rest of contemplation.

B. Centering Prayer

Thomas Merton, the author of *Contemplative Prayer*, was a leading figure in the renewal of ancient Christian contemplative practices. Unlike this manual's definition of prayer as inner asking, Merton used the term "contemplative prayer" to describe the contemplative practice of letting go of words and images in order to find the divine presence within the depths of one's own heart. Merton spoke of inwardly finding one's center within oneself and within God. From Merton's emphasis on finding one's center came the term "Centering Prayer" to describe a method for entering into the contemplative experience based on traditional Christian practices of inward seeking. In recent years Centering Prayer has become a popular contemporary approach to inward seeking. Trappists Basil Pennington, the author of *Centering Prayer*, and Thomas Keating, the author of *Invitation to Love* and *Open Mind, Open Heart*, are two leading advocates of the practice of Centering Prayer.

Through the efforts of Basil Pennington and William Menninger, the practice of Centering Prayer began as a monastic renewal originating at St. Joseph's Abbey in Spencer, Massachusetts, in the 1970s. This method that benefitted the monks was passed on to visiting priests and later to lay people. Workshops were offered, and Thomas Keating initiated an advanced workshop for the purpose of training others to become teachers of Centering Prayer. In the mid-1980s, Thomas Keating gave instruction in Centering Prayer to some New York parishes. From these parishes the practice of Centering Prayer reached greater numbers of religious and lay people. The Contemplative Outreach, Ltd. was created in 1984 as an outreach program to meet the needs of seekers who want to deepen their prayer life. This outreach program encourages not only individual practice of Centering Prayer, but also the formation of small mutual support groups that practice this method as a group experience.[3]

Like the practice of Christian Meditation, Centering Prayer employs the use of a sacred word (or words) as a focusing tool, but unlike Christian Meditation, Centering Prayer does not require the holding of the sacred word for the entire contemplative practice. In Centering Prayer the thought of the sacred word is held briefly at the beginning of your practice simply as a reminder of your intention to draw closer to the divine presence. You do not think about the meaning of the sacred word during your practice. The meaning of the sacred word is not relevant to your practice, because the sacredness of the word comes from being a symbolic reminder of your intention for inviting divine communion. Your intention is your willingness and choice to deepen your relationship with God.

You let go of the sacred word, which is only a symbol of your intention, in order to more directly invest in your intention itself for union with God. Various stray thoughts may pass by in your mind, and you can still be in a contemplative state of mind as long as you let each thought come and go without allowing your attention to be diverted from your intention of union with God. If you become preoccupied with distracting thoughts, it means you have forgotten your intention. Then you return your awareness to the sacred word to accomplish the dual purpose of turning away from distracting thoughts and returning back to your pure intention for the divine presence. After the sacred word has accomplished its purpose of calming the mind and reminding you of your intention, you can again let go of the sacred word in order to rest in the silence of the divine presence.

In contrast to Christian Meditation, which requires a greater degree of self-effort to hold on to the sacred word continuously, Centering Prayer relies to a greater degree on divine grace and produces what is sometimes called *passive contemplation* or *infused contemplation*. The words "passive" and "infused" emphasize that your work as a seeker is to get out of the way and do nothing to impede the action of the Holy Spirit. It is the divine impulse within the center of your being that accomplishes the real inner work of transformation. All that is required of you is to give your invitation to the Holy Spirit and to make every minute of your daily contemplative practice a renewal of your permission to allow the divine influence to bring about your inner transformation.

Centering Prayer has a basic premise similar to Christian Meditation, which is that the sacred word can direct the mind toward the presence of God and away from self-centered thinking. However, Christian Meditation places a premium on form being just as important as content in the sense that the form of the sacred word needs to be retained and continuously used as an expression of the content of the sacred word. The content of the sacred word is not the literal meaning of the sacred word; the content of the sacred word is your intention of seeking the divine presence. Centering Prayer emphasizes content over form in that the form of the sacred word is only a symbol that can be set aside and replaced entirely by the content of the sacred word, which is your intention. The form of the sacred word is only a tool to be used to bring your attention away from distracting thoughts and to simultaneously refocus on your intention. After having brought your attention back to your intention, you can set aside this refocusing tool, the sacred word. By setting aside the sacred word you can be aware of your intention alone that goes deeper than words. Instead of your sacred word being the primary focus of your spiritual practice, Centering Prayer places your intention of a closer union with God and your faith at the center of your spiritual practice.

Centering Prayer is also unlike Christian Meditation in that it has a very different basic premise regarding the nature of the mind itself. An underlying premise of Christian Meditation is that the nature of the mind is to actively multiply thoughts, producing a complex network of thoughts. Therefore, the sacred word needs to be constantly repeated to tame this tendency to multiply many thoughts. This is partially correct in that the mind guided by the ego is inclined to multiply thoughts. Yet it is incorrect to attribute this multiplication of thoughts to the mind itself. It is really the ego, the false perception of a separate self, that is the cause of the multiplication of thoughts. The multiplication of thoughts is actually an unnatural condition of the mind. Different from the view of the mind as a thought multiplier, Centering Prayer has a basic underlying premise that the mind itself is naturally simple and uncomplicated. Letting go of the sacred word allows the mind to rest in God and return to its natural state of being simple and uncomplicated, just as God Himself is simple and uncomplicated in His oneness.

The mind is naturally inclined toward rest and silence. However, if the sacred word is always repeated continuously as in Christian Meditation, how will you ever discover for yourself the simplicity of the mind that is its natural state? What is unnatural to the mind, which is the multiplication of thoughts caused by the ego, appears natural to you because of your identification with the ego. Likewise, what is natural to the mind, which is restful silence and simplicity, appears unnatural to you because silence and simplicity are unnatural to the ego, with which you are identified. Centering Prayer gives you the opportunity to become aware of the natural condition of the mind by learning to rest in the divine presence. This experience of objectless awareness in contemplation allows you to let go of ego identification and become increasingly identified with your true nature in God.

Your first experiences of contemplative resting in the divine presence will give you a frame of reference to distinguish between the natural simplicity of the mind and the unnatural state of the mind produced by ego identification. It would be nice if you could enter and stay in the restful state of contemplation consistently and continuously for your entire inward practice, but this usually happens only after many years of daily practice. Your practice will most likely become an experience of resting in the divine presence only for short intervals of time. Intruding on your rest will be distracting thoughts, and your sacred word can be used to redirect your mind back to your intention of divine communion. Sometimes these distracting thoughts can be very emotionally charged, and more about releasing these thoughts during Centering Prayer will be described below. In summary, Centering Prayer is a very helpful and effective method for entering into contemplation and making progress in terms of releasing inner blocks and therefore becoming a better reflection of divine love.

C. A New Approach to Contemplation

Centering Prayer is certainly beneficial as a spiritual practice that leads to contemplation. This manual advocates an equivalent spiritual practice, which is called *Inner Silence Meditation*. Centering Prayer is described with a slightly different emphasis and terminology than Inner Silence Meditation. For example, in Centering Prayer any word may be chosen as your sacred word or words, and for Inner Silence Meditation any affirmation may also be chosen, but the choice of the Divine Name of Jesus Christ is specifically emphasized and recommended.

These two methods offer slightly different recommendations for how to use the sacred word. Both methods acknowledge that the sacred word can be used as an aid in letting go of distracting thoughts and is a way of assisting you to reach deeper and deeper levels of awareness. Also, both methods say that you do not think about the meaning of the sacred word during your inward-seeking practice because the idea is to let go of discursive thinking in order to deepen your relationship with God and experience the divine presence. Both methods agree that the sacred word is a symbol of your intention. Although both methods agree on the *content* of the sacred word being a symbolic representation of your intention, they disagree about how to implement the *form* of the sacred word, such as the sound of the sacred word itself or the thought of the sacred word itself.

Advocates of Centering Prayer do not consider the form of the sacred word to be significant in itself because the content of your sacred word is what is important. Consequently, your purpose in Centering Prayer is to stay centered in your intention, of which your sacred word is only a symbolic reminder. Inner Silence Meditation maintains that the form of the sacred word is indeed primarily a reminder of the content of your intention. In addition, the form itself can play an important secondary role in your practice. The form of your sacred word can be a stepping stone to the content of your sacred word, which is your intention of deepening your relationship with God. In particular, repeating the form of the sacred word can be very helpful in setting aside distracting thoughts. Typically beginners have difficulty with mental distractions, so most beginners are likely to benefit from temporarily repeating the form of the sacred word in order to divert the mind away from distracting thoughts. Hopefully you will grow out of the need to repeat the form of the sacred word as you make progress in your practice of Inner Silence Meditation. Then you can rely only on your intention itself, which is an expression of your faith in God.

Inner Silence Meditation recommends repeating your sacred word at brief intervals to counteract distracting thoughts and calm the mind before letting go of the sacred word. Thomas Keating, in his book about Centering Prayer, titled *Open Mind, Open Heart,* does not specifically emphasize that you "repeat" the sacred word, but does say to "return"[4] to the sacred word and "to go back"[5] to the sacred word to remind yourself of your intention when you realize that you are thinking of something other than your intention. You do not go back to a predetermined form of your sacred word, such as the repetition of the word itself, but you do go back to the thought of the sacred word in whatever way it appears to you, as a reminder of your intention. Thomas Keating explains that Centering Prayer uses the sacred word as a symbolic reminder of your intention to fully open yourself to God. The emphasis on "returning to" the sacred word rather than "repeating" the sacred word is intended to distinguish Centering Prayer from repetitive practices. Centering Prayer is a receptive practice that does not require automatic repetition, in contrast to the continuous repeating of a Hindu mantra, which is a concentrative practice.

Thomas Keating describes below the process of using the sacred word:

> To start, introduce the sacred word in your imagination as gently as if you were laying a feather on a piece of absorbent cotton. Keep thinking the sacred word in whatever form it arises. It is not meant to be repeated continuously. The word can flatten out, become vague or just an impulse of the will, or even disappear. Accept it in whatever form it arises.
>
> When you become aware that you are thinking some other thought, return to the sacred word as the expression of your intent. The effectiveness of this prayer does not depend on how distinctly you say the sacred word or how often, but rather on the gentleness with which you introduce it into your imagination in the beginning and the promptness with which you return to it when you are hooked on some other thought.[6]

Ideally seekers can allow the sacred word to be used in the unstructured manner described above by Thomas Keating in order to let go of distracting thoughts and remind them of their intention, but most beginners find that it is difficult to let go of distracting thoughts. Because of this difficulty, Inner Silence Meditation includes an initial way of using the sacred word in a more structured manner in order to help you release distracting thoughts. This initial way involves repeating the form of the sacred word at brief intervals to counteract distracting thoughts, and at these intervals the sacred word is very temporarily used as a repeated mantra in meditation. This way of repeating the sacred word, which emphasizes form initially and then leads to the content of your intention, has been elaborated upon in previous descriptions of Inner Silence Meditation.

Four phases of using your affirmation in the practice of Inner Silence Meditation have already been identified in Chapters 5 and 7:

1. Mentally Pronouncing the Affirmation
2. Allowing the Affirmation to Be as It Presents Itself.
3. The Affirmation Leads to Faithful Awareness
4. The Affirmation Culminates in Resting in God

This list of the four phases includes not only the outer husk of the affirmation, which is the repeating of the form in words, but also the seed contained within. That seed is your desire for God and your acceptance of His presence in the darkness of faith. Your faith in turn leads you to the nourishing kernel of that seed, which is the resting in God that occurs during contemplation. The form of your affirmation points the way to the formlessness of contemplation, yet only divine grace makes the journey from form to formlessness possible. You can resist the divine grace of God drawing you to Himself. However, your affirmation serves the purpose of reminding you that you have decided to give up your resistance and have consented to the attraction of divine grace.

The first phase of using the affirmation, which emphasizes using the form of the affirmation in a structured, repetitive manner, is inconsistent with the practice of Centering Prayer, which does not encourage reliance on the repetition of the sacred word. This initial phase is recommended especially for beginners, but is optional and therefore may be omitted. The final three more advanced phases, which use your affirmation in a less structured way, emphasize reminding you of the content of your intention. This less structured approach is very similar to, if not identical to, the practice of Centering Prayer, although the terminology may be slightly different. In the practice of Inner Silence Meditation, if you choose to omit the initial optional phase of using the affirmation, your practice would actually be indistinguishable from the practice of Centering Prayer.

In spite of some terminology differences, Centering Prayer and Inner Silence Meditation can be considered as roughly equivalent practices at the functional level, because both use the sacred word as a reminder of your intention of deepening your relationship with God and both lead through faith to the experience of contemplation. Even though these two methods of inward seeking are equivalent in terms of their practice and their common goal of contemplation, there is a difference in how Inner Silence Meditation is recommended to be used in this manual and how Centering Prayer is recommended to be used by its advocates. Centering Prayer is recommended to be used alone for your entire attunement, but does not exclude the use of other methods of prayer and attunement at other times. In contrast to using Centering Prayer exclusively, the daily practice of Inner Silence Meditation is recommended to be used in coordination with other specific techniques to enhance its effectiveness.

Centering Prayer is a one-size-fits-all contemplative method that does lead to contemplation for those who learn to use it effectively. But what about those who do not seem to benefit from the practice of Centering Prayer? After encountering many seekers who have come very far along the spiritual path, Thomas Keating discovered that a large percentage of these maintain that they have never had the grace of a *felt experience* of the divine presence associated with contemplative practice. Many of these seekers have spent most of their lives in a monastery, as a place and community designed for them to be contemplatives. After practicing contemplative prayer for twenty or thirty years without having felt any inner experience of the divine presence, these seekers in their latter years wonder if they have failed in their contemplative profession. Having no outward sign to reassure them, they must rely on their faith, which after all is the centerpiece of all Christian spiritual seeking.[7]

Thomas Keating has concluded that it is inappropriate to determine the value of your experience of Centering Prayer based on whether or not you have a consciously felt experience of the divine presence sinking into your faculties and producing overt changes of a mystical nature. There is a connection between the practice of Centering Prayer and *divine graces*, which are free mystical gifts from God. Indeed, the resting in God of contemplation is a gift in itself, and there are additional divine graces that come as gifts with your openness to God's presence. Divine graces are not earned by your seeking since they are gifts. Yet without seeking and inviting God into your awareness, you would not be able to recognize and receive these gifts, which are so freely given. But not all gifts of divine grace, which may be called *mystical graces*, are consciously experienced. You can still be receiving mystical graces without being consciously aware of God's presence penetrating into your faculties to produce an inner transformation. Thomas Keating maintains that some seekers may have these consciously felt mystical graces, and others may have mystical graces that are not consciously felt, but in either case the seeker can be going through an inner transformation through God's grace.[8]

Even though it is true that there are many seekers who are receiving "covert" mystical graces instead of "overt" mystical graces, it is somewhat startling what Thomas Keating says about the numbers of cloistered contemplatives who are not having a felt experience of the mystical graces. According to Keating, "Less than five percent of cloistered contemplatives that I know have the mystical experiences that Teresa or John of the Cross describe."[9] He goes on to say, "Their consolations are few and far between."[10]

Many of these cloistered monks practice Centering Prayer for many years without experiencing overt mystical graces. It is remarkable that they persevere for so long, relying solely on their faith without any overt confirmation of the divine presence. Thomas Keating remarks that in his experience those who are in some form of active ministry or who are married seem to have the most fulfilling mystical life. He concludes that perhaps God gives more overt graces to those in the world because of their greater need for His help and that covert graces are sufficient to meet the needs of those who live in cloistered settings.[11]

How many seekers in the world would practice Centering Prayer for thirty years without ever having experienced overt mystical graces? Generally seekers in the world who practice Centering Prayer do so because of overt benefits, or they eventually will give up the practice. Similarly, people who practice hatha yoga or any other spiritual disciplines do so because they experience the overt benefits, and that is why they continue with their practice. Overt benefits may sometimes be outwardly apparent to others, but the word "overt" as it is used here simply means *inwardly apparent in an obvious way*. Thus in spite of the truth that Centering Prayer can produce covert benefits, the bottom line is that this method or any other method will typically be maintained if it produces inwardly noticeable results.

Exceptional seekers, such as some cloistered monks, will continue to practice Centering Prayer and graciously accept covert divine graces, if that is all God gives. But even those seekers, who only receive covert divine graces, will continue to want overt divine graces as a confirming sign of a closer communion with God. Obviously the covert experience of the divine presence is usually a second choice, and the overt experience of the divine presence is what is really wanted. Consequently, it seems appropriate to ask the question, "How can Centering Prayer become more effective and overtly beneficial to those who want to use it?"

To answer this question, it is necessary to define any shortcomings that could be corrected. A potential shortcoming of Centering Prayer is that this method may be too advanced for some seekers. Making the leap from being highly conceptually oriented to the nonconceptual experience of contemplation may be very difficult for Westerners who are accustomed to mental activity. There is a need for a *transition* to help bridge the gap between mental activity and passive resting in God produced by letting go of mental activity. Thus there is not a problem with the practice of Centering Prayer itself, but rather there is a need for enhanced preparation for the experience of entering into the restful divine presence.

Thomas Keating believes there are beneficial methods seekers can find within Eastern and Western spiritual disciplines to help calm the mind that would serve as a preparatory foundation for practicing Centering Prayer and entering contemplation.[12] In the Western tradition, he notes that during the Middle Ages a practice called "lectio divina" was used as a preparation for entering the restful state of contemplation. Lectio divina, which means "divine reading," consisted of four stages. The first part was "lectio," the reading or listening to scripture, which was then followed by "meditatio," discursive prayer, reflecting on the meaning of this scripture. This led to the third stage, "oratio," which is sometimes called "affective prayer," the inward and heartfelt spontaneous expression of the will directed toward God. In turn, this affective prayer in response to God ideally progressed to the final stage, "contemplio," resting in God.

Meditatio, oratio, and contemplio following the reading of scripture would often overlap, rather than being distinctly separate from each other. These overlapping inner experiences within the context of lectio divina evolved by the sixteenth century into separate spiritual disciplines. The mental approach of discursive prayerful reflection could be one's spiritual discipline apart from the other approaches. On the other hand, affective prayer could be practiced alone, or contemplation could become the seeker's means of inward seeking. There was no longer a transition framework like lectio divina in which the seeker could learn to allow expression of mental prayer to lead into the experience of contemplation.[13]

This lack of a smooth framework, which could lead one step at a time to contemplation, is still a problem today. One suggestion Thomas Keating makes is that some seekers may want to prepare for Centering Prayer by reviving the tradition of lectio divina. To do this, the seeker can read sacred scripture and then reflect on the meaning of the text. After this reflection the seeker can turn to prayer addressed to God and conclude this preparatory attunement time with the practice of Centering Prayer. The original version of lectio divina in the Middle Ages did not provide specific instructions in how to enter into the contemplio (contemplation) stage of resting in God. The modern-day contribution that Centering Prayer provides is a comprehensive "how-to" emphasis that describes the attunement process in detail.

However, there is still a problem with renewing lectio divina as the only means of preparing for Centering Prayer. The reading, the reflection, and the prayer aspects of lectio divina all rely on discursive thinking. Yet there is a large gap between using the mind for conceptual thinking and the letting go of conceptual thinking required for Centering Prayer. Certainly the discursive process of divine seeking is very helpful and necessary to instill the convictions of Christian faith. These serve as a conceptual foundation for progressing to contemplation. But the problem is with the attachment to holding on to this discursive approach so strongly that you cannot let go of it in order to experience contemplation.

The sixteenth-century mystic, St. John of the Cross, advises seekers to continue to use discursive reflection to approach God as long as seekers can do so effectively. St. John cautions that the time may come when God will take away the seeker's ability to use discursive reflection and express the will satisfactorily in prayer. In this case, God is calling the seeker to a deeper level of communication and relationship. Previously God gave His blessing to the seeker's reasoning and to his experience of the senses to help him communicate with Him in prayer. However, in this transition to a deeper relationship, God withdraws the assistance He provided to reasoning and to the senses during prayer, rendering these faculties ineffective and unsatisfactory as a means of divine communication. Seekers can become very discouraged by this state, called the "night of sense." Because of being unable to pray, they may be tempted to imagine either that they have abandoned God or perhaps God has abandoned them. St. John says that instead of resisting this condition, the seeker would be wise to embrace the situation since it is a sign that God is leading the seeker in the direction of nonconceptual contemplation.[14]

The night of sense is most likely to occur with those seekers who have practiced discursive methods of attunement for a long time, perhaps many years. Such seekers may simply run out of inspiring new thoughts and feelings so that their prayer life becomes stale. At this point, a new way of approaching God without concepts may become appealing. But it would be a mistake to think that a seeker must experience the night of sense as a necessary prerequisite to be open to a nonconceptual approach to God. Instead of experiencing the night of sense, many seekers today, unlike seekers of the past who were less informed, are willing to pursue a nonconceptual approach because of being better informed in this age of communication. Thomas Keating attributes the modern-day renewal of interest in nonconceptual contemplative practices to two factors. One is to the rediscovery of the teachings of St. John of the Cross and other early Christian mystics. The other is Western exposure to Eastern spiritual disciplines, which have become popular in recent years.

Thomas Keating acknowledges the Western bias of relying on the mental approach toward spiritual seeking and feels that the interest in the East is a sign of what is missing in the West. Thomas Keating does say some Eastern disciplines can serve as a preparation for Centering Prayer and the experience of contemplation, yet he does not elaborate on the specific Eastern methods. Advocating for Centering Prayer, he does not personally recommend the concentrative method of repeating a mantra continuously. But he does say that many Western seekers, especially beginners, who generally have an active disposition, benefit from this practice, which can serve as a preparation for Centering Prayer.

The new approach to contemplation advocated in this manual relies on looking to the East as a resource for preparing the seeker to enter Christian contemplation in a systematic manner. Why look to the East? Both the East and the West have the goal of leading seekers from conceptual awareness to a deep level of nonconceptual awareness. But the East does a better job of leading the seeker in a step-by-step manner from one technique to another, and then to still another technique. In addition, the East does a better job of including body awareness as part of the inward-seeking growth process, which will eventually bring the seeker beyond body awareness.

Zen Buddhism recognizes the need for learning meditation techniques in a sequence starting with more elementary methods and leading to more difficult methods. A Zen roshi will assign to a beginner the method of counting the inhalations and exhalations. The beginning seeker will count from one to ten, and then repeat this sequence continuously while also focusing on the navel area. The second method assigned at a later date is the counting of just the exhalations. The third method is the counting of just the inhalations.[15]

The Rinzai sect of Zen Buddhism then leads the seeker to repeat a koan. Examples of koans are "What is my face before I was born?" and "What is the sound of one hand clapping?" Another koan is "Who am I?" which is likewise found in some yoga traditions of self-inquiry. These koans are questions that cannot be answered by intellectual responses. The solution to the question can only be a direct experience of the Reality that is beyond dualism. These koans are assigned by a roshi to a student, with easier koans assigned first and more difficult koans assigned later. Unlike the Rinzai sect, the Soto sect of Zen Buddhism does not advocate the use of koans. The roshi belonging to the Soto sect guides the student in a systematic manner toward the practice of a nonconceptual approach to inward seeking, called *shikan-taza*. This spiritual discipline does not rely on holding on to any word, thought, or image and is an Eastern version of the objectless awareness of contemplation.[16]

Just as Zen Buddhist students are taught meditation techniques in a sequential manner, some yoga disciplines teach a sequence of focusing that leads in a systematic manner toward deeper levels of awareness. Similar to Zen Buddhism that focuses on the body, specifically the navel area, yoga techniques also focus on the body itself as a vehicle for spiritual transformation. Mantras are assigned for specific parts of the body, and the awareness is raised from the lower part of the body in a progressive manner upward toward the head. This is in sharp contrast to the traditional approach of Christian inward seeking that does not include body awareness as part of the process. There is a great deal that the West can learn from the East in regard to body awareness used as an aid to inward seeking. The importance of body awareness in meditation has been explained in Chapters 4 and 7.

Opening the Heart and Mind to Divine Love is the subtitle of this meditation manual in order to emphasize that the techniques presented in this manual are a means of leading you from lower levels of awareness to contemplation, which is an experience of divine love. There are *centers of awareness*, which are considered to be *spiritual centers*. These centers of awareness are like inner doors, which are normally closed. Specific meditation methods can be used in coordination with the action of the Holy Spirit in order to open these inner doors to create a doorway to contemplation, which in turn leads to higher consciousness. These inner doors are associated with parts of the body along the cerebral-spinal axis and ideally open from the bottom upward.

In Eastern philosophy these centers of awareness are called *chakras*. In the West the best symbol for these centers of awareness is the story of Jacob's ladder. In the Old Testament story, Jacob had a dream of angels descending and ascending on a ladder extending from the earth to Heaven. The rungs on Jacob's ladder symbolize the different levels of awareness that lead in a step-by-step progression from earthly awareness to heavenly awareness. In this manual the image of the rungs of Jacob's ladder can symbolize different techniques used in sequence that help to awaken higher and higher levels of awareness leading to contemplation.

Using this image of the rungs of Jacob's ladder as the techniques leading to higher awareness, Centering Prayer centered on contemplation is a single high rung on this ladder, and concentrative forms of mental focusing for inward seeking are very low rungs on this same ladder. Concentrative forms of attunement involve holding on to one or more spiritual thoughts. Contemplation involves the letting go of all thoughts and resting in the Spirit. Holding on to thoughts and letting go of all thoughts are two very different processes. Thus there is a large gap between the lower conceptual rungs of Jacob's ladder and the higher nonconceptual rung of contemplation. Many seekers are not successful in being able to bridge this gap and experience contemplation. To assist seekers in bridging this gap, what is needed is a sequence of rungs that can serve as steps leading to the experience of contemplation. One of the purposes of this manual is to provide a specific series of steps to fill this gap in order to make it easier for the seeker to let go of relying on mental activity and make the transition to contemplative resting in God.

Consequently, the major method recommended in this manual is Progressive Meditation, in which there is a sequence of four specific methods that are rungs on Jacob's ladder. The first three techniques lead toward the experience of contemplation in the practice of Inner Silence Meditation, which is equivalent to the practice of Centering Prayer. This sequence of methods in the practice of Progressive Meditation is designed to serve as a systematic series of steps for learning how to enter into contemplation.

D. Divine Healing

The previous section explains how a series of less advanced techniques can provide the preparation to lead the seeker to experience the more advanced state of resting in God during contemplation. The four methods of Progressive Meditation can meet this need for seekers, who have never meditated or who have tried techniques but have been unable to overtly experience mystical graces that would confirm their faith in the divine presence within. However, would the sequence of techniques in Progressive Meditation be of any significant benefit to you if you are already an experienced meditator, who perhaps uses Centering Prayer? Would Progressive Meditation be helpful for you if you have already experienced mystical graces and the divine presence in contemplation?

To make this determination requires discussing the internal process that can be called "divine healing," which would include spiritually guided psychotherapy. Divine healing is a process of letting go of inner blocks. These obstacles may be triggered and released during meditation, and even deeper blocks can be released through experiencing contemplation. During Centering Prayer your intention to enter the divine presence is not just an invitation to be at peace and rest. More importantly, it is also an invitation for transformation. Typically during meditation your mind will alternate between times of contemplative rest and distracting thoughts. If you are a beginner in practicing meditation, your mind may be so unruly that distracting thoughts may dominate your meditation period. Because you are a beginner, these thoughts usually are the ordinary thoughts, judgments, and concerns of everyday living. After some time you will be able to let go of these passing mundane thoughts and discover contemplative intervals of peace and increase the frequency and duration of these peaceful intervals. You will still have to deal with distracting thoughts, but there will be a balance between the peaceful intervals and the distractions. The remainder of this section will assume that you have already gone through the beginning phase of learning how to let go of everyday thoughts and that you have experienced intervals of peace during your attunement practice.

As you become a more experienced meditator, you will continue to encounter ordinary distracting thoughts, but in addition you will perhaps experience stronger thoughts that have a certain force behind them and therefore present a greater potential for distraction. These distracting thoughts may carry with them tension and emotions that have been suppressed. These emotionally charged thoughts may originate from immature childhood emotions and experiences that were hidden in the subconscious mind, rather than being fully resolved and released. The movement of these distracting thoughts from the subconscious mind into the conscious mind intrudes on your restful contemplation, but needs to be understood as being part of a divine healing process.

Since your true nature is love, the divine presence within you acts as a healing influence, helping you to return to the awareness of your love nature. Your times of resting in God create an inner mental environment conducive to healing. Inner healing is produced by releasing blocks to love. But you cannot generally release inner blocks while you are still hiding these blocks from your conscious awareness. Only after bringing your inner blocks to your conscious awareness can you then give these blocks to the Holy Spirit for inner healing to occur. Sometimes seekers mistakenly think that becoming aware of unresolved and immature emotions and tensions is a step backward spiritually. In fact, this is a sign of spiritual maturity, showing that the seeker is strong enough to face inner fears with divine assistance.

Ideally when these previously hidden thoughts and emotions are released into the conscious mind, you will be able to allow them to come and go without paying attention to them. Hopefully you will be able to remain centered on your intention to be aware of the divine presence. However, if you are distracted by these emotionally charged thoughts, you can simply return to repeating your sacred word as a reminder of your intention and as a way of diverting your mind away from the distracting thoughts.

Nonetheless, the ideal way of handling emotionally charged thoughts doesn't always work in practical experience. After making some progress with your practice of Centering Prayer, you may discover that instead of reducing distracting thoughts, you spend most or even all of your attunement practice being distracted. If this happens, you may find that emotionally charged thoughts have such an increased force and effect on your mind that they dominate your inward awareness. The reasons for these thoughts, such as unresolved childhood experiences or other inner conflicts, may not come to your conscious awareness. Even though the reasons may not be apparent, the tension, anxiety, and emotions can monopolize your attunement period. You may have to repeat your sacred word continuously in order to turn your awareness away from these disturbing thoughts, and even this practice may not succeed in calming the mind. As an aftereffect, you may become depressed for short or even long periods of time. All this unloading of the subconscious mind may be seen by you as proof of going backward in your spiritual life, rather than as a necessary step in your process of divine healing.

Your practice of Centering Prayer expresses your intention of having a closer personal relationship with God. In addition, manifesting your intention involves surrendering to God's Will, allowing Him to take you by the hand and lead you through whatever it takes to form a deeper relationship. What is required is not so much your willingness to face God, but rather your willingness to face your *self*—or more specifically to face your *shadow*. What is your shadow? It is a collection of thoughts in your subconscious mind. These thoughts represent the parts of yourself that you have deemed unacceptable and so have denied. This shadow is not objectively real and not part of your true Self. However, by hiding these emotionally charged thoughts away in your subconscious mind, you have given these thoughts a subjective reality within the private world of your own mind. You can change your mind about these thoughts and let go of them by giving them to the Holy Spirit for disposal. But first you have to bring this shadow portion of your mind out into the light so the divine presence can shine away the shadow. Because the emotionally charged thoughts in the shadow portion of the mind involve raw emotions, such as fear, anger, or pain, it takes courage to face these stark emotions. It also takes faith in the strength and love of God to support you during this purification process.

Facing this shadow part of your mind may occur only intermittently as part of your daily attunement practice over several years and may not overlap into your daily life, except occasionally. On the other hand, you may go through many short periods of depression that come and go because the shadow is being confronted and released at a deeper level. In your daily life experiences, conflicts or disturbances may occur that are a reflection of your inner turmoil. The outer experiences are another way for you to participate in your purification process with the help of divine grace. It is possible that you may even experience long periods of depression as you go through facing the shadow within. There is even the potential that at some time you may experience a spiritual crisis and turning point in what St. John of the Cross calls the "dark night of the soul," which is described in greater detail in the next chapter. This whole purification process may sound a bit daunting to you. A consoling factor is that you will face only as much of your shadow side as you are willing to look at. You will gain the growth that you are seeking and will go as far along the path as is appropriate to meet your needs at that time.

Suppose for a moment that you are very dedicated, and you want to travel very far along the contemplative path. In this case, it will be very important for you to be willing to confront the shadow at a deep level. Yet the typical Christian approach to releasing inner blocks may not be the best way to face and release the shadow. It is helpful to realize that you have alternatives, just as there are alternative routes of climbing a mountain to reach the peak.

The West and the East take different inward seeking routes, which can be illustrated by the following analogy: A man buys a flat field with a large tree in the middle. He decides to cover the entire field with cement, which surrounds even the base of the trunk of the tree. Then he decides to cover the entire tree with a large black tarp. Next he sells the field to a second man, who decides to take the black tarp off of the tree. The tree flourishes for a while in the sunshine. But after some time passes he sees that the tree is wilting because the heat of the sun is drying up the tree, so he puts the black tarp back on the tree. Next he sells the field to a third man who decides to break up and remove all the cement on the field. After the cement is removed, the tree can receive the nourishment of rainwater coming upward through the roots. Because of the water coming upward, the previously wilting tree is revived, and there is no longer a concern about the tree withering because of the heat of the sun. Thus he takes the tarp off, and the tree flourishes because of the harmonious combination of the rainwater rising up and the sunshine descending down.

This analogy is based on the premise that, generally speaking, there are three primary levels of transformation and healing that need to occur in order to return to wholeness. The top level is associated with mental transformation and the top of the body, the head. The middle level is associated with emotional transformation and with the middle level of the body, especially the heart. The bottom level is associated with physical transformation and the lower part of the body, including the navel area, the generative organs, and the base of the spine. In the analogy, the tree as a whole symbolizes the seeker. The branches and leaves represent the top-level mental transformation. The trunk represents the middle-level emotional transformation. The roots represent the bottom-level physical transformation.

The first man in the story, who puts the black tarp over the tree and places cement on the field, symbolizes the activities of separation that oppose harmony, integration, and unity. The second man, who takes the black tarp off the tree, symbolizes the typical Christian "top-down" orientation to divine healing and transformation. Removing the tarp from the top of the tree represents uncovering the mind first and disregarding the lower levels. Just as the tree prospers at first because of the descending sunshine, the seeker flourishes at first with this entirely mental orientation. Like the excessive heat from the sun that eventually becomes oppressive to the tree, the exclusively mental orientation can eventually cause problems for the seeker. The cause of the tree's problem is that the ground level has been covered over by cement. Therefore, the tree cannot receive water coming up from below for nourishment to balance the heat descending from above. Likewise, the seeker relying exclusively on the top-down mental approach cannot receive nourishment from the lower level energy rising up from below to create an inner balance.

Examples of the top-down orientation are both Centering Prayer and Christian Meditation, which are mental practices that focus on thoughts alone and disregard body awareness. Although Centering Prayer leads to the nonconceptual awareness of contemplation, it is included here as a mental method of transformation because it is designed to change the mind, and its practice totally disregards energy rising upward from the lower part of the body awareness. The practice of Centering Prayer brings many benefits in the beginning, just as the tree at first flourishes in the sunlight. Yet eventually so much of the shadow can be released during Centering Prayer that the seeker can become overwhelmed and depressed. This is similar to the tree in the analogy that wilts because it is oppressed by heat from above and not physically nourished by water coming upward through its roots. The lofty top-down orientation to transformation without adequate integration of the emotions and physical body can eventually stagnate and produce the spiritual crisis of the "dark night of the soul," described in Chapter 9. This turning point can certainly be met and overcome with faith and perseverance. However, it is very important to understand that this is certainly not the *only* route to divine healing and transformation.

The third man, who breaks up the cement first and removes it so the tree can get water for nourishment, symbolizes the typical Eastern "bottom-up" orientation to divine transformation. Breaking up the cement and removing it represents starting first by placing emphasis on the lowest and most concrete level that needs transformation, which is the physical level. For example, in Zen Buddhism the meditator focuses on the navel area, and in certain kinds of yoga meditation disciplines, the seeker focuses first on the *kundalini* at the base of the spine before raising his awareness to higher levels. In the analogy the breaking of the cement allows water to nourish the tree, and similarly Eastern yoga methods facilitate raising the kundalini energy from the base of the spine upward.

Of course, the kundalini can be improperly raised by extreme spiritual disciplines and produce very traumatic results. Such negative experiences have given the kundalini a bad name in the West, but actually the kundalini can be raised through moderate meditation methods in a slow and gentle manner. The kundalini acts as a means of bringing attention to inner blocks in a systematic way as it rises and helps to remove these blocks. Instead of becoming overwhelmed with blocks as can happen in the top-down orientation, the bottom-up orientation deals with releasing blocks in a piecemeal manner that follows a natural and somewhat predictable manner. This natural process helps you face your shadow through using a step-by-step manner in which each step builds on the previous step in a strengthening manner. As is the case with the top-down orientation, all the emotions will have to be addressed, including depression, but there is less potential for being overwhelmed by depression in this approach.

The sequence of four methods combined in the practice of Progressive Meditation is an effective means of fostering the bottom-up orientation to inward seeking and manifesting the piecemeal removal of inner blocks. If you are practicing Centering Prayer exclusively, you may run into difficulties with your practice because of forceful distracting thoughts and emotions due to the release of too many unresolved parts of your shadow all at once. In this case, because you have no alternate attunement practice, you will just have to continue with your practice of Centering Prayer, even if your practice is totally dominated by distractions. In contrast to having only one meditative practice, the four techniques of Progressive Meditation provide flexibility. If you have difficulty with Inner Silence Meditation because of too many unruly, distracting thoughts, you can choose to spend more time on the previous three techniques. The first three techniques of Progressive Meditation focus initially on calming the body, then calming the emotions, and then calming the mind. This sequence of inner calming, which is a bottom-up orientation, provides a preparation for entering the silence of contemplation. After becoming calmer within, you will be better prepared to proceed to Inner Silence Meditation and enter the rest of contemplation. When your practice of Inner Silence Meditation improves and your intervals of resting in God increase, you can decrease the time for the preparatory first three methods and increase the time for Inner Silence Meditation.

The four techniques of Progressive Meditation have been described previously as Jacob's ladder, leading the seeker one step at a time from lower levels of awareness to higher levels of awareness. In Jacob's dream image of a ladder, the angels are ascending and descending between earth and Heaven, but from the perspective of the seeker, his approach obviously has to be a bottom-up orientation. Even though the seeker may receive divine blessings from above, he has to start his journey in the lower level awareness of the earth where he is now and from the earth move upward.

What may not be so obvious about the dream image of Jacob's ladder is that the ladder that leads from lower levels of awareness to higher levels of awareness is within the body itself. The Kingdom of God is literally within one's self. Jacob's ladder has its base in the earth, which in the body is the base of the spine where the kundalini lies sleeping and waiting to be awakened in order to trigger higher levels of awareness as it rises. The top of Jacob's ladder is in Heaven, which in the body is the crown of the head or some would say just above the head. The raising of the awareness of the seeker is a natural process of the kundalini rising in a progressive manner from the base of the spine upward along the center of the body to the top of the head.

As has been emphasized, the typical mistake made by Christian seekers is to ignore this bottom-up natural process and to focus only on the top part of Jacob's ladder. As mentioned previously, Thomas Keating offers the theory that cloistered Christian seekers are less successful in experiencing overt mystical graces than seekers in the world. This is because God gives more grace to seekers in the world, who need more divine help. Yet if this theory of God giving more grace to seekers in the world is accurate, then it would logically follow that Eastern seekers in monastic settings would have less of a mystical life than Eastern seekers in the world. But it is generally believed that Eastern monks have a robust, mystical, spiritual life. My own opinion is that Eastern monastic seekers take the bottom-up approach to contemplative seeking that simply produces better consciously felt results.

This Eastern bottom-up approach facilitates the rising of the kundalini, the removing of inner blocks, and the revealing of the divine presence. In contrast to this, Christian cloistered monks use the top-down contemplative approach that ignores body awareness. Their restrictive lifestyle tends to deny and suppress the creative energy, which has the potential to be used for sexual purposes or to be raised up for higher spiritual purposes. The setting aside of sexual desires for moral reasons can be an asset to spiritual growth as long as this abstinence is accompanied by a corresponding raising up of the same creative energy for spiritual purposes. However, the problem for cloistered monks occurs when the sexual energy is suppressed and also the creative energy is suppressed instead of being raised up for spiritual purposes. It is this suppression of creative energy that prevents the majority of cloistered monks from experiencing felt mystical graces.

The limitations of the cloistered lifestyle tend to deny and hide inner blocks, especially blocks related to the middle and lower part of the body. The denial of inner blocks prevents these obstacles from being revealed, confronted, and surrendered to the Holy Spirit. Implementing a bottom-up approach to contemplation could correct this situation by helping to raise creative energy and by helping to reveal inner blocks so they can be offered to the Holy Spirit for healing. The drawing on page 203 identifies the various blocks that need to be faced and released and shows the parts of the body and spiritual centers generally associated with these blocks.

Christian seekers in the world who likewise use a top-down approach are more successful at having consciously felt mystical experiences than cloistered monks because their lifestyle is more conducive to expressing creative energy. Not being in a structured monastic setting, Christian seekers in the world are exposed to a greater variety of relationships and life experiences that tend to prevent the seeker from being in denial about his inner blocks. The revealing of these inner blocks in life experiences forces the seeker to directly confront these inner blocks and to release them with the help of the Holy Spirit.

Both Christian cloistered monks and Christian seekers in the world would benefit by a Christian bottom-up approach to contemplation. The sequence of four techniques of Progressive Meditation is designed as a contemplative bottom-up approach to contemplation. Centering Meditation, the first technique in this sequence, brings the awareness to the lower part of the body and invites the Holy Spirit in coordination with the gentle rising of the kundalini to release inner blocks at the physical level. Heart Meditation, the second technique, brings attention to the heart and invites the Holy Spirit along with the rising of the kundalini to remove inner obstacles at the emotional level. Brow Meditation, the third technique, focuses attention within the head and invites the Holy Spirit in coordination with the rising of the kundalini to release inner blocks at the mental level. The fourth technique invites the Holy Spirit to integrate the physical, emotional, and mental levels of your being to produce the unifying influence of your divine oneness. This fourth technique is Inner Silence Meditation (equivalent to Centering Prayer) that leads to contemplation.

Like the rungs of Jacob's ladder, each method builds on the previous technique and smoothly leads to the next technique. Collectively the first three techniques form a solid foundation for entering contemplation during the fourth method, Inner Silence Meditation. The advanced state of resting in God during contemplation is an experience of surrendering to God. In this surrender you give your consent to the activity and the presence of God. This is not a lifelong commitment. It is only a moment to moment surrender and an incomplete surrender. The inner blocks of the human condition make it extremely difficult to surrender your whole self to God even for a few moments.

Temporarily surrendering all of yourself, including your thoughts, is difficult to do since it requires a willingness to be vulnerable and naked before God. Intimacy with God, similar to intimacy at the human level, requires a gradual transition from friendship to intimacy. You can best learn to surrender to God by surrendering piece by piece before a deeper surrender can be made. The first three methods of Progressive Meditation are really a sequence of surrendering yourself in parts as a preparation for surrendering yourself more completely to God in contemplation. Through practicing this sequence of methods you surrender the physical, the emotional, and the mental parts of yourself to God. These partial surrenders prepare you for experiencing the more holistic surrender that occurs in contemplation during the practice of the final technique, Inner Silence Meditation.

The partial surrenders of the first three techniques of Progressive Meditation involve a release of inner blocks in a natural manner, which corresponds to the rising of the kundalini that helps to facilitate this purification process. The rising of the kundalini, when it is guided by the Holy Spirit, helps you to release inner blocks of tension, anxiety, and emotions from the subconscious mind. Blocks are released from all parts of the body. At first lower blocks in the body may be released first and then higher blocks may be released in a natural process, but often the release of blocks does not follow this upward sequence. Blocks may be released from any part of the body at any time during meditation or contemplation depending on the willingness of the seeker and on the action of the Holy Spirit. The four techniques of Progressive Meditation are just four rungs on Jacob's ladder to higher awareness. There are other helpful rungs below these, such as various forms of prayer and devotion, as well as various hatha yoga postures and breathing practices that can assist your growth. There are also rungs of attunement above the techniques of Progressive Meditation. Examples of these more advanced methods are presented in Chapter 11, which emphasizes learning how to open to light and love.

---

1. Thomas Ryan, C.S.P., *Prayer of Heart and Body: Meditation and Yoga as Christian Spiritual Practice* (New York, NY/Mahwah, NJ: Paulist Press, 1995), pp. 41-42.
2. Ibid., pp. 65-67.
3. Thomas Keating, *Open Mind, Open Heart: The Contemplative Dimension of the Gospel* (New York, NY: The Continuum International Publishing Group, 2001), Copyright 1986, 1992 by St. Benedict's Monastery, reprinted by permission of The Continuum International Publishing Group, pp. 143-144.
4. Ibid., p. 48.
5. Ibid., p. 48.
6. Ibid., p. 110.
7. Ibid., p. 10.
8. Ibid., pp. 10-11.
9. Ibid., p. 11.
10. Ibid., p.11.
11. Ibid., p. 11.
12. Ibid., p. 29.
13. Ibid., pp. 20-21.
14. Ibid., pp. 28-29.
15. Philip Kapleau, *The Three Pillars of Zen* (New York, London, Toronto, Sydney, Auckland: Anchor Books, Doubleday and Company, 1965, 1980), pp. 35-41.
16. Ibid., p. 49.

9

CONTEMPLATION AS A PATH OF DARKNESS

~ • ~

A. Contemplation as Imageless Self-Awareness

This chapter will focus on seeking God through contemplation in the darkness of pure faith. Although this is the path of darkness that requires pure faith, this road to awakening ultimately culminates in a profound transformation of consciousness that involves a transcendent experience of divine light. However, the contemplative path itself described here consists of the steps you take along the way, not the culmination.

Contemplation is a wordless form of communication with God that does not involve focusing on body awareness and that comes by grace. During contemplation the Holy Spirit overshadows you as you rest in a state of *inner absorption*, which may also be called a state of *imageless self-awareness*. While in this state, there is no desire to use any of the functions of the rational mind to unite with God. Contemplation is not something that you can do, but rather something that happens to you by the action of the Holy Spirit. Contemplation occurs after using various forms of meditation for some time and is a manifestation of grace.

While in the state of contemplation, the mind is fully alert and at the same time empty of all desire for any thoughts. Thoughts themselves may appear, yet there is no desire for them. These thoughts may float through the mind, but they are not possessed. To possess a thought is to judge it, or even to recognize it, by thinking, "This is my thought." Thoughts come and go as garbage floating in a river. As the garbage floats in front of you, you do clearly see that garbage. Nevertheless, you do not look upstream to see where the garbage is coming from, nor do you look downstream to see where the garbage is going. You let the garbage come and go without paying any attention to it.

As progress is made in contemplation, even these thoughts that float by also disappear for intervals of time. The mind is totally alert and yet empty. Your mind does not reflect on itself as to how it feels or how it thinks, but rather simply rests in the state of imageless self-awareness. This form of wordless meditation should not be confused with an idle stupor of the mind. It is really a state of keen awareness, though not intellectual thought-awareness. Neither should contemplation be considered to be a state of thought suppression. The very effort to suppress thought would stir up more thought. Some people foolishly attempt to counterfeit true contemplation by "blanking out" the mind in a state of thought negation. Manipulating the mind in a mechanical way that negates thought may actually succeed only in dulling the mind rather than bringing about the heightened awareness produced by contemplation.

The initial stage of contemplation can be facilitated by a technique, such as Inner Silence Meditation. But contemplation itself, especially in its deeper stages, should not be thought of as a method of emptying the mind, nor can it be taught. During contemplation the mind is indeed emptied, but this state should be more clearly understood as a filling of the Holy Spirit, which silences the functioning of the rational mind. Since contemplation is not a technique, but rather a gift of grace from the Holy Spirit, contemplation itself cannot be taught. Yet you can be taught how to prepare yourself to be receptive to this gift. This preparation consists of learning how to practice various preliminary spiritual activities or disciplines that form a foundation for experiencing contemplation.

If you desire the gift of contemplation, you need to prepare yourself to receive this grace first by performing good works in the active life. You cannot receive the inner peace of contemplation without first learning to live at peace by serving your brothers and sisters. In addition to purifying the heart through service to others, you need to also prepare a clean dwelling place for the Holy Spirit through prayer and meditation, which will help to overcome negative emotional factors and mental distractions. Consistency in practicing prayer and meditation is very important. The best prayer is to do God's Will in all the activities of daily life, yet in order to do that, you need to establish a daily habit of prayer and meditation, the effects of which carry over into outward activities.

Just as there are many methods of meditation, there are many ways of praying. You can practice forms of prayer that are most spiritually moving for you, including formal prayers such as the Lord's Prayer, or prayers of petition, spontaneous prayer, group prayer, worship services, and many other ways of communicating with God. These forms of prayer increase your devotion, faith, and humility, and along with meditation they prepare the soul for contemplation.

Besides attracting spiritual graces, the effect of prayer and meditation techniques that use words is that these words create and instill strong positive impressions in the mind. Through repetition practiced over a period of time, these positive word impressions have a stronger impact on the mind than the negative impressions of past memories. If you were to attempt to go directly into wordless contemplation without first having built a solid foundation of positive word impressions, you would be opening yourself to a potentially harmful situation. In your wordless meditation, you might be confronted with negative past impressions and/or suppressed emotions, which you might not know how to handle. However, with a store of positive impressions, you have a means of counterbalancing and overcoming these negative impressions.

All forms of communication with God can help to build this positive foundation. Nevertheless, techniques such as Progressive Meditation that include the repeating of an affirmation of your spiritual ideal are especially effective in establishing a firm foundation of positive mental impressions. Your affirmation, perhaps in the form of the Divine Name, is your best tool for dispelling negative past impressions and at the same time attracting divine grace.

With the first three methods of Progressive Meditation, you use your affirmation with body awareness methods. However, after meditating with your affirmation and with body awareness, then you may practice letting go of your affirmation and letting go of body awareness to allow yourself to be moved by the Holy Spirit at a level beyond words. This way of meditating is Inner Silence Meditation, the fourth and concluding method of Progressive Meditation. As has been described previously, the purpose of Inner Silence Meditation is to lead you from a technique of stillness toward contemplation.

As you use your affirmation, without trying to use the rational mind to intellectualize about its meaning, and then let go of your affirmation, occasionally contemplation may occur. You may drift into and out of the contemplative state of self-awareness without images and at times without thoughts. For intervals when you let go of your affirmation during Inner Silence Meditation, all thought may stop. You will have an intuitive self-awareness, but you will not be able to analyze this state intellectually while you are in it. As you drift out of this state, you may attempt to use your rational mind to comprehend where you have been. Instead, let your intellectual thoughts simply be a reminder for you to return to repeating your affirmation. Where you have been can only be experienced. It cannot be explained satisfactorily in a purely intellectual way even to yourself.

Meditation, in general, attempts to lead you from a state of "doing" to a state of "being," but since Inner Silence Meditation is a technique, there is still at least some sense of "doing" something to empty the mind and to feel the divine presence. Contemplation relies to a greater degree on just "being," and allowing the Spirit to be the doer within you. It is the difference between subtly attempting to possess God and freely allowing God to possess you. Therefore, to allow contemplation to happen by divine grace, you need to be completely passive and only receptive to God's initiative of love without taking any initiative of your own.

When you practice Inner Silence Meditation, if you find that your attention is drawn toward stray thoughts of the rational mind, then return to the repetition of your affirmation. However, when your mind becomes calm, you can let go of your affirmation to enter inner silence. As you rest in inner silence, if you find yourself naturally absorbed into the state of imageless self-awareness, then continue in this way as long as stray thoughts do not divert your attention.

Inner Silence Meditation guides you toward contemplation, but it should be mentioned that contemplation can occur spontaneously at any time with any meditation method. For example, contemplation may occur when you are practicing any one of the body awareness methods of Progressive Meditation. After you have let go of your affirmation and while you are still focusing only on a particular focusing area in the body, you may be drawn into the contemplative state of imageless self-awareness. If this contemplative state presents itself spontaneously, you can let go of focusing on a part of the body and rest in the inner absorption of imageless self-awareness. If you become distracted by stray thoughts, you can return to your affirmation and to the focusing area appropriate for the body awareness technique that you are using.

Although you are practicing techniques in which contemplation may occur, it is important to realize that this state of imageless self-awareness is not really caused by any technique. It is a gift. The experience itself of imageless self-awareness will not be the result of calling on the Name of God or any other method. It is because God is calling you. His calling of you has moved you to call on Him, first with words and then at a level beyond words.

Contemplation, as a gift of being overshadowed by the Holy Spirit, is not like human gifts, which are given intermittently. It is a divine gift given constantly. Like many spiritual gifts, it is a present that is always available to you, yet awaits your opening. You open this gift by meeting four necessary conditions. These four conditions were initially introduced in Chapter 5 and then described in Chapter 7. Now for emphasis this chapter will elaborate upon the nature of these four conditions.

Learning to meet the conditions of contemplation may be compared to learning to float in the ocean. The buoyancy of water is what enables you to float, and buoyancy is always present, awaiting your meeting of the conditions that would allow you to float. You need to meet four conditions. The first condition is to produce a calm body and mind, which is necessary for floating to occur. Just as with your practice of meditation, you calm yourself for floating by allowing the body to be as motionless as possible, by slowing down your breathing, and by calming your mind, allowing your body to be surrounded by water. The second condition is to have the desire to float. The third condition is your consent, which expresses your free will to accept being in the water to make floating happen. The fourth condition is to have faith in your ability to float. Before you actually have the experience of floating yourself, you need to have faith that this process of placing yourself in the uncertainty of being horizontal in the water will result in you actually being able to float. After calming yourself, desiring to float, and giving your consent to accept this process that would make floating possible, the last requirement is your faith. Through implementing your faith that this process will actually work, you meet all the conditions necessary to make floating possible. Meeting all four of these conditions allows the natural buoyancy of water to create a lifting effect on your body, resulting in floating.

The lifting effect produced by the buoyancy of water is always there, waiting for you to meet the following four conditions: calming yourself, expressing your desire, giving your consent, and offering your faith to trust that floating will occur. Similarly, the uplifting spiritual effect that is produced by the Holy Spirit is always there, waiting for you to meet the conditions of calming yourself, expressing your desire, giving your consent, and offering your faith that contemplation will occur. The first condition for receiving the gift of contemplation is a calm mind. The calmer your mind becomes, the more you can open yourself to contemplation and the deeper your experience of contemplation will be. Your meditation practice is designed to calm the mind sufficiently enough to open you to contemplation. The second condition is your desire for God expressed in words by your affirmation, which focuses your intention to open to God. The third condition is your consent to accept His presence. When you let go of your affirmation, you allow your desire and consent to be expressed in inner silence at a deeper level beyond words where you are guided by your pure faith in God, which is the fourth condition for contemplation to occur.

In summary, in order to float, you calm your mind, make your body motionless, express your desire to float by sinking into the water, give your consent to accept being encompassed by the water, and finally express your faith that you will float by surrendering to the whole process. The result is that you experience floating. Likewise, for contemplation to occur, you will need to calm your mind, make your body motionless, express your desire by sinking into the Spirit, give your consent to accept being encompassed by the divine presence, and finally allow your faith in God to allow you to surrender to the Spirit. Having met the necessary conditions, you will experience the gift of contemplation.

The result of meeting the conditions of floating is the natural state of floating, and the result of meeting the conditions of contemplation is the natural state of contemplation. But the contemplative state appears to be an unusual state, not a natural state. This is because the idea of being separate from God seems natural and the idea of being with God seems unnatural. Ironically it is your idea of separation from God that is what stands between you and your awareness of God. You are joined with God every moment, just as God is joined with every object and every form of existence. Yet your idea of separation, which is your ego, keeps you preoccupied with attachments and compulsions that appear "natural" to you because of conditioning and familiarity. Your preoccupations divert your mind from its true, natural inclination to be open to your divine nature. By learning to let go of your thoughts that pass by in your mind, you release, even if only temporarily, your attachments and compulsions. You are willing to engage in this process of letting go of thoughts, because you have faith that beyond these thoughts there is a divine presence. You desire to become more aware of this divine presence, and you give your consent to accept this presence being revealed to you and being expressed in you. Thus the combination of the four conditions listed below results in the experience of contemplation:

The Four Conditions of Contemplation

1. Calmness of the mind
2. Desire for God
3. Consent to the divine presence
4. Faith invested in God

The degree of calmness in the mind, the degree of your desire, the degree of your consent, and the degree of your investment in faith determine both the depth and the consistency of your contemplative experience. The practice of Progressive Meditation is important as a means of increasing the degree of your calmness, desire, consent, and faith, so your contemplation will be experienced deeply and consistently. Using the first three techniques of Progressive Meditation, you give your consent to accept the divine presence by opening to God at the physical, the emotional, and the mental levels of your being.

During the fourth method, Inner Silence Meditation, you give your consent to accept the Holy Spirit, allowing the unification of these levels and expansion of your awareness. With your continued consent, the Holy Spirit acts through all your centers of awareness. This action of the Holy Spirit opens you to His World, a dimension transcending the physical world. Entering His World brings about the dynamic inner absorption of contemplation. This contemplative experience produces what is described in greater detail below as the "cloud of unknowing," because your rational thinking (your normal way of knowing) is not at home in His World.

Your desire for God and your consent to accept the Holy Spirit are important conditions for contemplation to occur. Of course, the other conditions of achieving a deepening of calmness in your mind and implementing your faith also need to be present for contemplation to occur. Another term for a calm mind is a "unified mind." Sometimes when the word "mind" is used, it refers only to the discursive thinking portion of the mind. But the word "mind," as it will be used now, has a broader meaning that includes the ability of the mind to be aware of levels of consciousness beyond just rational thinking. The mind is naturally simple rather than complex, unified rather than divided. The mind has a divine origin, and its natural inclination toward simplicity and unity is a reflection of God, Who is Oneness, simple and undivided. One way of describing contemplation is to say it is a natural state of consciousness in which the mind is simple, unified, and open to Spirit by your consent.

Even though contemplation is a natural state of mind, at first it seems unnatural. In contemplation you enter His World, which seems unnatural, and you leave your world, which appears natural to you only out of familiarity. But the truth is that in your daily life you live in an unnatural world where the mind is divided between the worldly thoughts of the ego and the desire for union with God. The mind that is divided becomes complex as it becomes preoccupied with ego-based thoughts that produce tension. As you let go of ego-based thoughts in meditation, the mind becomes increasingly free to pursue its natural inclination toward simplicity and unification. When the mind reaches a certain degree of simplification and unification, the mind no longer presents an obstacle to the natural occurrence of contemplation.

Although any meditation technique can help you to calm the mind, Progressive Meditation is especially helpful in bringing about a unified mind. Calmness of mind is produced through a cumulative effect of systematically emptying both your conscious mind and subconscious mind of your ordinary ego-based preoccupations. Progressive Meditation is a comprehensive and systematic means of releasing your attachments and compulsions at the physical, emotional, and mental levels, forming a foundation for spiritual development. Also, Progressive Meditation opens your awareness to your intuitions and produces an integration and unification of your faculties. This in turn brings the mind to a deeper level of calmness that facilitates the deepening of your experience of contemplation.

Your first experiences of contemplation require only a momentary consent, calming of the mind, and expression of faith. Correspondingly, they produce a fleeting experience of contemplation. By practicing Progressive Meditation, you extend your consent to the Holy Spirit to act on all of the levels of your being, allowing a release of subconscious clutter and tension. This release of inner blocks and tension and also the integration and unification of your centers of awareness produce a deeper level of calmness and a greater investment in your faith. By expanding your consent, increasing the application of your faith, and reaching a deeper level of calmness, you are bringing about a simplification and unification of the mind. Continuing to practice Progressive Meditation will increase the consistency and quality of your contemplation.

Progress in your meditation cannot be solely viewed by how calm your mind is during your practice. Every practice in which you are assailed by stray thoughts is your continuing opportunity to relieve the subconscious mind of its attachments and compulsions. The subconscious mind has its own ego-based value system that is programmed into you from your early childhood. As you attempt to let go of your thoughts in meditation, you may encounter at times highly charged thoughts and emotions, which are extremely challenging for you to face. It is these difficult encounters with your subconscious clutter that can be very helpful for your overall growth, even though it may appear to you that for the time being you have failed in calming your mind. There comes a time, and realistically it may take years, when the subconscious clutter in your mind has been largely evacuated to the point where your experience of contemplation becomes deep and consistent. Instead of contemplation being a fleeting few moments at a time, you can make progress so that you can climb up the ladder of your consciousness, enter contemplation, and stay there on the rooftop of your awareness for most or all of your daily practice.

B. Going Beyond Self-Awareness

Contemplation has been described previously as a restful and yet dynamic inner absorption, a state of imageless self-awareness. But this is not the deepest level of contemplation. The goal in contemplation is not "awareness of" but "awareness" itself. "Awareness of" means you are the possessor of the awareness of some object from which you are separate.

In this case, the self is present and the object is present, and each appears to be separate from the other. The result is always self-awareness. In contemplation you want to eventually be able to transcend the self so you can experience "awareness" alone rather then "self-awareness."

Self-awareness, even though it can be experienced without thoughts or images, is still really self-centered. What remains in this self-awareness, after the thoughts and images have passed away, is a naked knowledge of your own self. This naked knowledge, just as Adam's knowledge of his nakedness, is what separates you from God. It is the first knowledge Adam experienced in separating himself from God and also the last knowledge you need to dispense with before returning to God, because this knowledge of yourself is not the knowledge of your true nature in God. It is the elemental knowledge of your ego, your separate self.

Unfortunately you can become so preoccupied with your own self (as you think of yourself, which is your ego) that, considering yourself as the subject of meditation, you mistakenly believe the experience of self-awareness to be the all-important experience. This is unfortunate because, whereas previously the self was attached to the senses of the body and the ordinary thoughts of the mind, now the self is attached to spiritual experiences as well. If there is to be spiritual progress, however, you need to drop this idea of yourself as the subject of meditation, which has in turn made God into an object of meditation. It is equally wrong for you to look on yourself as an object on which God is working, as though you are a separate object that does not already exist within the Being of God. The forms of prayer and meditation already mentioned, including imageless self-awareness, are helpful techniques of drawing closer to divine union, but such methods continue to perpetuate the ego's subject-object division between you and God.

God is nothing and He is not worthy of your belief, unless He is everything and infinitely more than your highest conception of what everything is. He is the Being that transcends your being, since He is the cause of all that exists and His Being is the being of all that exists. Thus you do not have a being distinctly separate from God. Because you have an ego, a false perspective of yourself, you do not realize that God is the being of everything, and God is therefore your own being, your own existence. Your ego tells you that you are alone, yet the truth is that God is always with you and you can never be alone. Your true relationship with God is beyond the subject-object division, which views God as something other than your own being. If you wish to experience God most intimately, you need to be willing to first admit that you, as you currently think of yourself, are only a shadow of your true Self in God.

You may acknowledge that the ego is a lie and that your soul exists in the Being of God, but this is only intellectual agreement. It is the ego that says "Yes" intellectually and yet says this from a perspective of separation. Thus this needs to be experienced, not from an intellectual viewpoint based on the ego, but rather from an inner awakening of consciousness. This awakening would be an experience of yourself as being inseparable from God and existing totally within His Being. The only thing that prevents this realization as an experience is the ego itself. The ego ultimately needs to be given up.

This does not conflict with learning to deal with and accept the ego on your spiritual journey. As long as you live on earth with a body and a mind, you will have an ego. You must not try to get rid of the ego. Ideally you will dedicate the ego to doing God's Will as a service. For most people, the opportunity to completely give up the ego will come at the moment of death. When your body is about to die, you imagine that you are dying. However, your true Self that exists within the being of God cannot die. Therefore, what is dying with the body is only what you have imagined yourself to be, which is a body and a rational mind limited to the body. If throughout your life you have trained the self to be a servant of God's Will in order to allow your true being Self of love to flow through the vehicle of the body and mind, then you will be prepared to give up the ego and be united with God when the moment of truth called death arrives.

In your spiritual journey, a realistic goal is to release inner ego-based blocks that hide your true nature of love and after many years perhaps reach what can be called "the plateau of self-acceptance." This is a state of mind in which you have learned to accept the ego but, more importantly, accept your divine nature. While you are accepting the ego, you still recognize it is an illusion and so you place limits on your ego-based desires in order to let your divine nature shine through in your life. When you reach this plateau of self-acceptance, you have released many inner blocks. Thus you will be able to calm the mind sufficiently to experience contemplation for longer periods of time on a much more consistent basis. In addition, you may occasionally reach a deeper level of contemplation beyond imageless self-awareness. It is a wonderful accomplishment for you to reach the plateau of self-acceptance, and this is recommended as a realistic goal for anyone who wishes to grow spiritually. The next chapter explains the plateau of self-acceptance in more detail.

Perhaps at times your experience of contemplation will go beyond imageless self-awareness. If this happens, you will be going to a deeper level of letting go of the self. This deeper letting go of the self during contemplation occurs spontaneously. If you realize it is happening, your realization itself will be enough to bring you out of this state. Obviously self-awareness has returned when you become aware that you have given up the self, so you can only reflect back on this state after it has already happened. However, realistically not everyone is called to go beyond contemplation with self-awareness to contemplation without self-awareness.

Likewise, not everyone is called to enter the deeper levels of the "dark night of the soul." Just because there are deeper levels of renunciation does not mean that you are meant to pursue these deeper levels. It is important for you to carefully evaluate yourself to determine if you have the degree of desire, renunciation, and determination to pursue deeper levels of letting go of the self. After evaluating yourself and receiving inner guidance, you may be led to pursue a deeper level of letting go of the self. If God's Will has called you to experience the deeper levels of contemplation, the ego must be given up at least for the time of the contemplation. If God's Will has called you to the deeper levels of the "dark night of the soul," you will have to undergo an even more radical giving up of the ego.

Why is it necessary for the ego to be given up for the occurrence of deep contemplation that goes beyond self-awareness and for undergoing the "dark night of the soul"? Why can't you think of the ego as an identity that is expanding and that will reach a higher state of fulfillment? It is because the ego is nothing more than a false idea of separation. As a lie, it cannot co-exist with the truth. While you are experiencing imageless self-awareness or other forms of meditation, you may feel the peaceful presence of God within you. However, there is still a division that exists between you and God by the very fact that you consider God to be working on you as an object, as though God were something other than your own being. This false idea that you are an object in separation from God and that God is not your own being is the very foundation of the ego. Since the ego is the idea of separation from God, this idea of yourself must be given up in order to go beyond self-awareness.

Man's false belief in the ego is like the false belief that the sun revolves around the earth, which mankind believed to be the truth in the times of the earthly ministry of Jesus. Gradually, a few men said that the earth revolves around the sun, but they were not believed. They met disbelief because most men were deceived by appearances since the sun appeared to revolve around the earth as it rose and set every day. Today, mankind knows that the earth revolves around the sun and that the false belief, which mankind was clinging to, is actually a lie.

The way this relates to man's belief in the ego is that mankind continues to be deceived by appearances. The body and mind appear to be separate from God, and the ego-based belief in a separate self is confirmed by the appearances of this world. A few men have directly experienced God as their own existence, as the cause and ground of their being. These men have realized that man is not a separate body and mind, but rather that man is a spiritual being made in the image and likeness of God. These men then have told other men that the ego is only a false perception, which mistakenly views man as the center of consciousness, when in reality God is the center and very being of man.

Though these few men have spoken the truth, they have likewise met with disbelief, just as the men who said the earth is not the center of the universe were disbelieved. There are different kinds of disbelief. The obvious kind of disbelief is the viewpoint of the atheist that says, "You are a body and mind imagining that you are a spirit." This is in direct opposition to those few men who have directly experienced God and have spoken the truth by saying, "You are a spirit thinking that you are only a body and a mind limited to the body."

There is another more subtle kind of disbelief that distorts the truth by compromising the truth. The truth is compromised by combining a false idea with a true idea. In this case, the compromise takes the form of the idea that says, "You are a body and a mind separate from God and also simultaneously you are a spiritual being." The truth in this statement is the words "...you are a spiritual being," but that truth is compromised by the other words in the statement. What is true and what is false are mutually exclusive. Therefore, you cannot accept both what is true and what is false simultaneously without compromising the truth.

The convenient compromise of combining the belief that you are both an ego and a spirit is created because most people find it just too hard to let go of the belief that says, "You are a body and a mind separate from God." If this is your belief, it isn't particularly harmful in a practical sense for you because it allows you to function comfortably in this world where this idea makes perfect sense. You can even hold on to this belief and make a great deal of progress spiritually by dedicating your body and mind to God's service in this world.

But what if you want to experience deep contemplation in His World? From the perspective of His World, do you think God looks on you as a body and a mind separate from Him? No, that's how you view yourself mistakenly. God looks on you as you are. He sees you as a spirit made in His image and likeness, and He sees Himself as joined with you as your source and substance. Any other viewpoint is your illusion about yourself.

Consequently, when a false statement, such as "You are a body and a mind separate from God," is combined with a true statement, such as "You are a spiritual being," the result is a compromise of the truth. You cannot combine a true statement with a false statement and have the combined statement remain true. If you are really seeking the truth, you will need to give up any false ideas that would compromise the truth. For example, could mankind believe in both the old false belief of the sun revolving around the earth and in the new truth of the earth revolving around the sun at the same time? No, of course not, since before the new truth can be accepted, the old false belief must be acknowledged as an error and be given up.

You may ask, "How can I give up the false perception of the ego in order to experience God as my own source and substance?" In answer to this question, "you" cannot do that since the you—meaning the you that you think you are—is the you that needs to be eliminated. Another question you may ask is, "What method should I use?" In answer to this second question, no method can bring you directly to God. To do that, God must take you by the hand and truly empty you of all things in the darkness of faith. He will not show you His Light in its full mystical brightness because your ego could not bear it, and so He takes you into a mystical darkness and emptiness. In this manner, He helps you to surrender your ego by showing you that what you think you are is absolute darkness and nothingness. During contemplation He will lead you from the state of self-awareness into the Void, where the self will feel lost and afraid. Faith must be very strong to step into the Void, because the soul has nothing to call its own. The soul is surrendering the old, familiar, ego-centered consciousness. The soul with both detachment and faith needs to wait passively and patiently in mystical darkness and nothingness. This is what the sixteenth-century mystic St. John of the Cross refers to as the "dark night of the soul." St. John of the Cross describes the detachment necessary to pass through this dark night in order to move on toward divine union when he says:

> A soul is greatly impeded from reaching this high estate of union with God when it clings to any understanding or feeling or imagination or appearance or will or manner of its own, or to any other act or to anything of its own, and cannot detach and strip itself of all these…. Wherefore, upon this road, to enter upon the road is to leave the road; or, to express it better, it is to pass on to the goal and to leave one's own way and to enter upon that which has no way, which is God. For the soul that attains to this state has no longer any ways or methods…. [1]

To further clarify this, another mystic writer, John Tauler, states:

When we have tasted this in the very depth of our souls it makes us sink down and melt away in our nothingness and littleness. The brighter and purer the light shed on us by the greatness of God, the more clearly do we see our littleness and nothingness. In fact, this is how we may discern the genuineness of this illumination; for it is the Divine God shining into our very being, not through images, not through our faculties, but in the very depths of our souls; its effect will be to make us sink down more and more deeply into our own nothingness.[2]

Thomas Merton comments on these two previous quotations in his clear-sighted book, *Contemplative Prayer*, by saying:

There are two simple conclusions to be drawn from this. First, that contemplation is the summit of the Christian life of prayer, for the Lord desires nothing of us so much as to become, Himself, our "way," our "truth and life." This is the whole purpose of his coming on earth to seek us, that He may take us, with Himself, to the Father. Only in and with Him can we reach the invisible Father, whom no man shall see and live. By dying to ourselves, and to all "ways," "logic" and "methods" of our own we can be numbered among those whom the mercy of the Father has called to Himself in Christ. But the other conclusion is equally important. No logic of our own can accomplish this transformation of our interior life. We cannot argue that "emptiness" equals "the presence of God" and then sit down to acquire the presence of God by emptying our souls of every image. It is not a matter of desire, of planned enterprise, or of our own spiritual technique.

The whole mystery of simple contemplative prayer is a mystery of divine love, of personal vocation and of free gift. This, and this alone, makes it true "emptiness" in which there is nothing left of ourselves.[3]

Many would like to experience the illumination that Christ experienced, but how many would like to experience His cross? To follow Christ into the depths of mystical contemplation means a sacrifice of the small self, a total self-surrender to the Will of God. If you wish to follow Jesus, in the beginning you need to desire sincerely to be illuminated by the Light of Christ. Yet in the deepest mystical contemplation, you must surrender even the desire for illumination. Why? Because, who is it that wishes to express such a desire? It is the ego that wishes to make even illumination into an object that it can grasp and hold on to. The ego, which tries to manipulate all things to revolve around itself, is the first to apply as the candidate for illumination, as though it were something to be possessed. But the small self that applies for illumination is not the same Self that receives the gift of illumination. Yet the ego is allowed to see itself as it really is, which is darkness and nothingness in contrast to the true Self that is revealed in God's Light after the small self is completely surrendered.

If you are called to mystical contemplation, you may not even cling to the desire for illumination as something that you might possess. If you surrender yourself entirely to the Will of God, you will find that one desire will remain within you. That one last desire is the pure desire to love God. The pure desire to love God is not an ordinary desire that originates within the self, for such a desire can bear no fruit since its origin is in the self and therefore is not pure. Rather, this pure desire originates in God, who infuses the soul with this desire of pure love for Him. The Will of God has no other purpose than to elevate the soul to a union of love with Him. The person who is bound by the lie of the ego can be filled with the love of God by His grace. The effect of such a love is that the person who is faced with the choice of experiencing himself as he presently imagines himself to be, or experiencing God as He is, will choose not to experience himself. Thus denying himself and forgetting himself, he will wait in nothingness and emptiness until God chooses to reveal Himself.

C. The Cloud of Unknowing

An unknown Christian mystic of the fourteenth century wrote two books—*The Cloud of Unknowing* and *The Book of Privy Counseling*.[4] These two books are recommended as spiritual manuals for those called to contemplation. In *The Cloud of Unknowing*, it is explained that between the individual and God stands a barrier called the "cloud of unknowing" and to pierce that cloud with love, you need to proceed by way of a "cloud of forgetting."

Those who are called to contemplation are advised in both of these spiritual manuals to drop all conceptualization by allowing all thoughts to be absorbed by the "cloud of forgetting." To do this, *The Cloud of Unknowing* suggests using an affirmation as a tool of meditation. The idea is to take one word in which you can place all your desire for God alone and to choose a simple word, which can be retained easily by the mind and which is especially meaningful for you personally. The book explains a specific procedure to be followed after choosing your word:

Then fix it in your mind so that it will remain come what may. This word will be your defense in conflict and in peace. Use it to beat upon the cloud of darkness above you (referring to the cloud of unknowing) and to subdue all distractions, consigning them to the cloud of forgetting beneath you. Should some thought go on annoying you, demanding to know what you are doing, answer with this one word alone. If your mind begins to intellectualize over the meaning and connotations of this little word, remind yourself that its value lies in its simplicity. Do this and I assure you these thoughts will vanish. Why? Because you have refused to develop them with arguing.[5]

You may use an affirmation if you desire to do so. But whether an affirmation is used or not, *The Cloud of Unknowing* states that there is only one basic requirement for contemplation. Most of all, you need to simply raise your heart to God with a single naked desire for God alone. In this regard, *The Book of Privy Counseling* gives the following advice:

See that nothing remains in your conscious mind save a naked intent stretching out toward God. Leave it stripped of every particular idea about God (what He is like in Himself or in His works) and keep only the simple awareness that He is as He is. Let Him be thus, I pray you, and force Him not to be otherwise. Search into Him no further, but rest in this faith as on solid ground. This awareness, stripped of ideas and deliberately bound and anchored in faith, shall leave your thought and affection in emptiness except for the naked thought and blind feeling of your own being.[6]

If you are called to a deeper level of contemplation, both of these spiritual manuals advise you to go beyond the use of an affirmation and likewise to go beyond the naked feeling of your own being, which has been described previously as imageless self-awareness. *The Book of Privy Counseling* explains this as follows:

But now I want you to understand that although in the beginning I told you to forget everything save the blind awareness of your naked being, I intended all along to lead you eventually to the point where you would forget even this, so as to experience only the being of God. It was with an eye to this ultimate experience that I said in the beginning: God is your being. At that time I felt it was premature to expect you to rise suddenly to a high spiritual awareness of God's being. So I let you climb toward it by degrees, teaching you first to gnaw away on the naked, blind awareness of your self until by spiritual perseverance you acquire an ease in this interior work; I knew it would prepare you to experience the sublime knowledge of God's being. And, ultimately, in this work, that must be your single abiding desire: the longing to experience only God. It is true that in the beginning I told you to cover and clothe the awareness of your God with the awareness of your self, but only because you were still spiritually awkward and crude. With perseverance in this practice, I expected you to grow increasingly refined in singleness of heart until you were ready to strip, spoil, and utterly unclothe your self-awareness of everything, even the elemental awareness of your own being, so that you might be newly clothed in the gracious stark experience of God as He is in Himself.

For this is the way of all real love. The lover will utterly despoil himself of everything, even his very self, because of the one he loves. He cannot bear to be clothed in anything save the thought of his beloved. And this is not a passing fancy. No, he desires always and forever to remain unclothed in full and final self-forgetting. This is love's labor; yet, only he who experiences it will really understand. This is the meaning of the Lord's words: "Anyone who wishes to love me let him forsake himself."[7]

Forsaking yourself, which is the giving up of the ego, is not a suicidal running away from yourself. Also, it is not a struggle between a good self and a bad self, which is the root of all forms of false asceticism. You only have one Self that is the real you. But your one true Self is obscured by a false idea you have about your true nature. There is a separation in your mind, which is divided in its allegiance between the Truth and your false perceptions of your own being. Truth is Wholeness and Oneness. Truth can only be recognized in a whole mind that is not separated—not divided in its allegiance. You can only find the Truth by letting go of what is false. Learning to identify with your true Self cannot be accomplished directly until you learn first to "disidentify" with your false perceptions. This first requires a stripping of all thoughts of the rational mind so that you may have the most direct and elemental experience of your own naked self-awareness. Then you need to realize that this naked self-awareness that you have experienced is a false perception with which you are bound as a bird in a cage.

Self-awareness may be so comfortable that encountering the falseness of self-awareness can be painful. This can become an especially painful experience when you realize that self-awareness alone separates you from a union of love with God. Nevertheless, it is only by being confronted with the painful wretchedness of your false condition of ego-centered awareness that you are prepared for divine union. This is elaborated upon in *The Book of Privy Counseling* in the passage below:

> Yet do not misunderstand my words. I did not say that you must desire to un-be, for that is madness and blasphemy against God. I said that you must desire to lose the knowledge and experience of self. This is essential if you are to experience God's Love as fully as possible in this life. You must realize and experience for yourself that unless you lose self you will never reach your goal. For wherever you are, in whatever you do, or howsoever you try, that elemental sense of your own blind being will remain between you and your God. It is possible, of course, that God may intervene at times and fill you with a transient experience of Himself. Yet outside these moments this naked awareness of your blind being will continually weigh you down and be a barrier between you and your God, just as in the beginning of this work the various details of your being were like a barrier to the direct awareness of yourself. It is then that you will realize how heavy and painful is the burden of self. May Jesus help you in that hour, for you will have great need of Him.
>
> All the misery in the world taken together will seem as nothing beside this, because then you will be a cross to yourself. Yet this is the way to our Lord and the real meaning of His words: "Let a man first take up his cross" (the painful cross of self) that afterward he may "follow Me into glory," or, as we might say, "to the mount of perfection." But we listen to His promise: "There I will let him savor the delight of My love in the unspeakable experience of My divine person." See how necessary it is to bear this painful burden, the cross of self. It alone will prepare you for the transcendental experience of God as He is and for union with Him in consummate love.[8]

D. Contemplation as a Loving Interior Absorption

In the *Ascent of Mount Carmel*, St. John of the Cross describes the degree of detachment from self that is required of anyone who truly wishes to take up his cross and follow Jesus wholeheartedly. On this pathless path, only God Himself can be the guide, and the soul must be passive and open to His promptings. St. John of the Cross, in his book *Living Flame of Love*, explains how the soul is delicately anointed with the Spirit, who gradually draws the soul closer to union with God in a step-by-step process.

The first taste of contemplation may occur while a meditator is practicing Inner Silence Meditation. Likewise, this first experience may happen when using any meditation technique, as well as, surprisingly, even when not meditating. By God's grace you may find that you are spontaneously overshadowed by and filled with the Holy Spirit. If this happens during meditation, you can let go of thoughts effortlessly and feel like an object on which God is working His grace.

St. John of the Cross describes this initial stage of contemplation as a state in which the contemplative is led into the silence of the Father and feels a *loving awareness* of God. St. John referred to this loving awareness as a "loving knowledge" or "passive loving receptivity," meaning an inner listening in which the heart opens to God.

The contemplative is advised by St. John not to be attached to any feeling or desire, but rather to be completely open to whatever way God would guide the soul. Thus, in general, the Spirit would prompt the contemplative, as previously stated, to spontaneously feel this loving awareness. But then the contemplative needs to be willing to release even this loving awareness. St. John of the Cross referred to the letting go of this loving awareness, which he termed a "loving advertence," in the following way:

> When this comes to pass, and the soul is conscious of being led into silence, and harkens, it must forget even this loving advertence of which I have spoken, so that it may remain free for that which is then desired of it; for it must practice that advertence only when it is not conscious of being brought into solitude or rest or forgetfulness or attentiveness of the spirit, which is always accompanied by a certain interior absorption.[9]

Thus there is a "loving advertence," meaning "loving attention," that leads to an "interior absorption." Progressive Meditation can help you to allow yourself to be drawn into this interior absorption because it is an aid in opening to love by removing the blocks to love in a systematic order. The first three methods use body awareness to form a foundation for practicing the fourth method, Inner Silence Meditation. The purpose of Progressive Meditation is to serve as a transition from methods to no methods and from active participation to the passive inner absorption of contemplation.

A contemporary of St. John of the Cross and another mystic, John of St. Samson, refers to the interior absorption as a simple, naked "gaze" beyond methods, as follows:

> In this state the soul is in a simple, naked and obscure condition, without even knowledge of God. The spirit is elevated above all inferior light to the state where it is unable to act with its interior

faculties, because they are all willingly drawn and fixed by the power of their unique and simple Object, God. They remain fixed in a supereminent view at the highest point of the spirit. All this is accomplished in the depth of the All-incomprehensible in nakedness and obscurity. There, all that is sensible, specific and created is dissolved in unity of spirit, or rather, in simplicity of essence and spirit. Within, all powers look steadily and attentively upon God who engages them uniformly in contemplating him. They are quite simply absorbed by the action of his continual gaze which he maintains in the soul, and which the soul mutually maintains in him.[10]

The term "gaze" does not refer to the picturing of a visual mental image in your mind. It is a term to describe the drawing of your wholehearted awareness toward God and brought about by God Himself. Ideally this simple and naked gaze may become established as one's regular and consistent experience in contemplation of God, but often this is instead a momentary experience that may come and go. To make this gaze a constant practice requires a dedication to inward seeking over a long period of time. It also requires a giving up of active methods by being passively receptive and a willingness to set self aside. Like St. John of the Cross, John of St. Samson also stresses the need to die to self, which leads toward divine touches. He describes this when he writes:

> Here the condition of dying constantly is appropriate for the soul, because, by this means, it follows that which it knows not and sees not. Due to a very simple gaze that is lost in God, the soul has an active and joyful inclination which places it in a most singular and supereminent repose. One infallibly leads to the other.
>
> In this state the soul begins to see God simply, without forms or images. All that is annihilated along with the soul's own life in this ardent, superessential center into which it is transfused. When the soul's active desire is entirely suppressed by the strength and simplicity of love, it begins to enjoy its Spouse purely in his essence by means of simple touches. These touches dilate and enlarge it in simplicity in a way that it has never experienced.[11]

In order to die to self, you must experience spiritual darkness. But this darkness that is experienced by the soul is actually excessive light that is mistakenly perceived as darkness. This is explained by another mystic, St. Symeon the New Theologian, in the following quotation from *Writings from the Philokalia on Prayer of the Heart*:

Like a man who, standing in a dark room with all windows and doors fastened, opens a window and the light streaming in suddenly envelops him in such a brilliant glare that, unable to bear it, he closes his eyes, wraps up his head and hides; so if a soul, totally imprisoned in the sensory world, lets its mind peep out into the supersensory world, as out of a window, it becomes bathed in the radiance of betrothal with the Holy Spirit, which is within it, and unable to bear the brilliance of the uncovering of Divine light, it immediately trembles in its mind, hides within itself and flees as though into a house, seeking cover in the sensory and the human.[12]

The abundance of divine light has the effect of causing blinding darkness and blocking understanding for anyone not accustomed to such excessive light, as is confirmed by John of St. Samson, as follows:

The divine darkness is the Divinity, which thus makes itself obscure to the soul, and especially to the understanding. This faculty is surrounded by it and dazzled by the abundance of its blinding light. There, it is divinely elevated and suspended in admiration at the ravishing beauty of the Object which fills it. The soul is transported with the greatest delight as it contemplates the divine Object in a superessential manner, that is, in a completely naked, abstract and simple manner, in the superessential unity of God. Quite often it is elevated to this state without knowing what it is or where it is. God caused this darkness for his own greater glory and for the soul's perfection.[13]

The soul needs to persevere in this darkness to be purified and learn to be open to the divine light. In order to encourage the soul, God elevates it by means of His divine gaze, as well as by intermittent divine "touches," mentioned above, and further described by John of St. Samson in this way:

Sometimes God knocks gently within the deepest part of the soul. Stirred by this very brief and sudden touch, it is completely renewed within and filled with strength, understanding, love and delight. By such frequent touches, God seems to be saying, "Behold me within you. Do not be afraid of losing me." This is so wonderful that the soul's faith in God and its belief in his awareness of it are continually renewed by this inspiring and exciting gaze and by his delightful and ardent touch.[14]

Then these divine touches and also even the divine gaze may be withdrawn altogether so that one is only aware of oneself again. These times of divine withdrawal are tests to see if the soul is seeking God alone and not just His pleasing gifts. But for the soul that perseveres and does not lose faith because of this time of dryness, an inner transformation happens that opens the soul to a deeper relationship with the divine. The darkness that oppressed the soul disappears with new inner experiences, as John of St. Samson writes:

> But finally, after so many sorrowful and touching aspirations, the Beloved, moved with compassion, returns suddenly in a momentary act, like a flash of lightning. In this encounter the soul feels completely renewed. Darkness vanishes and is succeeded by an infinite light. Its former multiplicity and distractions cease to exist and all is reduced to unity of spirit. Now it experiences a new attraction as it is transported and caressed by Jesus Christ, its Spouse and Lover. Profoundly dilated, it abides in his divinity in a state of complete liquefaction. All its anguished laments are completely forgotten, as if they never existed.[15]

In addition, the divine touches return to lead the soul toward deeper levels of inner transformation, as John of St. Samson explains:

> Often too, it is so deeply penetrated by a touch of love that it feels as though it were melted and completely transformed by the immense sea of fire which consumes it. It is so plunged and absorbed in this fire that it constantly becomes the same thing with it and in it, as well as one life with it.[16]

In the quotations above, John of St. Samson, like so many other mystics, refers to a consuming "fire" and to "light" as part of the spiritual transformation process. Christian mystics did not have the Eastern understanding of the term "kundalini," but their references to "fire" and to "light" are attempts to describe the experience of the activity of the kundalini. According to John of St. Samson, the experiences of the divine gaze and divine touches lead the soul toward the state of divine union. John of St. Samson describes this transforming union by writing:

> When thus favored, they are filled with every kind of happiness and perfection, and seem to be entirely overwhelmed by it even to the point of pouring it out upon others. But the highest and most intimate state in this degree consists in a very simple and intimate

exchange between God and the soul. The soul contemplates God constantly and is, so to speak, imperceptibly absorbed in what it sees and feels.[17]

The state of divine union may be easier to describe by what it is not than by what it is. Of this state, John of St. Samson writes:

In short, in this condition, there is neither creature nor created object, knowledge nor ignorance, all nor nothing, word nor name, past, future nor even present; not even the eternal now. All is lost and dissolved in this obscure mist which God himself produces.[18]

To summarize much of what has been said about contemplation, there is a consistent experience of "interior absorption" in God in which the Spirit leads the soul by the hand into various states of awareness of God. The soul remains completely passive and receptive, feeling like an object on which God is working, and because of this, there is still a feeling of separation. The soul is gradually purified and transformed as it is led to deeper states of contemplation. In these deeper states, there is an increased feeling of oneness that serves as a preparation for the spiritual marriage of the soul and God in divine union.

When divine union is achieved, the feeling of being an object on which God is working is entirely dissolved in oneness. In divine union the soul is in a state in which it can hardly draw distinctions between itself and God, Who is indisputably its Source. John of St. Samson says of this:

In this degree of transformation the soul says to its Spouse, "You are what I am, and I am what you are without there being any difference between us."[19]

A quotation from *Merton's Theology of Prayer*, by Father John Higgins, refers to the transformation process of divine union with God as follows:

In this transcendent experience it becomes evident that the individual subject really undergoes a radical change, an inner transformation, or what Merton refers to as a "transformation of consciousness" from an awareness of his empirical self (also called man's false self or ego-self) to an awareness of his transcendent self (also referred to as man's true self or his person). The individual is no longer conscious of himself as an isolated ego but sees himself in his inmost ground of being as dependent on Another or as being formed through relationship with God. By forgetting himself both as subject and object of reflection, man finds his real self hidden with Christ in God. And so his self-consciousness changes, the individual is transformed, his self is no longer its own center; it is now centered on God. There is death of the self-centered and self-sufficient ego and in its place there appears a new and liberated self who loves and acts in the Spirit. Man is now empty of all ego-consciousness; he is a Transcendent Self—a person who has gone beyond his individual self and has found his true self in the presence of God. Hence, it is through this dynamic process of inner transformation or transformation of consciousness that man empties himself and transcends himself, and thus ultimately becomes his true self in Christ.[20]

Deep contemplation is the highest expression of the Christian prayer life, but, as has been emphasized, it is a divine calling and is not expected of everyone. God wants everyone to be drawn to Himself in divine union, yet God is not so small in giving His grace that only contemplatives will reach such a high state of spiritual union. God brings each man closer to Himself by whatever gift of prayer He gives each individual. Prayer in its broadest and most important sense is the doing of God's Will in all the activities of daily living. You set aside special times for prayer and meditation only so that you may be strengthened inwardly by His Spirit to be able to follow His Will throughout each day.

Your prayer life is a necessary part of your life, yet you are certainly not justified by your prayers. It would be a mistake to think that anyone can practice contemplation, meditation, or prayer, and thereby "earn" divine union. Divine union with God is a free gift offered to everyone. But like so many spiritual gifts, it is a gift that has already been given and continues to be given. This gift is only awaiting your acceptance. It may take a lifetime of opening the door of your heart to receive this gift with thanksgiving. Most individuals are not called to unwrap this gift and fully receive it during their lifetime. However, everyone is called at the time of physical death to let go of the ego entirely and to receive the gift of divine union at that time. If you have lived your life with the desire for the gift of divine union, your passage out of this world of appearances will not be an ending, but rather a birth, awakening, and acceptance of divine union in His World.

What is the true nature of the gift of divine union, which is the gift of salvation? You are saved only from yourself. A more accurate way of saying this is that you are saved from your illusions about yourself. Because of the ego, you think you are a body and a mind that will one day be united with God in divine union. The words "divine union" are used to describe spiritual fulfillment, but these words are misleading because they imply two are becoming one. Actually divine union is not a union, but rather a subtraction. What really happens in divine union is all the illusions you have about yourself are eliminated. You are saved from the false idea that you are a body and a limited mind. What remains is not merely the understanding of who you really are, but rather the *realization* of who you are as an *experience* of your spiritual being.

When you let go of the ego and realize your spiritual nature, you will see yourself as God has always seen you. You will see yourself as part of God and understand that at no time have you *ever* been separate from God. When you were in your world of apparent separation, you thought you were a body and mind separate from God. But after entering His World, you will see that your separation was only an illusion of separation. You will understand that if you really had been separate from God, you would have ceased to exist. Your existence depends on union with God because God is existence itself and everything that exists is part of God. If you were not part of God, you would not exist. The dropping of your illusions reveals that you are now and have been all along one with God.

Salvation then is a change in awareness—a change of consciousness. Prior to divine union, you are not aware of your union with God, and when divine union occurs, you become aware of your union with God. Salvation then is ironically the revealing of the divine union that has existed all along, but which was hidden from your awareness.

It may be hard to accept that you are already united with God now, but are unaware of that union. Is it really necessary for you to accept this idea? No, it is not necessary. Many of the ideas presented here about the ego and about your true spiritual nature may be extremely challenging for you. After all, you are not now seeing yourself from the perspective of His World. Everything in your world says that you are a body and a mind and that you are separate from God. So why should you accept new ideas that challenge your perception of yourself? You are not being asked to accept these theological ideas. Traditional religious organizations require their members to accept a set of specific theological ideas as a dogma. But you are not being asked to join a religious organization. If you belong to one, you are not being asked to give up your present theological thought system. Fortunately your goal in meditation is not directly related to theological ideas. In fact, it would be best for you to set aside any ideas you find in this book that would create a stumbling block for you.

This manual is designed to encourage you to communicate with God. Challenging ideas are presented in this book because as you deepen your communication with God, you cannot do so without being confronted with the question *Who am I?* The answer that you will find in your world of outer appearances will be sufficient to help you to function in your everyday world. However, as you enter His World, you will feel a need to answer this question at a deeper level. Some theological ideas here address the question at a deeper level, but a book cannot give you the answer to this question. You will have to find the answer within yourself. It is not important if your conclusions are different from those presented in this book. It is only important that you continue to seek the divine within yourself as an experience rather than as an intellectual idea. Hopefully your experience of the divine within will provide your answer to the question *Who am I?*

---

1. St. John of the Cross, *Ascent of Mount Carmel*, edited by E. Allison Peers (New York: Image Books, a division of Doubleday and Co., Inc., 1958), p. 174f. This book was published by arrangement with the copyright holder and original publisher, Newman Press, which has been absorbed by Paulist Press, Mahwah, NJ.

2. John Tauler, *Spiritual Conferences of John Tauler*, translated by Eric Coledge (St. Louis, MO: 1961), in Sermon 52, p. 232.

3. Thomas Merton, *Contemplative Prayer*, cited from the paperback edition (New York: Image Books, 1971), pp. 93-94, from the original, hardcover edition, *The Climate of Monastic Prayer* (Kalamazoo, MI/Spencer, MA: Cistercian Publications 1969), p. 127.

4. These two books by an unknown author have been incorporated into one edition by Father William Johnston, who edited them and wrote the introduction (New York: Image Books, a division of Doubleday and Co., Inc., 1973).

5. Ibid., p. 56.

6. Ibid., p. 149f.

7. Ibid., p. 171f.

8. Ibid., p. 172f.

9. St. John of the Cross, *Living Flame of Love*, edited by E. Allison Peers (New York, New York: Image Books, a division of Doubleday and Co., Inc., 1962), pp. 105-106. This book published by arrangement with the copyright holder and original publisher, Newman Press, which has been absorbed by Paulist Press, Mahwah, NJ.

10. John of St. Samson, O. Carm., *Prayer, Aspiration and Contemplation*, translated and edited by Venard Poslusney, O. Carm. (Asbury, NJ: printed by Fr. Venard Poslusney, The 101 Foundation, 1994), p. 130.

11. Ibid., p. 129.

12. *Writings from the Philokalia on Prayer of the Heart*, from the Russian text, "Bobrotolubiye," translated by E. Kadloubovsky and G.E.H. Palmer (London: Faber and Faber, eighth edition, 1975), p. 118.

13. John of St. Samson, O. Carm., *Prayer, Aspiration and Contemplation*, translated and edited by Venard Poslusney, O. Carm. (Asbury, NJ: printed by Fr. Venard Poslusney, The 101 Foundation, 1994), p. 133.

14. Ibid., p. 128.

15. Ibid., p. 155.

16. Ibid., p. 120.

17. Ibid., p. 131.

18. Ibid., p. 130.

19. Ibid., p. 153.

20. John J. Higgins, SJ., *Merton's Theology of Prayer* (Spencer, MA/Kalamazoo, MI, 1971), p. 33f.

10

OPENING TO
INNER FEELINGS

~ o ~

A. Seven Inner Feelings

If you decide to continue with meditation on a daily basis, you may be asking yourself, "What will my experience be like in the future when my meditation deepens?" There are many kinds of unusual phenomena that may spontaneously occur and disappear during meditation. It is best to let these come and go without attachment or aversion. However, there are other positive experiences that may happen, and in some cases may happen consistently as meditation deepens.

Everyone's experience of deepening meditation is unique. If travelers are climbing a mountain, each may take a different route and yet arrive at the same point on the top of the mountain. But a wise traveler will take a map with various routes on it. Such a map will show guideposts to indicate where he is along the way. On your meditation journey, you may experience any of the following seven guideposts:

1. an inner feeling of love
2. an inner feeling of oneness
3. an inner feeling of heightened awareness
4. an inner feeling of light
5. an inner feeling of the divine presence
6. an inner feeling of peace
7. an inner feeling of joy

The most important guidepost is not mentioned above. That guidepost is a growth in pure faith. There are two basic ways in which meditation can deepen. One way is through pure faith that does not give you any "felt" experience related to contemplation. To practice the previous techniques of meditation that have been provided and to enter contemplation does not require any felt experience, just a willingness based on faith to be open to the hidden action of the Holy Spirit.

The second basic way that meditation can deepen also relies on pure faith, but in this case there is in addition a felt experience related to your meditation and contemplation. This felt experience has to do with the development of the intuitive level of your being. Pure faith itself is the highest form of intuition, but is too lofty of an expression of your intuition to be called an "inner feeling."

The inner feeling of the divine presence is a felt experience of being in the presence of holiness, which may be an experience of God, of Christ, or of the Holy Spirit. This kind of inner feeling of the divine presence is perhaps the inner feeling most closely associated with faith, since faith is the inner knowing of the divine being present within you. But faith is more than a sensing that you are in the presence of holiness. Faith is more than a compass that points in the right direction. It is also an indescribable inner impulse that allows you to reach out and actually contact and find the divine within you that you are seeking, even if you must do so with all your senses and faculties in darkness.

If your pure faith can be considered the ultimate expression of your intuition, the seven inner feelings identified above may be thought of as ordinary intuitions. Whereas pure faith is your most important guidepost and your indispensable form of intuition, these seven inner feelings are also guideposts that show progress yet are not necessary for your growth in meditation and contemplation.

These seven inner feelings are not mentioned to define the limits of your meditation experience, but rather to identify some of the possibilities that indicate the deepening of meditation. The term "inner feeling" refers to your intuition, meaning an inner sensing or inner knowing, which is not based on the normal, rational thinking process of the mind.

B. Purifying Emotions

Before elaborating upon the inner feelings related to your intuition, it will be helpful to discuss the process of releasing negative emotions that block your spiritual growth. Perhaps the most critical aspect of your spiritual growth is how you deal with your emotional nature. Initially your experience of meditation may bring spiritual consolations that encourage you to continue your spiritual discipline of setting aside time each day for deepening your relationship with God. But when God wishes to draw you closer to Himself, He may take away the sweetness of meditation in order to purify and elevate the soul. Then meditation will seem to create turmoil, when actually it is performing a cleansing.

For example, you may own a swimming pool that does not have a filtering system. The water in the pool may appear clean toward the top, but on the bottom of the pool there may be a great deal of mud that can only be seen if you take a deeper look. In order to clean the pool, a pump and a filter must be installed. When the water is pumped through the filter, the flow of the water stirs up the dirt on the bottom. Then the dirt that has been stirred into the water is circulated through the filter and caught in the filter. An observer who is not aware of the cleansing process may look at the pool and imagine that it is in much worse condition than before, because he sees only the dirtiness of the water. Such an uninformed observer does not understand that it is part of the cleansing process to stir up the water so that it can be purified.

In this analogy the filter is your meditation practice that includes your affirmation. As this filter is used more intensely, it creates a strong flow (like the water pump). This stirs up the waters of the mind and reveals subconscious thoughts and past emotional impressions that prevent you from being as kind and loving as you would like to be. But you should not be like the uninformed observer and imagine that when such thoughts or emotions appear, this means the condition is worsening. On the contrary, you need to realize that these are being stirred up and brought to the conscious mind so that they can be confronted and released by the power of the Holy Spirit.

Bringing your subconscious thoughts or emotions to your conscious awareness is one aspect of how meditation serves as a purification process that releases physical, emotional, and mental tension. By handing this process over to the Holy Spirit, you can be certain that tension will be released in the most appropriate and timely manner. After practicing meditation on a daily basis over a period of time, a sensitivity to tension within the body may develop. Previously the tension was present but not in your awareness. However, meditation can expand your awareness to include the conscious experience of tension as it is being released.

If you use Progressive Meditation, you may discover that while you hold the awareness in various parts of the body, you feel an automatic movement of energy upward from the navel area to the center of the chest. Then you may feel the energy in the chest move upward into the head. Also, if you practice other methods, you may have a similar spontaneous upward movement of energy, perhaps feeling energy rise up in the spine. Yet having such an experience is not a standard of what "should" happen. Actually most meditators do not experience energy movements nor are these conscious experiences necessary for your spiritual growth. But for those who do spontaneously experience such an energy movement, it is helpful to know that there are usually two basic reasons for these energy movements. One reason is because the energy of the body is naturally being raised up and transformed into energy to be used for spiritual purposes because of your intention to express the divine within you.

The other reason is that the energy movement may be a conscious awareness of tension being released. The tension that is released is the result of your shadow side coming to light so it can be released piece by piece. Your subconscious mind is filled with defense mechanisms, negative thoughts, emotions, and anxiety that are stored there because you simply do not want to look at them. Some of these come from traumatic childhood experiences that have left emotional scars and unresolved issues. Normally you cannot release these unhealthy elements of your subconscious, but when your mind becomes calm in meditation and contemplation, you are ready to face the hidden side of your psyche. In addition, because of your spiritual purposes and willingness to surrender to the Holy Spirit, you allow yourself to be open to bringing portions of your shadow side to the light.

Meditation on particular parts of the body, in sequence from bottom to top, helps you raise creative energy for spiritual purposes, but as part of this same process tension is released. Previous descriptions of Progressive Meditation have mentioned that this sequence of methods addresses the release of inner tension, anxiety, and repressed emotions in a systematic manner. The concluding method in this sequence, Inner Silence Meditation, leads you toward contemplation. As contemplation deepens, the mind becomes so restful that the purification process can go to a deeper level by triggering the release of additional subconscious ego-based thoughts and emotions.

Just as the body has its own way of eliminating unwanted waste, this is the psyche's attempt to clean out unwanted mental and emotional waste that is stifling your inner development. At first in your meditation practice, you will perhaps only be dealing with the release of tension that is related to your emotions, but which is not as intense as raw emotions themselves. As your practice of meditation deepens, your purification process will go from releasing tension only to releasing at times the deeper underlying emotions and negative thoughts themselves that are causing the tension.

The subconscious waste from your psyche may present itself to your conscious awareness during meditation or contemplation as very highly charged thoughts and emotions that attempt to grab your attention. You can learn to let go of these highly charged thoughts and emotions by dealing with them in the same way that you would respond to any other thoughts during your practice of meditation or contemplation. Through your daily practice, you learn to relate to your thoughts in meditation as if they are garbage floating by in the river of your mind. You do not look upstream to see where the garbage is coming from nor do you look downstream to see where the garbage is going. This detachment from your thoughts is a process of *letting go and receiving*. You are letting go of thoughts and receiving the Holy Spirit to strengthen you in the process.

This letting go and receiving process for your ordinary thoughts prepares you to respond similarly when tension-filled thoughts come to your conscious mind. These tension-filled thoughts may have a certain amount of energy and emotional burst. The sudden appearance of these tension-filled thoughts and emotions may initially produce an uncomfortable feeling. If, for example, you are using Inner Silence Meditation and have let go of your affirmation, ideally you can just continue your normal practice by letting these thoughts and emotions pass by in your mind without your attraction or aversion. But because of the highly charged nature of these thoughts and emotions, it is likely that your mind will become distracted.

When this occurs, you simply hold on to your affirmation as a way of focusing your mind positively and preventing distraction. You can remain unaffected by the highly charged thoughts and emotions by placing your full awareness on your affirmation, thus ignoring these thoughts and emotions. By not paying attention to them, they fade away like any other thoughts. You have faced them by allowing them to surface in your consciousness, and you have let them go by not fighting with them. By having neither an attraction nor an aversion to these thoughts, you release the emotional charge these thoughts formerly had. Thus there is no more need to hide these thoughts in your subconscious mind. You have given up your identification with these thoughts and emotions so they are no longer your possessions. The thoughts and emotions in essence become meaningless to you and therefore you no longer need them, so they dissipate.

Frequently tension-filled thoughts and emotions are released from the subconscious mind and presented to the conscious mind as a generalized feeling of anxiety. However, sometimes the tension-filled emotions that surface may involve anger, pain, fear, or some very traumatic experiences that are so strong and emotionally charged that you are unable to let these thoughts go as you would any other thoughts. You may be filled with the emotional charge of these thoughts, so you are reexperiencing the trauma that caused them. Sometimes the specific source of the traumatic emotion will be presented spontaneously in the form of a psychological insight. Nevertheless, in most cases you will not have an intellectual understanding of this trauma—only the raw emotion itself. When you try to focus on your affirmation or on any other focusing object, you may be unable to do so because the emotional impact is just too strong for you to focus your mind.

If you find that your emotions are so disturbing that you cannot focus your mind even on your affirmation, you can consider another option. You can practice an inner meditative discipline just like the mental discipline described previously of placing your full attention on emotions that occur in your daily life to avoid repression and avoid acting out. During this inner meditative practice, instead of placing your awareness on an affirmation in order to divert your mind away from your emotions, you allow yourself to join with your emotions. Therefore, you become one with whatever you are experiencing by fully sinking into your feeling nature and placing your entire awareness on your emotion itself.

You join with the emotion that you are feeling. By not running from it, you absorb its emotional charge fully and defuse it by your acceptance of it. It is only by struggling with thoughts that you prolong them. Your willingness to face your emotions and experience them fully allows them to fall away since you are no longer afraid of them. There is no need to hide these thoughts in your subconscious mind because you have dealt with them and seen them in the light, finding they cannot harm you.

Ideally it is helpful for your overall growth to have intellectual insights into the psychological nature of these emotions, yet it is still possible to release emotions without having that intellectual understanding. This form of release involving joining with your emotions is not an intellectual process, but rather a feeling process. You are meeting your emotions at the emotional level and accepting what you find. You can dissolve intense anxiety, raw emotions, and even physical pain by accepting them in the act of becoming one with whatever you are experiencing. Your focusing object becomes your emotions until they dissolve, and then you can return to your regular meditation practice. You will be surprised to find out that often it may take only a minute or two of joining with your emotion before it is dissipated.

Yet there are deeper emotional patterns that may take longer to dissipate. These patterns are whole networks of thoughts that are highly charged with emotions. These emotional patterns may be produced by one traumatic experience, in some cases originating from childhood. But usually the emotional patterns are established as a result of repeated exposure to situations or experiences that elicit a particular emotional response from you, such as pain, fear, anger, or some other emotional reaction. Through habit these emotional patterns become ingrained in your personality, so when similar situations occur, you automatically react emotionally. Releasing these kinds of habitual reaction patterns may take more time than less ingrained emotions. These habitual emotional patterns may be dissolved a little bit at a time. Emotional patterns that are being released in this piecemeal manner will reappear intermittently. Over time these emotional patterns will appear less frequently and with less intensity until, with repeated meditation practice, they will disappear altogether.

An example of an ingrained emotional pattern for some people would be the fear of pain from dental procedures. Some dental clients, because of a reaction pattern, begin to be fearful even at the anticipation of going to the dentist's office. Removing this kind of reaction pattern may be challenging since it is a habitual emotional pattern that involves intense emotions related to physical pain and the fear of physical pain. Becoming one with your emotions can be a very effective means of releasing this kind of intense emotional pattern.

One meditator I know practices Centering Meditation when he goes to the dentist and accepts no injection to numb his feelings. He diverts his attention to his affirmation and to the navel area and away from feeling the pain of dental procedures. However, when the pain becomes so intense that he can no longer focus his attention, he lets go of the affirmation and of focusing on the navel area and instead places his full awareness on the pain itself. By making the pain the object of his awareness, he disempowers the pain so it no longer has any effect on him. What he is really doing is releasing not only the pain by joining with it, but also releasing any fear of pain. Without the fear of pain, the experience of pain is just another passing experience. Also, he is releasing his aversion to pain, which is in itself a form of attachment to pain.

This is an extraordinary example of becoming one with an intense emotion in order to face and overcome that emotion. Since this process can work successfully for facing and releasing an intense emotion, such as the pain of a toothache being drilled, would it work for letting go of less intense emotions? Yes, it can work equally effectively for the less intense experience of facing the highly charged thoughts and emotions that may surface during your practice of meditation and/or contemplation. Just as in the example of overcoming dental pain, when you become one with a highly charged thought or an intense emotion during meditation, you are also releasing fear as well as any tension that may be associated with what is being released.

But sometimes you may attempt to become one with your emotions and find that the thoughts and emotions are so highly charged that you are unable even to sit still in a meditative posture. On some occasions even experienced meditators find themselves unable to calm the mind during meditation because of overwhelming emotions. If this happens to you, do not condemn yourself for this, or think that you have left your path toward God. During this difficult time, you can let go of becoming one with your emotions as a meditative practice. Although you do not practice sitting meditation at this time, you can either continue to become one with the emotions you are facing as a mental discipline in your daily life, as has been described previously, or you can simply take a time out and rest. Another option is that you can temporarily turn from meditation to prayer. If you decide to face your emotions, you can offer your prayers directly to God and ask for His guidance and help. You can give your emotions to God since He is not burdened by them. You can put all your emotions to use by turning to God with them and becoming one with the emotions you are feeling. Also, you can turn to God indirectly through seeking out a trusted friend to express your emotions, since the Holy Spirit can speak to you and assist you through your brothers and sisters.

If your emotions involve grief or pain, the most precious prayer you can offer to God is your tears. You only cry with people with whom you feel intimate. What better way to become intimate with God than to give Him your tears? At such times, you cry out from within for God's help. You can reach out to God in this way without words, or you can use whatever words may come spontaneously. You may imagine you are alone at such times, but you are not abandoned for certainly the Holy Spirit helps you in your weakness, as the Bible testifies:

> Likewise the Spirit helps us in our weakness; for we do not know how to pray as ought, but the Spirit himself intercedes for us with sighs too deep for words.[1]

This prayer works when no one and nothing else can help. The aftereffect is a feeling of relief. Crying to God with tears is the dissolving of selfishness within. This is one way to release subconscious blocks and serves to renew spiritual intents and purposes, so that you can return wholeheartedly to meditation.

C. Four Categories of Emotional Blocks

Emotions are gross expressions of your feeling nature. Emotional reaction patterns are stored in the subconscious mind and correspondingly in parts of the physical body producing tension. As you release the unconscious emotional clutter in your mind and the tension in the body, your feeling nature becomes more refined. Therefore, you are less likely to have emotional reactions. Instead of emotional reactions, you become aware of your feelings without being controlled by them. Through your practice of meditation you are able to purify your feeling nature so that you can be responsive to others with your feelings. In addition to being aware of your feelings, your meditation may deepen even further so you can become at times sensitive to your inner feelings that are intuitions. These intuitions are not a direct experience of the divine. Rather, they are only by-products of approaching your true spiritual nature.

What kinds of emotional blocks will you encounter as you make progress in meditation? Your emotional blocks will generally fall into four categories: *denial, anger, guilt,* and *depression.* Each of these general categories involves letting go of fear related to them. These categories are associated with specific spiritual centers in the body, as is illustrated on the next page.

You may go through a growth stage in which you mainly face and overcome denial issues. In this stage, you learn to rely on faith in God. Also, you become willing to change. You become aware of the false nature of the ego that had been hidden from your conscious awareness, and you learn to increasingly trust in your true spiritual nature in oneness with God. Releasing emotional patterns of denial involves letting go of blocks from the gonad center and navel center. Centering Meditation as part of Progressive Meditation is especially helpful in releasing denial patterns and fears associated with denial.

You may experience a growth stage in which you mostly face and overcome anger issues. In this stage, you learn to become aware of anger without being controlled by it. You accept full responsibility for all of your experiences. Thus you let go of projection so you do not blame others. Letting go of emotional patterns of anger is related to releasing blocks from the adrenal center. Heart Meditation as part of Progressive Meditation is an effective way of facing and overcoming the *fight or flight syndrome* of the adrenal center, meaning releasing emotional blocks of anger and fear.

Heart Meditation as part of Progressive Meditation is also helpful for releasing guilt and depression because these emotional patterns are related to the heart. You may experience a growth stage in which you mainly face and overcome guilt and depression issues. As you succeed in overcoming guilt and depression issues, you develop a non-egotistical self-love. Guilt and depression are based on the false belief that you deserve punishment. By releasing guilt and depression, you accept the belief that God is Love, and as one of His children, you deserve only love and not punishment. The process of releasing guilt and depression fosters forgiveness of others and yourself, as well as an increasing sense of gratitude.

Inner Silence Meditation helps you to enter contemplation and release denial, anger, guilt, and depression, along with associated fears, at deeper levels. These releases open you up to divine love. After you practice daily meditation for many years, you will make progress experiencing various stages of growth involving issues of denial, anger, guilt, and depression. Then you will reach the stage of development, which can be called the *plateau of self-acceptance.*

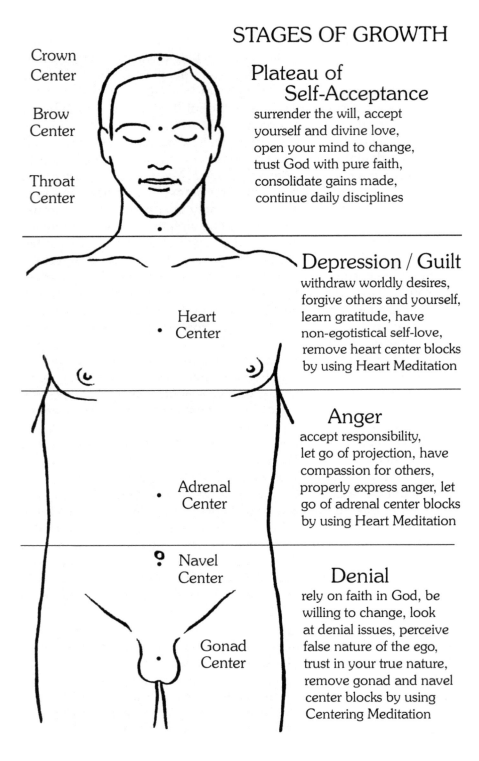

STAGES OF GROWTH

Crown
Center

Brow
Center

Throat
Center

Plateau of
Self-Acceptance

surrender the will, accept
yourself and divine love,
open your mind to change,
trust God with pure faith,
consolidate gains made,
continue daily disciplines

Depression / Guilt

withdraw worldly desires,
forgive others and yourself,
learn gratitude, have
non-egotistical self-love,
remove heart center blocks
by using Heart Meditation

Heart
Center

Anger

accept responsibility,
let go of projection, have
compassion for others,
properly express anger, let
go of adrenal center blocks
by using Heart Meditation

Adrenal
Center

Navel
Center

Denial

rely on faith in God, be
willing to change, look
at denial issues, perceive
false nature of the ego,
trust in your true nature,
remove gonad and navel
center blocks by using
Centering Meditation

Gonad
Center

D. The Plateau of Self-Acceptance

A realistic long-term goal for your spiritual journey is reaching the plateau of self-acceptance. It is a state of mind in which you release many inner ego-based blocks that hide your true nature of love. At this stage in your spiritual development, you identify increasingly with your true divine nature. However, you have learned to accept the ego so you are neither fighting against it nor encouraging its influence. You realize that the ego is an illusion and so you place limits on your ego-based desires. When you have reached the plateau of self-acceptance, you will be able to improve your ability to focus the mind during meditation. You will be able to calm the mind sufficiently to experience contemplation for longer periods of time on a consistent basis.

After releasing many emotional patterns of denial, anger, guilt, and depression, you will gain a deeper sense of self-worth and maturity. Then you will arrive at the stage of the plateau of self-acceptance. When this happens, you will feel a new sense of freedom from habitual reaction patterns and a detachment from the physical, emotional, and rational world that had previously monopolized your consciousness. You will encounter some situations that would have elicited from you a particular emotional reaction pattern if they had occurred in the past. But because of your growth, these same situations will no longer affect you emotionally in a negative way. You will be able to respond to situations instead of reacting. You will be able to gracefully handle circumstances that would have been difficult for you in the past. You will gain confidence in your ability to be a problem solver and will have emotional reserves to handle even stressful or emergency situations. Of course, you will have ups and downs, but not dramatic mood swings. You will still make mistakes, but you will be able to correct mistakes without condemning yourself. You will be more patient with others and yourself and quick to forgive others and yourself.

Your plateau of self-acceptance will be a consolidation period of your gains. Your consciousness has been significantly restructured so you will feel like a more whole and well-rounded person. You will know that you will still have to continue on your spiritual journey, yet you will be able to rest to a certain degree in a more peaceful overall consciousness. Your subconscious mind has become relieved of so many emotionally charged thoughts that your meditative practice of opening to His World will generally be experienced as less challenging than in the past. After removing so much emotional clutter, you will become increasingly open to experiencing the previously described seven positive inner feelings that begin to surface. In your meditation you will find that it will be easier for you to enter into contemplation and to remain for longer intervals of time resting in the Spirit without distraction.

Your plateau of self-acceptance means accepting to a greater degree your true divine nature of love. Yet it also means a greater acceptance of the ego. Acceptance of the ego means knowing it is a false perspective of yourself and at the same time allowing it to be. Therefore, you neither deny the power of the ego nor surrender to its power. You deal with your ego by following a middle path of setting reasonable limits on the ego that neither entirely suppress ego desires nor entirely give in to ego desires. You will find that the divine love in you can manifest even in your ego expressions by doing God's Will to the best of your ability and understanding. In this way, you will become a servant of God's Will, even in your ego condition.

To reach the plateau of self-acceptance, you will have to let go of many blocks of denial, which are associated with the gonad and navel centers and which Centering Meditation will help you to release. You will have to let go of many blocks of anger, which are associated with the adrenal center and which Heart Meditation will help you release. You will have to release many blocks of guilt and depression, which are associated with the heart center and which Heart Meditation will help you release. Inner Silence Meditation can take you to a deeper level of releasing all these blocks and the fears associated with each of them.

Although the plateau of self-acceptance is a time of consolidation of your gains, it is not a time for complacency. You will still have lessons to learn in this stage. The stage of the plateau of self-acceptance does not mean that you will no longer have any blocks in the lower centers. Thus all of the four methods of Progressive Meditation will still help you to release inner blocks. For example, you will still have some denial obstacles that can be released with Centering Meditation. Also, you will have blocks of anger, depression, and guilt that can be released with Heart Meditation. And you will still a have a variety of blocks to divine love that can be released with Inner Silence Meditation.

The obstacles that surface during the plateau of self-acceptance may be deeper and more subtle aspects of these blocks that come to your conscious awareness so you can release them. For instance, you may find yourself learning to let go of all forms of judgment through practicing Heart Meditation. Judgment in the form of overt negativity toward others, such as blaming, is a block of anger. But more subtle types of judgment are released during the plateau of self-acceptance. These more subtle kinds of judgment consist of any evaluations of others based on the ego perspective of separation. These judgments value a person based on whether or not he or she is pleasing to the ego. It is a common personality trait to make negative judgments about other people and then to base decisions on these judgments. Letting go of judgment allows you to release making your own decisions based on the perspective of what is best for your ego. By not relying on ego-based judgment, you can allow the Holy Spirit to make your decisions for you based on what is best of everyone from a divine perspective.

Also, ego-based judgment is a dishonest and inaccurate appraisal of your brother, who is just as divine as you are. Judgment produces guilt, and your negative appraisal of your brother becomes your negative appraisal of yourself. Judgment consciously appears to be about judging your brother but is actually a judgment of yourself. Because the plateau of self-acceptance is about accepting yourself, this means it must be about not judging yourself. The way to escape from judging yourself is to let go of judging others, which will also allow you to let go of the guilt that comes with your judgment of others. Of course, you will still need to have some way of evaluating situations and making decisions, if you let go of your judgments. You can learn to rely on the Holy Spirit to meet this need. The Holy Spirit can give you the divine perspective of situations and show you what decisions would be most helpful.

Many of the ego-based patterns have been released prior to reaching the plateau of self-acceptance, but this releasing of blocks and undoing of the ego is a lifelong process. Besides letting go of obstacles that are still in the lower centers, there will also be the necessity of releasing blocks in the throat center, the brow center, and the crown center by practicing Brow Meditation and Inner Silence Meditation as part of Progressive Meditation.

E. Guideposts of Meditation

The inner feelings of love, oneness, heightened awareness, light, the divine presence, peace, and joy may surface at any time in your growth. But inner feelings are more likely to surface consistently and at a deeper level after you reach the plateau of self-acceptance. This is because a lot of your emotional garbage has been eliminated, which enables you to reach a deeper level of meditation and contemplation in your practice of Progressive Meditation. After removing so many blocks to love and after reaching the plateau of self-acceptance, you will experience a greater openness to inner feelings and to divine love in particular.

The most important inner feeling that you can encounter is the inner feeling of love. Since divine love can be defined as oneness, there may be a question about why the inner feeling of love and the inner feeling of oneness are indicated as two separate inner feelings. It is because love has many facets and can be experienced in different ways. For example, when you are meditating with a primary focus on the heart, you can experience an "inner feeling of love" that is personal, intimate, and devotional in nature. However, when you are meditating with a focus in the head, you will not have the same kind of personal and devotional feeling. It will be more of a universal "inner feeling of oneness."

The inner feeling of heightened awareness is a feeling that your consciousness is being raised in some manner. Consciousness is closely related to what Eastern philosophy calls "prana," vital life force energy. Thus one possible way you may experience the feeling of heightened awareness is to experience feelings of energy or movements of energy during your practice of meditation. Both consciousness and prana are associated with light, and the life force energy of prana may be considered *light-energy*. Thus the energy or movements of energy that you feel during meditation may be experienced not only as energy, but also as the inner feeling of light.

As your meditation experience deepens, you may experience one or more of these seven inner feelings. You may already be experiencing some of these inner feelings, but continued meditation practice will increase the depth of your experience of these inner feelings. Although these guideposts are described separately here, they may overlap so any combination of these inner feelings may be experienced simultaneously.

These inner feelings, as guideposts, reflect the reality of God's presence, yet cannot reveal His presence directly. As indirect perceptions, these inner feelings serve as signs that point to the reality of seven qualities of God. While the attributes of God are as limitless as He is, the qualities of God that are most important in relation to deepening meditation are the following seven: totally pure love, endless oneness, infinitely heightened awareness (pure consciousness), boundless light, immeasurable peace, unconditional divine love, and the divine presence that permeates all of existence. If, by divine grace, you would have a direct and complete experience of any one of these seven qualities, you would automatically be experiencing all of these qualities in union with God.

For now it is only necessary to know that meditation is an indirect perception of these qualities. It would be incorrect to think that when you meditate, you can create these qualities, because then you may deceive yourself into trying to manufacture feelings of these qualities. What actually happens during meditation is that you inwardly become aware of these qualities of God that are already within you, but which you are unable to experience directly. Thus the best you can do is to become increasingly sensitive to the feeling of the qualities that are hidden within you.

At first in meditation you may indirectly perceive the qualities of God only mentally. The significance of the seven guideposts of inner feelings is that they are signs of moving to a deeper level of experiencing the divine within. During the beginning experiences of meditation, there is the goal of controlling the stray thoughts of the mind, so the focus is on the mental process of letting go of thoughts. Therefore, you learn to hold one thought of the affirmation and to let go of the many other distracting thoughts. But as you gain the ability to hold one thought firmly, the direction of your growth may change from thought to feeling. This is because with the distracting thoughts removed, you are able to tune into inner feelings that you never knew were there. It's like adding a fine-tuning device to a radio. The tuning device blocks out static and allows you to discover channels that were not available to you before.

The question of if, when, and to what degree you may experience any of these inner feelings cannot be predetermined. You may not experience these inner feelings at all. If you do have these inner feelings, it will depend primarily on the spontaneous action of the Holy Spirit, but also requires your willingness and openness to receive the awareness of inner feelings.

There are different theories about how to respond to these inner feelings when they occur during your meditation experience. One way to respond is to continue to hold on to your affirmation and just allow these inner feelings to come and go without attachment or aversion. Taking this approach treats these inner feelings just as you would respond to thoughts that are seeking to grab your attention, so you use the affirmation to prevent your mind from being distracted. This approach of releasing inner feelings is recommended for Inner Silence Meditation. Letting go of inner feelings can also be used for other techniques of meditation and may be most effective at times when these inner feelings present themselves as short bursts of awareness that appear and disappear suddenly.

However, letting go of inner feelings is not generally recommended in this manual because these inner feelings are not like the thoughts that are seeking to grab your attention during meditation. Instead, these inner feelings are given to you to lead you beyond thought in the direction of increasing your awareness of your divine nature. Therefore, instead of ignoring these inner feelings and holding on to your affirmation, it is recommended that you let go of your affirmation and allow yourself to focus on these inner feelings if they appear.

The recommendation to "focus" on these inner feelings does not mean to evaluate, analyze, or think about them. Just as you can focus on the experience of breathing without intellectualizing about the breathing, you can focus on the experience of inner feelings. This focusing on the experience of inner feelings occurs in the present moment, rather than as an intellectual reflection of looking back on these inner feelings immediately after the fact. Consequently, this focusing means to direct your awareness to being open to these inner feelings as they occur. Also, focusing on inner feelings does not mean to try to hold on to them, but rather to direct your awareness by faith toward allowing these inner feelings to embrace you. This is an expression of openness to allowing the divine radiance to encompass and penetrate you.

If the inner feelings disappear and you become distracted by stray thoughts, you can return to the repeating of your affirmation. This is the approach to be taken during the first three techniques of Progressive Meditation. These three techniques focus on body awareness, but focusing on inner feelings can take you to a deeper level beyond body awareness. You can let go of the affirmation and body awareness, and then you can be aware of these inner feelings as long as they last.

But focusing directly on inner feelings is definitely *not* recommended for practicing the final method of Progressive Meditation. The final technique, Inner Silence Meditation, is designed to lead you toward contemplation, which will require you to let go of clinging to anything, including inner feelings. Of course, inner feelings may spontaneously present themselves during Inner Silence Meditation or contemplation. If this happens, you do not hang on to these inner feelings and you do not try to resist them. You let them come and go just as you would allow thoughts to come and go. But you do not directly focus on these inner feelings because your goal is inner silence that leads to contemplation. Any form of clinging, even to positive inner feelings, would be a diversion from your goal of coming to God with an open mind and heart. By not clinging to any thought or inner feeling you can proceed in pure faith.

Progressive Meditation can provide the opportunity to focus on the awareness of inner feelings for the first three techniques, if these inner feelings spontaneously occur. However, focusing on inner feelings is not used for practicing Inner Silence Meditation. In addition to responding to inner feelings that spontaneously occur during meditation, there is also a proactive approach that can be taken toward these inner feelings. You can choose to practice particular techniques that are designed to focus on specific inner feelings. You can choose inner feelings that you would like to experience at a deeper level and experiment with techniques that will help you move in that direction.

Some meditation methods that focus on inner feelings are described in the next chapter. These techniques emphasize using the inner feeling of love and the inner feeling of light as focal points for your meditation experience. These methods are particularly effective if you are already intermittently experiencing inner feelings spontaneously and if you would like to experience these inner feelings on a more consistent basis.

Remember, however, that experiencing these inner feelings is not your final destination. These inner feelings, as guideposts, are only signs that point in a direction. Would you worship a sign and not move in the direction it is pointing? A wise traveler decides his destination first before setting out on a journey. This is the reason why you have chosen your spiritual ideal. It is your final destination—the top of the mountain. Your destination is a state of oneness with your ideal that is called "divine union." You need to remember that techniques of meditation cannot bring you to the final destination of divine union. These can only help prepare you to receive this gift of God's grace.

F. Growth in Divine Love

Meditation is simply a device to help you to experience God's Love. Hopefully this message has not been clouded over by the descriptions of various techniques and other aspects of meditation. This section will review parts of what has been already stated about divine love and add a few new concepts to clarify the role of divine love in relation to meditation.

Spiritual growth is a matter of learning to love. Perhaps you may not consider yourself to be a very loving person, so the idea of becoming more loving may be a bit overwhelming and even disheartening. But do not be discouraged. Your recognition that you lack love is in itself an indication that you are ready to change. Those who are justified in their own eyes do not realize their need for love. Openness to divine love comes from the awareness of your need for love. The very fact that you are reading this book and considering meditation as a step in your life is itself a sign that God's Love is motivating you to draw closer to Him. It is His Love within, which you may not even yet feel, that will guide you to the form of meditation that will help you discover God's Love for you. Or if you are already aware of His Love, it will help to deepen your awareness of that Love.

For your initial encounter with meditation and even if you already have some experience practicing meditation, Progressive Meditation has been recommended for one reason: It is really a method that aids you to grow toward fulfilling the commandment that Jesus gave and that was also the cornerstone of the Old Testament:

And you shall love the Lord your God with all your heart, and with all your soul, and with all your mind, and with all your strength.[2]

To understand how this relates to Progressive Meditation, you may view the physical body as the temple of your worship, since that is exactly what it is. Within this temple you may consider that you have four altars. The first altar is the navel center, where you can learn how to open yourself to loving God with all of your strength. You do this in Centering Meditation, the first method of Progressive Meditation, by focusing on the navel area and letting the body's physical functioning be given over to the action of the Holy Spirit. Through this receptivity to the Holy Spirit, you are revitalized at the physical level and can offer the strength of the physical body to God's purposes.

The second altar of the temple of your body is the heart center, where you learn how to be receptive to loving God with your whole heart. You do this in the second technique, Heart Meditation, by focusing on the heart area to offer your feeling nature to the Holy Spirit. This produces the quality of devotion. At first, this may not be felt, but gradually you begin to develop the qualities of compassion, sharing with others, and a deeper desire for union with God based on love and thanksgiving.

The third altar of the temple of your physical body is the brow center, where you learn how to open yourself to loving God with your whole mind. Through Brow Meditation you can hold your awareness at the brow area and offer the activity of the mind to the divine influence. Thus the mind becomes the loving instrument of the Holy Spirit. The brow area, associated with the mind, may be considered the doorway to higher consciousness that leads to the fourth altar.

Inner Silence Meditation, the last method of Progressive Meditation, involves opening your spiritual awareness. Perhaps the most important spiritual awareness that is awakened is the inner feeling of love, which is more than human love. This spiritual awakening is a revealing of your true nature of love in union with God. For this practice you let go of body awareness to transcend your temple and enter the Holy of Holies. As you do so, you reach into a deeper level of His World and by faith increase your awareness of His silent, loving presence. When His Spirit draws you into the state of deep contemplation, you will be able to love God with your whole strength, heart, mind, and soul.

The first awareness of love in relation to God is invariably not your love for God, but rather God's Love for you. It is for this reason that meditation may be considered inner receptivity to the Holy Spirit that allows you to be open to receiving God's Love. Meditation, regardless of what method you choose, allows you first to accept the love that God has for you and then in turn allows you to offer this love back to God. Progressive Meditation is especially helpful in regard to increasing your awareness of receiving love from God and expressing love to God.

In addition, a technique called *Inner Love Meditation* is described in the next chapter for your consideration as a means of opening to divine love. This method is recommended as an alternative to your regular meditation, or it may even become your regular practice if you are drawn to using it. It may be practiced while sitting, but you may also use this method in the lying-down position to help you relax and open to God's Love for you and your love for God.

After you inwardly express your love for God, you are better able to dedicate yourself to doing His Will of Love and to offer yourself as a channel of blessing to others. This will encourage you to take the next step after meditation—which is to pray for others. Through your prayers for others the love that has been enkindled within you is given back to God as a blessing to your brothers and sisters in accordance with God's Will. Of course, the real challenge then is to allow that loving feeling that has been awakened within you to carry over into your thoughts, words, and activities of daily living so that you can be a blessing to all those whom you meet. In this way you can fulfill the second great commandment: "You shall love your neighbor as yourself."[3]

Meditation, when properly understood and consistently practiced, is a reminder that more important than anything else in your spiritual life is a growth in love. You have a deep-seated psychological need to love yourself and to love others in the same way, but you have an even deeper spiritual need to feel the Love that God has for you. Without that Love, all these meditation techniques would run the risk of being only an exercise in egotism and self-will. However, with that Love, techniques can be used to purify yourself so that you will be better able to know and do God's Will.

The word "love" is used in many different ways, yet have you ever asked yourself to define "love"? It might be helpful for you to take a moment right now, before reading further, to ask yourself how you would define love, with the understanding that there is no right or wrong definition. The various definitions of love could easily fill a book and still would not exhaust all the facets of what love is all about. But a definition of love will be offered now that may help to clarify and encompass much of what has been stated so far in this book.

Love can be defined as *oneness*. Consider what this means. The single most important truth about spiritual growth is this: Love is your own true nature. Love, meaning oneness with God, is the condition in which you exist. Yet this most important truth is likewise the most difficult truth for you to understand and accept. Your ego condition contradicts this truth by telling you that you are separate from God and so you must become united with Him. Since you are not yet aware of your natural state of oneness with God, the idea of love as oneness does not meet your needs for a definition of love that will help you in a practical sense in your everyday life to grow toward your spiritual aspirations. If you accept that you are already united with God, how can you possibly "grow toward becoming" united with Him? In fact, your growth does not "manufacture" divine union, but rather you are learning to let go of the ego's false perception that imagines that you are separate from God.

Although the definition of love as oneness expresses the truth of your condition theologically, the definition does not help you in a practical sense to let go of your false ego-based perspective of separation. Thus as a concession to the ego condition, a second definition of love can be used that takes into account that you are not yet aware of your natural state of oneness with God. As a practical aid for spiritual growth, you may define love as the desire and the manifesting of *two becoming one*. The first definition of love as oneness is an acknowledgment of the being state of love. This second definition is an expression of the principle of love in action. Love defined as oneness is the end result of union, but love defined as two becoming one expresses your desire for union and is a more useful definition for the entire process of bringing about that union.

Using this definition, you can see why love is so important to spiritual growth. Meditation properly applied is an expression of love because it is the manifestation of the desire for the meditator and the spiritual ideal to become one. Through love, not techniques, you may reach the highest level of communication with God beyond duality. Duality is based on your self-awareness that imagines that you and God are separate. It is love that bridges this gap out of the desire for a true oneness with God.

Of course, this gap between you and God does not really exist except in your own rational thinking mind, which has an attachment to the ego and to the belief in separation. Since you are already united with God and cannot be separate from Him, the idea of two becoming one must in fact be an illusion. Nonetheless, it is a helpful illusion because the illusory idea of joining with God is an important motivational factor in discovering the truth that you already are one with God.

Love as two becoming one can be seen in your daily life also. It is reflected in the most intimate human relationships between a man and a woman. To a lesser degree it is demonstrated in your spontaneous desire to hug your relatives or friends as an expression of oneness. But if you look carefully behind these expressions of human love in your daily life, you will see that God is showing you His Love for you. His Love is not so much shining *on* you as His Love is shining *in* you. It is His Love in you that reminds you that from His viewpoint you are already two as one. Your world is a world of only apparent separation. From your perspective it may be difficult to see that your world is overlapped by His World and that you truly draw your very existence from His World, which is a world of oneness. No definition can adequately define God by saying He is this only and no more. Yet keeping the inadequacy of defining God in mind, it may be helpful here to describe God in His unmanifested state of Being as both Love and Oneness. Since God, as Love and Oneness, is everywhere and in everything, it is impossible for Him to be separate from anyone. The challenge is to realize that you are not separate from Him. If you were apart from God, how could you exist, since His Love for you keeps you in existence? Because He is in each individual, you have the opportunity to see Him in every person you meet, if only you have "eyes to see and ears to hear."

Many years ago while I was visiting Philadelphia, I was invited to a small gathering of spiritually minded people and was asked to conclude their meeting with a meditation. I talked for a few moments about the Jesus Prayer and about Christian techniques of meditation, which we practiced together. After the meditation was completed, several people came over to talk with me, but I noticed a young man in a wheelchair who was being ignored as everyone else was socializing. I went over to him and looked in his eyes. I felt very close to him, and I hugged him. He hugged me back, almost like a drowning man would clutch a life preserver. He continued hugging, and then he started crying. Yet I could feel his tears were tears of joy, of being accepted, and of being loved.

Within myself I felt the same feelings—joy, acceptance, and love. When we separated, he pointed to a card with the letters of the alphabet written on it. He couldn't speak, so he pointed to letters in succession in order to spell—"G..O..D....L..O..V..E..S....Y..O..U." I pointed to him and said, "God loves you." He smiled broadly and pointed to letters on the card again—"G..O..D....L..O..V..E..S...U..S."

This brief encounter had a great impact on me. I felt I could see right through that crippled body, and there was a perfect child of God, perfectly Loved by his Creator. I could feel love for him, too, not the sympathy that perhaps he sometimes got. I could see he sensed what I was feeling. He could also see that I accepted his love for me and that I accepted him as my equal before God. He was teaching me, too. In case I might miss the message, it was being spelled out for me that God loves me. It's a message that everyone has to learn—and relearn daily.

The message is everywhere, just as God is everywhere in His creation. But are you able to see Him and His message? It takes so long to go from birth to the age of reason that somewhere along the way you forget that everything around you is a miracle constantly in the process of unfolding. The sun rises every day, but you fail to see the miracle because you and everyone around you have collectively taken it for granted. God is there in every breath of air you breathe, yet you have become accustomed to it, so there seems to be no miracle. Every part of creation is working together like a perfect symphony to keep you alive. Why? Because it is God's way of saying He loves you.

You may mentally believe that God is in everyone and everything, but in your daily life it is often difficult to see God in other people or to see God's Love in creation. Even if you have the perception to see God in these ways, it will never satisfy your deepest yearning, which is to recognize His presence within yourself, and ultimately to become one with God in divine union.

Techniques of meditation cannot bring about divine union. However, they can be a significant aid in becoming receptive to that gift. While techniques can aid you in your spiritual growth, in the final analysis you can not base the true value of your meditation experience on how successful you may be in your practice. The real importance of practicing meditation is that it serves as a way for you to express your *desire* to be one with God. It's not your meditation results, but rather your desire for God's presence and His saving grace that will bring about divine union. Techniques of meditation, while not necessary for everyone, are helpful for those who are drawn to them as a means of crystallizing their desire, as a preparation for divine union. Since divine union is a spiritual marriage, it requires a desire and willingness on the part of the soul to create the bond of love, because God will not impose Himself on anyone. From this you can see that if you have developed great mental abilities through years of meditation, but do not have love, you are wasting your time. On the other hand, if you are a poor meditator or have never meditated, and yet you have love, you are richly prepared to receive the gift of divine union.

The story of the prodigal son is a good reminder of divine love. It is easy to identify with the prodigal son. He squandered all of his inheritance and experienced suffering. Then he decided to go back to his father and offered to be a lowly servant. "But while he was yet at a distance, his father saw him and had compassion, and ran and embraced him and kissed him."[4]

In this same way, God responds to you whenever you wish to change your life and make one little step toward Him. He makes ten running strides to you and touches your heart with His embrace. This is how it will be for anyone who decides to take the step of using meditation as a way of drawing closer to God. Even if you feel that you are able to make only limited progress in your meditation practice, God will still shower many spiritual blessings on you for your effort. As far as God is concerned, it is your sincerity of heart that matters.

1. Romans 8:26.
2. Mark 12:30.
3. Mark 12:31.
4. Luke 15:20.

11

TECHNIQUES OF
LIGHT AND LOVE

~ • ~

A. Inner Light Meditation

If you experience one or more inner feelings during meditation, there are different ways of responding. Initially when these inner feelings present themselves to you in meditation, you may have an inappropriate attachment to them simply because they are pleasant, and you may be starved for spiritual sweetness. You may want to cling to these pleasant feelings, and your ego may attach a prideful significance to having these feelings. Your attachment may actually prevent these inner feelings from recurring more frequently. You may make the mistake of valuing your meditation experience based on whether or not these feelings occur. Yet the most valuable meditations you have may be the ones that appear to be a struggle for you, but in which you are facing and removing inner blocks.

When these inner feelings first begin to appear, it may be best to treat them like any other thoughts. You can focus on your affirmation and let these inner feelings come and go without attachment or aversion. Some approaches to meditation teach that this is always the way you should respond to these inner feelings. This is really a safe approach because when you are seeking God, you must rely most of all on pure faith that does not require your having a felt experience to confirm your faith. This approach prevents you from mistakenly interpreting these inner feelings as evidence of having a direct experience of God Himself, instead of correctly realizing that they are only signs that point the way to God.

Nevertheless, there comes a time in your development when you understand that these inner feelings can be used as a means of drawing you closer to God without being a distraction or attachment. Your inner feelings are not like other thoughts that grab your attention during your practice of meditation because inner feelings are guideposts reminding you of your divine nature. As long as you remain centered on your faith in God, you do not have to ignore these inner feelings and therefore disregard the message that these inner feelings have for you.

One way of accepting your inner feelings as an aid to your practice is to let go of your affirmation and focus your awareness on your inner feelings when they appear. This focusing does not mean thinking about your inner feelings, but rather placing your attention on the experience of these inner feelings as they occur in the present moment. You can focus on any one inner feeling or any combination of inner feelings that comes to your awareness. If the inner feelings disappear and your mind becomes distracted, you can return to using your affirmation. You can apply this same approach to the three techniques of Progressive Meditation that focus on body awareness. You can let go of your affirmation and hold your awareness in the focusing area within the body appropriate to the technique being used. While focusing on body awareness, you can also focus on inner feelings when they present themselves. When the inner feelings leave your awareness, you can return to just focusing on body awareness, or if your mind becomes distracted, you can return to focusing on both your affirmation and body awareness. A description of how to respond to inner feelings during the practice of Inner Silence Meditation and contemplation is provided in the next section in this final chapter.

The approach that has just been explained relies on responding to inner feelings when they occur spontaneously without your consciously attempting to uncover these inner feelings. After you have made progress in removing subconscious emotional clutter, your mind may become calm to the degree of allowing more of these inner feelings to surface. If you notice that inner feelings are naturally surfacing more frequently, you may want to take another approach that may allow you to experience these inner feelings consistently. For your new approach, you can decide to proactively initiate uncovering these inner feelings. The rest of this section focuses on initiating the opening of yourself to experiencing the inner feeling of light, the inner feeling of love, and other inner feelings.

If you want to increase your awareness of the inner feeling of light, you may be guided to create your own meditation technique related to the awareness of light. Some meditators, who imagine white light to be surrounding and filling the body as a preparation for meditation, find this process so effective that they continue to focus on white light throughout their meditation. Other meditators find it helpful to focus on a candle flame with the eyes open, and then closing the eyes, they focus on the light within. Some imagine a sphere of light like the sun within the head and imagine light radiating outward from that sphere. There are also meditators who can actually see a steady inner light and meditate on that light. The ability to see light within may occur spontaneously or may be learned. One way of learning this ability is to first close your eyes during meditation and focus on seeing blackness. Within that blackness you can look for the slightest bit of light. Then you focus on that tiny bit of light. Gradually after repeated practice, the amount of light you can see will increase until ideally you can consistently see an inner light.

There is a technique of focusing on light, which does not use the imagination and does not use the visual experience of seeing light. This method is called *Inner Light Meditation*. For this method you are aware of feeling the presence of light and allow that inner feeling to be the focus of your meditation. Sometimes you can feel this light as it moves through the body. It is quite different from imagining white light because it appears to be something happening to you in your receptive state of mind, rather than something you are actively attempting to produce through your imagination. Oftentimes this inner feeling of light seems to carry with it other feelings as well, such as an inner feeling of the divine presence, love, or peace. It may also be accompanied by a feeling of heightened awareness, which may be experienced as expanded consciousness or as energy.

Initially the presence of light may be felt as a temporary experience within the body that comes and goes of its own accord. Consequently, this inner feeling may at first be difficult to use as a consistent focus for meditation because of its spontaneous coming and going. But there is one area of the body where this feeling of inner light can be experienced most consistently. This area is the location of the physical heart. The exact location is not the whole area of the physical heart, but rather a very small area on the left side of the chest that can be felt intuitively during meditation. If you develop a sensitivity to this inner feeling, you will experience a light emanating from this area. This sensitivity cannot happen through a forceful effort of the will. In order to feel this light, you literally need to open your heart. In other words, the light in the heart can only be felt by you when you are in a loving state of mind.

When you first start your practice of Inner Light Meditation, your practice is just like Heart Meditation in that you repeat your affirmation and hold your awareness in the heart area. When your mind becomes calm, you let go of the affirmation and only focus on the heart area. For Inner Light Meditation, you specifically hold your awareness on a very small area of the heart. It may take many meditation periods before you are able to tune into the light and love that emanate from the heart. When you do experience the inner light and/or love, you focus on the heart and also on that inner feeling as long as you are able to do so. You can eventually make this a consistent focus for your meditation, rather than an intermittent focus.

In the area on the left side of the chest where the light is felt, there may also be a subtle energy or very slight pressure without pain that pinpoints the exact spot. This spot is referred to by St. John of the Cross in his book *The Living Flame of Love* when he speaks about the presence of a divine inner flame. In fact, the phrase "living flame of love" perfectly describes this spot in the heart where divine love is waiting to be awakened. This phrase is usually interpreted as only a literary metaphor used by St. John of the Cross. However, this loving and living flame is the exact description of what can actually be experienced in meditation. It truly feels like a flame of subtle energy that is alive and actually sending out light and love. It really is an eternal flame that is in every individual heart. The flame can be limited to only a tiny spark of light and love, but it can never be extinguished. Invariably it is covered over by the cares of the world so that you do not notice it.

As you focus on this area and perhaps can feel the presence of this flame, your meditation will deepen, and your feeling of light, love, and energy will increase. Eventually after awakening the flame in the heart on a consistent basis, it will be quite natural for the light, love, and energy to expand outward from the heart. Gradually the light, love, and energy will expand to the whole chest, especially to the center of the chest.

With continued practice, the light, love, and energy naturally rise upward through the neck and into the head. The light, love, and energy may go up the front of the head but are more likely to first go up to the lower portion of the back of the head. Finally the head may become filled with light, love, and/or energy. Typically these inner feelings are experienced in the body as taking an upward path. However, some meditators experience these inner feelings as descending from over the head and moving downward within the body.

Inner Light Meditation may be employed as part of a variation of Progressive Meditation, which is described in the next section. In this variation Inner Light Meditation replaces Heart Meditation. So when the light, love, and energy rise from the heart center into the head, you can shift your awareness to the brow area for Brow Meditation, as part of this variation, which is called *Expanded Progressive Meditation*.

When practicing Inner Light Meditation, you may feel energy currents rising upward from the base of the spine into the head while focusing on the light and love in the chest. In addition, there may be jolts of energy that suddenly rise upward through the neck and jerk the head somewhat. Regardless of whatever occurs on a form level, you will need to remain focused on your intent of maintaining a loving state of mind and seeking the divine within.

It is important to remember that experiencing inner light is fueled only by remaining in a love state. If the mind becomes distracted by unloving thoughts, the light will literally go out and very quickly at that. If the feeling of inner light disappears, you can focus on an affirmation, such as "Christ Light" or "Jesus Christ Light," and hold the awareness in the heart area. If your mind becomes calm, you can release the affirmation and hold your awareness in the heart area, just as you would do in Heart Meditation. When the awareness of inner light returns, you can focus on the heart area and also focus on the inner feeling of light and love.

Since the cares of the world literally cover over the flame in the heart, it is necessary to have a purity of purpose if you intend to uncover this flame. The goal should not be the attainment of an experience, but the desire for God Himself. Also, once the flame is initially uncovered, there are still many inner blocks that would hinder your progress in meditation. These inner obstacles are the ego-based concerns of the world that are like a dark cloud around the flame. This dark cloud lifts as you release inner blocks by focusing on the heart with the help of the Holy Spirit.

After releasing blocks over an extended period of time, you will notice an increased sensitivity to being aware of light, love, and energy within. You may find that when you attempt to hold your awareness on the flame in the heart, your awareness instead goes to the center of the chest where you feel a strong light, love, and energy emanating. If this happens, feel free to allow the center of the chest to be your ongoing focusing area for your regular practice of Inner Light Meditation.

Hopefully you will be able to open both your physical heart and the center of your chest to the divine love that is your true nature. For your practice of Inner Light Meditation, you can hold your awareness on whichever of these two locations draws your attention, as you are in the process of literally opening your heart to the divine influence.

Through practicing Inner Light Meditation, as part of Expanded Progressive Meditation, you will eventually have an increased ability to be aware of light, love, and energy filling the chest, the head, and then the whole body. Eventually your increased awareness of light and love can help bring about a noticeable inner and outer transformation. The results of this transformation are not only a significant deepening of meditation, but also an enhancement of your personality that increases your outer expression of love to others. By removing many inner blocks while focusing on the inner feelings of light and love, you will experience a deep peace and an inner sense of well-being. Discovering the light and love within your own heart is indeed a wonderful blessing.

For the practice of Inner Light Meditation, you may experience any combination of the feelings of inner light, inner love, and heightened awareness, which can be felt as an expansion of your consciousness or more tangibly as a subtle energy within the body. Also, you can focus on any one of these inner feelings.

B. Expanded Progressive Meditation

If you have been consistently practicing Progressive Meditation for a long time and would like to increase your awareness of inner feelings, you may want to consider using a variation of your regular practice. This variation is called *Expanded Progressive Meditation*. This practice includes all of the methods of Progressive Meditation with the exception of Heart Meditation, which is replaced by Inner Light Meditation that also focuses on the heart area.

The first method of Expanded Progressive Meditation is Centering Meditation. This method is practiced exactly as in your regular practice of Progressive Meditation. There is no particular emphasis on opening to inner feelings during Centering Meditation because first you want to establish a relaxed breathing pattern and begin your practice just as you always do when using Progressive Meditation. Nevertheless, if you do feel light, love, and or/energy rising from the bottom of the spine or moving upward from the navel area, you have the option of focusing on these inner feelings. One adjustment in your practice of Centering Meditation may be changing your affirmation if you feel that a new affirmation would help you to open up to your inner feelings. For example, you may choose an affirmation such as "Christ Light" or "Christ Love."

For your second method of Expanded Progressive Meditation, you practice Inner Light Meditation, which focuses on a specific area of your physical heart and on the inner feelings emanating from this area. These inner feelings of light, love, and/or energy become your focus for meditation, as has been described previously. But if your awareness is naturally drawn to the inner feelings of light, love, and energy in the center of the chest, you may focus your awareness there instead of in the location of the physical heart. Under ideal circumstances you will experience the light, love, and/or energy from the heart expanding and filling the chest and then rising into the head, which will be the best preparation for practicing the next method, Brow Meditation.

For your practice of Brow Meditation, a change from your regular practice of this method is that when you focus on the brow area, you also focus on the inner feelings of light, love, and/or energy in the brow area. You place your focus entirely on the brow area for this practice. But without consciously intending to do so, you may feel light, love, and/or energy in the heart area or in the center of the chest as a result of previously practicing Inner Light Meditation. You continue to focus at the brow area even though you may feel the light, love, and/or energy rising up from the heart or from the center of the chest and into the head. Whether or not you can feel light, love, and/or energy rising up from below, the goal is to allow your mind to be a loving instrument of the Spirit. You can use an affirmation if you become distracted, yet as you make progress, the affirmation will be needed less and less.

For those meditators who specifically feel energy in the body while practicing Expanded Progressive Meditation, it may be helpful here to review the ways that energy may manifest itself during the practice of the first three techniques. The energy that is being felt is prana and can be felt in many different ways. It can be felt as concentrations of energy in each focusing area in the front of the body or as the energy of tension being released in any part of the body. It may also be felt as movements of energy up the front or the back of the body that may be experienced as slow, steady movements or sudden, jerky movements.

By opening your mind to the Spirit, you may feel the partial rising of the kundalini in the body as energy manifesting in various ways. One possible specific way in which the partial rising of the kundalini can occur in Expanded Progressive Meditation will be described now. This specific partial rising goes all the way up to the crown area, but is partial rising in terms of intensity, since it is only a small portion of the full kundalini force that is being raised up. The way this may manifest is that some of the coiled prana at the base of the spine rises very slowly up the spine as the meditator is holding his awareness in the navel area, the heart area, and the brow area during the first three methods of Expanded Progressive Meditation. Some meditators can feel the prana as it rises slowly up the spine, then to the lower part of the back of the head at the medulla oblongata, and finally to the crown area.

Some meditators cannot feel the energy rising in the spine, yet can feel the crown area being activated by this rising energy. In some cases the crown area can be felt as a circular "opening" or simply as an increase of energy at the top of the head. In general, most meditators do not feel the energy rising in the spine or the energy in the crown area. But the rising of energy in the spine and activation of the crown area can certainly occur without the conscious awareness of the meditator. When some of the inner blocks are removed and a certain amount of the creative energy rises up to the top of the head, the creative energy flows into this circular crown area and allows an integrating energy to descend downward into the whole body, coordinating all the centers of awareness. This rising creative energy and resulting descending energy is due to the activity of the kundalini. The kundalini removes blocks as it rises and integrates the spiritual centers as it descends. This brings about the experience of the seven inner feelings described in Chapter 10.

Those who can feel the integrating energy from the crown center as it descends downward may first feel the energy come down into the center of the chest and then feel the entire body being filled with energy. The Twenty-third Psalm makes a reference to this overflowing energy:

> Thy rod and thy staff, they comfort me. Thou anointeth my head with oil. My cup runneth over, surely goodness and mercy shall follow me all the days of my life.

The "rod" is the endocrine glands in the front of the body. The "staff" is the nerve plexuses in the spine plus the medulla oblongata and also the crown area that creates the curve to the top of the staff. The "cup" is the crown center. The anointing with "oil" is the oil of God's grace that takes the form of the creative energy filling the crown center and overflowing, just as a cup can be filled to overflowing. This overflowing energy integrates the physical, emotional, and mental levels of your human nature, bringing them into accord with your spiritual nature. Even though most meditators do not feel this coordinating effect as a consciously felt experience, this integration can still occur without your conscious awareness of it.

During the first three methods of Expanded Progressive Meditation, you have the option of releasing body awareness altogether and briefly focusing only on the inner feeling of light, love, and/or energy as a transition to the next method, which is Inner Silence Meditation. For this fourth and final method, you release your focus on light, love, and/or energy, and you practice Inner Silence Meditation just as you would ordinarily for your regular Progressive Meditation practice.

If you become consciously aware of energy in the body, such as feeling energy rising in the spine and descending from the crown center, you may feel energy throughout the whole body. This can present a slight problem in relation to your practice of Inner Silence Meditation. Practicing Inner Silence Meditation requires releasing body awareness altogether, but if you feel your whole body filled with energy, it may be difficult to let go of body awareness.

If you are unable to let go of body awareness, you will need to let go of your desire to feel energy in the body. You can still rest in inner silence and contemplation while you are experiencing body awareness and energy awareness to some degree, as long as you can let go of your desire for these. You can let go of your desire by setting aside both attraction to energy awareness and aversion to energy awareness. Since the faculty of your will is not involved, you can let energy awareness come and go of its own accord without your invitation or rejection. In this way you may experience energy awareness *passively*. Since you are not using this awareness of energy as a focusing object, you will be able to practice Inner Silence Meditation without being distracted.

For Inner Silence Meditation, the fourth and final technique, you let go of body awareness as much as possible and open yourself to resting in the divine presence. As with all four methods of Expanded Progressive Meditation, you can repeat an affirmation at those times when your mind becomes distracted. If the crown center of awareness has been opened by using the first three methods, the crown center will ideally continue to be open for Inner Silence Meditation. Hopefully you will be receptive to the unifying effect of the Holy Spirit acting through the crown center of awareness. With your consent the Holy Spirit will assist you to calm and to unify the mind enough for you to enter contemplation. During contemplation you can rely on your pure faith alone, which is the highest form of intuition that goes deeper than your inner feelings. Your faith is a reliance on your inner knowing of the divine presence, which may not be felt experientially. During your contemplation you are drawn into an inner absorption that allows you to let go of mental distractions.

Your faith is essential to bring about the overshadowing of the Holy Spirit and to enter contemplation. Although your faith does not require a felt experience to confirm the divine presence, it certainly does not exclude having a felt experience of the divine presence. Thus because of your openness to your inner feelings during your practice of the previous three techniques of Expanded Progressive Meditation, you may find yourself continuing to experience the inner feelings of light, love, and/or other inner feelings as you rest in inner silence. If these inner feelings, including the feeling of energy, spontaneously present themselves, you can be open to them and feel them as long as they last, without feeling as though you need to cling to them or push them away.

The previous three methods of Expanded Progressive Meditation focus directly on the inner feelings of light, love, and/or energy. Yet when you release your affirmation during Inner Silence Meditation, you do not focus specifically on these inner feelings. These inner feelings may come to you anyway, but during Inner Silence Meditation you want to be completely open to the action of the Holy Spirit so that you exert no initiative of your own directed toward what you would like to experience.

You learn to let go in order to reach a deeper level of receptivity. You will need to be willing to let go of yourself, as you think of yourself. This includes releasing your own desires, even self-chosen spiritual desires. In order to succeed, you will need to have faith that you will be supported by the Holy Spirit in your process of letting go. Your trust in the Holy Spirit will be rewarded. You will be supported, but not necessarily in the way in which you expect. You will receive from the Holy Spirit whatever you truly need to make progress spiritually, rather than what you may consciously want.

The body awareness methods of Expanded Progressive Meditation allow you to proactively direct your awareness toward experiencing inner feelings. However, this proactive expression of the desire for experiencing inner feelings is counterbalanced by the nonattachment of Inner Silence Meditation, in which you do not consciously direct your awareness toward revealing your inner feelings. It would be helpful here to mention some differences between meditation and contemplation in order to explain why you do not use your inner feelings as a focusing object during the practice of Inner Silence Meditation, which leads to contemplation.

Meditation is communication with God, which always has an object as the focus for meditation, so in meditation you are the one deciding to hold on to that object. Consequently, you can have your inner feelings of light and love as your focusing object for your meditation. In contrast to meditation, contemplation is communication with God in which you do not have a focusing object. Thus during contemplation you cannot direct your mind toward your inner feelings as a focusing object. But you can experience whatever inner feelings present themselves as they come and go, but without any feeling that you must hold on to them or push them away. This approach allows you to let go of your own desires and leaves you entirely open to the divine influence.

Directly focusing on inner feelings when practicing techniques that use body awareness can work for the lower rungs of the ladder to higher consciousness. Yet when you want to let go of body awareness and enter contemplation, a greater degree of nonattachment is required. The reason for emphasizing the need to let go of directly focusing on inner feelings during Inner Silence Meditation is that holding on to inner feelings represents a form of possessiveness that reinforces the false self. The ego survives by its ability to possess not only material things, but also by possessing thoughts and feelings, even spiritual thoughts and feelings.

You may be so starved for spiritual experiences that when inner feelings occur, you may want to hold on to them in a clinging fashion. But this clinging itself is a fear of loss, which will close off your openness and trust and thus shut down your experience of inner feelings. When you can let go of the clinging to these inner feelings, you will no longer be under the influence of the aspect of the ego that seeks spiritual experiences for the sake of spiritual pride. In doing so you will not close the door to spiritual sweetness, but rather you will have only given up your possessiveness that is so characteristic of the ego. Ironically it is by giving up this very possessiveness that you actually remove a hindrance to having spiritual consolations come to you spontaneously.

God cannot be possessed in the way that the ego is accustomed to possessing objects. *But you can allow God to possess you.* By allowing the Holy Spirit to come over you in contemplation, you are allowing yourself to be embraced by the nourishing Spirit of God and His Love. Being embraced by His Spirit requires that you possess nothing, letting thoughts come and go without attachment to them. Likewise, you let your inner feelings of spiritual sweetness come and go of themselves.

After you learn to let go of any sense of possession regarding inner feelings, you may discover that when inner feelings do spontaneously occur, it feels as though the inner feelings are possessing you. When the Holy Spirit overshadows you in contemplation, inner feelings may come as well. Generally these inner feelings come and go. Yet after you have been exposed to contemplative experiences over a long period of time, you may notice that these inner feelings stay without your exerting any initiative for this to happen. After you have released many inner blocks and reached the plateau of self-acceptance, these inner feelings that stay may last for most of your practice. When these inner feelings stay with you, it may appear to you that these inner feelings are holding on to you.

Inner feelings are from God, but they are not God, just as sunlight is from the sun but is not the sun. These inner feelings are the radiance of God. When these inner feelings persist without you exerting your will for this to happen, it appears to you that you are being possessed by God. It feels as if you are an object that God is embracing with His Light and Love, even if it is only an indirect embrace.

Earlier, when you were trying to possess these inner feelings, you viewed yourself as a subject, who is the one possessing these inner feelings, and you viewed your inner feelings as the object you were possessing. In this more advanced state, you perceive the object to be yourself, who is being possessed and perceive the subject to be God, Who is indirectly possessing you. But this view of yourself as an object upon which God is radiating is still an illusion that perpetuates the subject/object division between you and God. This illusory division is caused by the ego, which is the thought of division. In reality, it is only your lack of awareness of your true nature and your investment in the ego that prevents you from realizing that you are one with God.

Your contemplative experience of the Holy Spirit overshadowing you is a state of *imageless self-awareness.* You give up your possessiveness, but there is still the awareness of yourself as the observer of the parade of both thoughts and feelings. Your awareness is not totally unified so you may actually be experiencing different levels of awareness at the same time. For example, in what might be called the "foreground" of your awareness, you may be experiencing inner feelings, and in what might be called the "background" of your awareness, you may be dimly conscious of the stream of thoughts passing by in the mind. You are the observer placing most of your attention on your inner feelings and to a lesser degree noticing unwanted thoughts pass by, but without paying attention to them. It may happen that even the passing unwanted thoughts disappear entirely from your awareness, so you experience only inner feelings. But even in this state, you would still be aware of yourself as being the observer.

The next step on the ladder to higher consciousness is going from contemplation with self-awareness to the experience of contemplation without self-awareness. This deeper level of contemplation beyond being aware of yourself may be called *pure awareness* or *pure consciousness*. In the state of self-awareness, you are aware of yourself as the one who is seeking and who is separate from what you are seeking. In the state of pure awareness or pure consciousness, you let go of yourself, as you think of yourself. You let go of the false self, the ego, which means you let go of the illusory idea that you are separate from God.

You cannot exert the force of your will to bring yourself into the deeper contemplative state of pure awareness, because this state occurs spontaneously of itself by divine grace. Nonetheless, you can prepare yourself for this by letting go of the desire for spiritual experiences. After all, if you are seeking spiritual experiences of inner feelings as possessions for the ego, how will you be able to let go of the false self in order to be in a state of pure awareness?

If you have decided that your final destination is divine union, you need to recognize that your divine union is far beyond any temporary experience you may have in your journey toward your destination. If you have set your course on reaching a mountaintop, you can stop for a few minutes to refresh yourself by drinking from a natural spring that you find along your way. However, then you need to continue on your journey in order to reach the top of the mountain. Releasing the need to hold on to the inner feelings that may come and go will give you a new freedom in which spiritual experiences are not a concern, but still can be accepted without attachment or aversion. In this way your heart can remain truly devoted to God alone, Who can meet your every need.

The final technique of Expanded Progressive Meditation is not much different from your regular practice of Inner Silence Meditation, except that you may notice an increase in the number and depth of inner feelings that spontaneously occur during your practice. Your increased awareness of inner feelings will be the result of having opened yourself significantly to the Spirit during the previous methods that used body awareness. Through your increased openness to the Spirit, you may find that during your practice of Inner Silence Meditation you are able to experience contemplation more consistently and at a deeper level.

C. Inner Love Meditation

While all meditation methods help you to increase your awareness of God's loving inner presence, *Inner Love Meditation* in particular helps you to be receptive to God's Love. Using the imagination has not been recommended for the meditation methods in this book. However, this technique is the exception to that rule, as will be explained shortly. Before attempting to use this technique that does focus on love, it is helpful to look at your own perceptions of what love means to you.

Your perception of love is influenced by your perception of yourself. The ego-based self tells you that you are a limited mind and a body that is separate from God. This false self is how you normally perceive yourself. Although this perception is what separates you from your awareness of God, you cannot reject the self as your enemy. Actually you need to accept the mask of self and indeed love that mask, because in doing so you are allowing your true Self, your true nature of love, to be expressed. You are conditioned to think it is selfish to love yourself. In reality, it is *only* by accepting and loving yourself that you are able to accept and love others. In fact, Jesus said that you must love your neighbors in the same way that you love yourself. This means you must love yourself without allowing your self-love to make you think you are better than your neighbors, since this is pride. Having a healthy self-love for yourself means accepting the mask of self and loving yourself with the love that God has for you.

Loving your mask does not mean that you approve of the selfishness of the ego condition. Rather, it means that you are loving the limited form through which your true Self is now expressing itself. You accept the fact that sometimes your limited form will produce selfishness, but basically you love that limited form in the same way that you would love a child. When a child misbehaves, you neither approve of the inappropriate behavior of the child nor do you condemn the child for his inappropriate behavior. You know that the child's misbehavior is part of his normal process of growing up. Therefore, you don't love the child's misbehavior, but you do love the child. Similarly, you do not specifically love the selfishness of the ego condition, but you can in a general sense love your mask. You love the mask, not because of what it is in itself, but rather because of your true Self in union with God that stands behind that mask and gives it life.

Inner Love Meditation can be used to help you develop a healthy self-love. The first step in learning to love yourself in the right way is to realize that God loves you unconditionally. For this reason, in the beginning of Inner Love Meditation, you relax and imagine a blessing of God's Love is coming down over the top of the head and filling the entire body. Instead of feeling a descending blessing, you may choose the option of focusing on God's blessing emanating from the heart, then filling the entire body.

The manner in which you perceive the blessing occurring is not as important as your attitude of openness and willingness to receive this blessing. You focus on accepting this blessing of love for no other reason than being alive. It is essential to not put any conditions on this love, even though you may normally only allow yourself to accept love when you are "good," which trains you to condemn yourself when you are "bad."

By focusing on a feeling of being loved and nourished, you accept God's Love. To intensify this love, an affirmation is repeated, such as "God loves me," "Love," "Thank You, Lord," or "This is how God feels about me."

For most Christians, God's Love can be experienced most intimately through an openness to Jesus Christ. If you wish to develop receptivity to Christ's Love for you, then you may want to use an affirmation that includes His Holy Name, such as "Jesus loves me," "Jesus Christ Love," "Christ Love," or simply "Jesus," with a feeling of being loved.

For Inner Love Meditation, you set aside all feelings of how you feel about yourself, and think only of yourself as one who is being loved. At first, repeating the affirmation and imagining yourself accepting love will seem to be mechanical and not really felt. But slowly, the inner feeling of being loved will begin to manifest and grow. Some meditators imagine that God's Love for them is expressed through the vehicle of light, so if you are drawn to imagine yourself being filled with both love and light, feel free to do so.

As you practice Inner Love Meditation, you will learn to accept this love as God's Love for you and you will experience it. After your "imagined" feeling of God's Love for you changes to an inner feeling that God really is in fact loving you, you will discover that you will genuinely be able to love God in return. Unfortunately most people, even people who are actually very loving, do not consider themselves to be very loving. If you question your ability to love in general or if you specifically question your ability to love God, you are not being asked to imagine your love for God. If you were being asked to imagine your love for God, you might feel that you are faking your love and creating a manufactured love that is not genuine.

Consequently, instead of being asked to imagine your love for God, you are being asked to imagine God's Love for you, which by faith you know is a reality. Then when you actually do feel the presence of God loving you, you can allow His Love to affect you while you remain passive. Spontaneously and naturally His Love will come forth and eventually will draw forth a loving response from you.

First you will feel yourself as one who is being loved by God. But gradually you will feel the ability to return your love to God. Then there will seem to be two loves—an apparently external love coming from above the head and filling the body and an inner response to that love that inspires you to love God in return. However, perhaps on a rare occasion brought about purely by God's grace, the apparently external love and the internal love may at least temporarily merge into a loving state of being that just *is*.

Some people use visualization to help them use their imagination. Yet the term "imagination" as it is used here does not mean the visualization of mental pictures. To imagine something is to make believe—to make something so real to you that you can feel its presence. The key to using the imagination in meditation is that you must choose to imagine only those things that do in fact have a reality behind them—but a reality that is hidden from you and is therefore only accessible through the imagination. After you imagine something to be real, then the reality behind that something shines through so you can become aware of the presence of that reality.

Although you begin Inner Love Meditation by imagining God's Love, this is not a manufactured experience or a "power of positive thinking" experience. You are simply using the imagination to tune into the reality of love that is really there, and then the reality becomes apparent. You can accept love since love is your true nature and power. As you accept love, your love nature manifests spontaneously in a way that can be experienced directly. As an aftereffect of this experience, you can learn to love yourself in your everyday life as one who is loved by God.

Imagining God's Love is the exact opposite of the kind of "imagining" you are doing in your present ego condition. Actually right now you are "imagining" that God does not love you. Since God is Spirit, and you imagine yourself to be only a body and a mind, you imagine that you are separate from God and separate from His Love. You may have some ideas about God loving you, but these ideas are permeated with contradictory ideas of separation that restrict your openness to His Love. Because of your ego, you imagine an illusion of separation, a false reality, which seems to be confirmed by your experiences of separation in everyday life. Since you are imagining a false reality, it makes sense to also use the imagination to counteract the illusion that you have created. You can do this by giving yourself permission to imagine the true reality of God's Love for you, as is suggested in Inner Love Meditation.

All four techniques of Progressive Meditation are designed to help remove blocks that prevent you from becoming aware of God's Love. The primary block related to the crown center is the fear of losing one's ego. This fear of losing the ego is actually the *fear of God's Love*. This block needs to be released in order to become completely open to God. Why is this block so important? It is important because of what God's Love means to your ego. God is infinite and eternal, and so His Love is also infinite and eternal. The ego is finite and time limited. To the ego, the infinite and eternal Love of God means annihilation. The ego and the full force of God's Love are mutually exclusive, so you can have one or the other but not both. Practicing Inner Love Meditation is not a means of producing a full acceptance of God's Love and the complete giving up of the ego, which can only occur as a result of divine grace. The total acceptance of divine love can happen during a deep experience of illumination or at the moment of truth that comes at physical death.

The fear of God's Love and the parallel fear of your own love for God are hidden from your normal awareness by defense mechanisms of the ego. The fear of God's Love is a very large inner obstacle that can only be overcome by divine grace. Nevertheless, a portion of that grace is allowing you to release tiny bits of that block in a gradual manner. Although Inner Love Meditation is not a means of removing the entire block, the repeated practice of this method can assist you through the action of the Holy Spirit to remove little pieces of your block to God's Love. Through this piecemeal process, you can learn to accept a small amount of God's Love for you and accept a small amount of your love for God. In this gradual process of learning to accept love, you are correspondingly letting go of little bits of your ego-based thoughts of separation that had previously blocked your awareness of love.

Since releasing the fear of God's Love also involves letting go of the ego, another way of describing the fear of God's Love is to call it the *fear of losing your individuality*. The illustration on the opposite page shows the primary blocks related to each of the seven spiritual centers. This illustration indicates that the major block related to the crown center is the fear of losing your individuality, which is the same as the fear of losing one's ego and the fear of God's Love. In your current everyday life, you falsely believe your individuality rests in the ego. Your ego has taught you that being separate from others makes you individual. Because of your false identification with the ego, you believe that you

INNER
BLOCKS

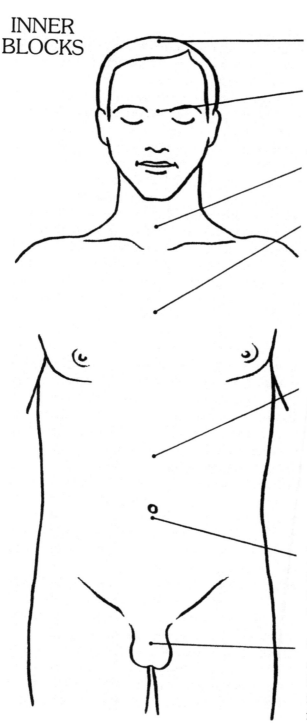

Crown Center
fear losing individuality

Brow Center
mental blocks,
lack of openness

Throat Center
misuse of the will

Heart Center
depression and guilt,
fear of punishment,
losses, selfishness,
lack of self-worth,
self-condemnation,
lack openness to love

Adrenal Center
inner or outer hostility,
passive aggressiveness,
judgment, blaming,
complaining, revenge,
attack thoughts,
projection

Navel Center
fear of meditation,
misusing imagination,
sexual fantasy

Gonad Center
sexual issues, laziness,
inconsistency, apathy,
insecurity, confusion,
fear of death

will lose all of your individuality if you merge with God. You believe you would be like a raindrop falling into the Ocean and then have no individual nature. But the truth is that your true individuality is found in your loving union with God. As an analogy you can think of your true nature as an individual branch on a tree in which God is the trunk nourishing you with the life-giving sap of His Love. In the practice of Inner Love Meditation, the imagining of love descending from over the head downward is a way of helping to reduce this block associated with the crown of the head and freeing up divine love to manifest more fully as it descends upon the body.

This form of meditation may be practiced while sitting. Yet it may also be practiced while lying down, but only if reclining does not cause you to become drowsy. To avoid drowsiness the best time of day to use the lying-down position is in the middle of the day, rather than at the start or end of the day. Inner Love Meditation is suggested to be practiced as a lying-down alternative to your regular form of sitting meditation. This technique is especially recommended if you are going through a difficult period in which you are so unsettled that you are unable to practice your regular meditation in a sitting position.

For using the lying-down position, you place the hands one over the other at the navel area. The tips of the thumbs can be placed together so they are gently touching each other just below the navel. If placing the hands over the navel area feels uncomfortable, you can place the hands along the sides of the body with the palms turned upward.

After Inner Love Meditation is completed, you may want to pray for others to allow the love that has been received from God to be passed on as a blessing to others. Inner Love Meditation can be used as part of the kind of healing prayer that includes the laying on of hands. As you feel God's Love for you, you can allow that loving feeling to pass through your hands and into the person receiving the healing. You may want to also coordinate your breathing while doing the laying on of hands. For this option you let yourself inhale and feel yourself absorbing God's Love, and then exhale to feel God's Love flowing through your hands and into the other person. Regardless of what technique is used, the secret of healing others is in caring about them and allowing God's Love to flow through you. The source of all forms of healing is God's Love. His Love facilitates healing by awakening the divine love nature that is already within the person who is receiving the healing.

Whether Inner Love Meditation is used as a meditation method or for healing, it should be used only if it feels inwardly right to do so. For example, you may feel uncomfortable with imagining God's Love for you because of a concern about fabricating an artificial experience created by yourself. In this case, instead of using the imagination, you might want to request God's help with an affirmation, such as "Lord, help me to feel Your Love." Another approach is to focus on your mental knowledge of love, rather than your feeling of love. With this emphasis on mental awareness, you can use a statement for your meditation that affirms your knowledge of God's Love. Another option is to focus on the word "acceptance" rather than love. Thus you can choose an affirmation of God's acceptance of you, or even your own acceptance of yourself.

Any method that uses the imagination is subject to distortion. Thus Inner Love Meditation is recommended to be used only temporarily as a stepping stone to increase your awareness of love within and as a preparation for using other methods that do not use the imagination, such as Progressive Meditation. While you are practicing Inner Love Meditation, you may hear the inner humming sound, and then you can let go of your affirmation and switch to practicing Inner Listening Meditation. Since the inner humming sound originates from a spiritual source, you may discover that listening to this inner tone actually helps you to feel the divine within as a loving presence.

D. Concluding Thoughts

Congratulations on reading this book to express your openness to practicing various meditation methods. My first meditation experience started with reading a book on Zen Buddhism and practicing Counting Meditation, the technique described on page 44. Back then in 1968, I thought that meditation was all about controlling my unruly mind. Now, after many years of using a variety of methods, I have learned that all of my spiritual growth is a process of becoming increasingly aware of the Ocean of Divine Love in which I live and move and have my being.

Ask yourself right now, "Do I live within an Ocean of Divine Love?" Did you hear a voice within that said, "No, I do not live within an Ocean of Divine Love"? If you heard that voice, it is the voice of the ego. The ego is a false idea about who you are, but it is not you. The ego's voice represents the majority of what is called "self-talk," which is your constant internal conversation. The ego claims that its voice speaks on your behalf. Yet the ego actually speaks on behalf of all your false beliefs about yourself. It tells you that you are very limited. It tells you that you are all alone in the world. Its voice focuses on the past and reminds you of guilt, shame, pain, anger, fear, and all sorts of worries and difficulties. The ego plays repeated tapes in your mind of negative experiences. It makes you fear that past failures will happen again in the future. It keeps your mind focused on yourself and your concerns, which it magnifies all out of proportion. Many people consider the ego's inner dialogue to be so much a part of themselves that they do not think they can do anything about it. Others seek self-help means to change, such as "the power of positive thinking." But positive thinking alone will not stop the ego from counteracting such efforts. To change your internal dialogue, you will also need *positive action*. Your positive action must bring results that you can see for yourself, serving as a reinforcement that tells you that you are actually changing for the better.

No matter what action you take, the ego will not stop speaking to you. It speaks loudly, and its voice always speaks first. Fortunately, there is a second voice that contradicts everything the ego tells you. That second voice is the Voice for God, the Holy Spirit. He speaks for your Father, saying, "I love you now and forever." Although it appears to you that you only live within a world of limitations, the Holy Spirit reminds you that you live and move and have your being within the Being of God. Since God is Love, you live within His World, which is the Ocean of Divine Love. The Holy Spirit reminds you that you are never alone because you are forever joined with God and joined with all your brothers and sisters whom God loves as much as He loves you. The Holy Spirit enables you to perceive everyone including yourself through the eyes of love and forgiveness.

You can learn to disregard the negative thinking of the ego's voice and instead listen to and believe the uplifting Voice of the Holy Spirit. The best positive action you can take is to learn how to meditate. If you are a beginner in practicing meditation, your mind will jump around in many directions, and your ego will do everything it can to convince you to give up your meditation practice. There is one belief that will be an anchor for your mind, helping you to continue your meditation practice in spite of the storms of the mind that the ego presents. It is the belief that God loves you. He created you as a love being and gave all of His Love to you. You are forever His Beloved, and nothing, not even your unloving actions, will ever change His Mind about loving you.

But you will need faith to disregard the ego's voice that tells you that you are alone and not loved. It will require your faith to believe in God's constant love for you. After you persist in your daily practice of meditation, you will see the results for yourself. However, all meditation manuals have an inherent limitation because no book can really be your teacher. The Holy Spirit Who has led you to read this book and begin practicing meditation is your true Teacher. In conclusion, I only want to encourage you to listen with the ears of faith to the Holy Spirit and follow His guidance. As the Voice for God, the Holy Spirit will lead you Home to your inevitable awakening in your Father's Embrace.

ABOUT THE AUTHOR

~ • ~

Donald James Giacobbe recorded his life story in his autobiography, *Memory Walk in the Light*. He was employed for sixteen years as a case manager serving developmentally disabled clients. The professional nature of his work limited his ability to express his spiritual motivations overtly, so out of necessity he served as an "undercover agent" for God.

A more direct approach to spirituality was facilitated by living with Zen Buddhist seekers and then being part of a yoga community. Later he was the director of the Aquarian Age Yoga Center in Virginia Beach, VA. He served as an instructor of meditation and yoga, teaching college courses and appearing on television. He specialized in providing yoga teacher training certification courses and leading meditation workshops and retreats. Don has attempted in his teaching of meditation to strip away the rituals of Zen Buddhism and yoga practices and transpose only the bare essence into a Christian context. Techniques of meditation inspired by Eastern sources open the mind to the influence of the Holy Spirit and enhance the use of traditional Christian practices, such as the "Jesus Prayer" and Christian contemplation. These techniques can be found in Don's book *Christian Meditation Inspired by Yoga and "A Course in Miracles": Opening to Divine Love in Contemplation*.

Don's goal is to do God's Will, be receptive to the Holy Spirit, and find Christ within the temple of his own heart. He is not affiliated with any religious group. Formerly Don used the term "Christian yoga" to describe his path, which combines following Christ with yoga disciplines. In recent years he has adopted the term "Miracle Yoga" to describe his type of Christian yoga. This spiritual path is a combination of yoga and the philosophy of *A Course in Miracles* that encourages seeing with "forgiving eyes" and perceiving Christ in everyone. Don seeks to maintain a balance between opening to divine love inwardly and allowing that love to be extended outwardly to others. You are welcome to contact Don at miracleyoga@gmail.com and read his teachings on the following websites:

www.miracleyoga.org
www.christianyoga.org
www.christianmeditation.org

Lightning Source UK Ltd.
Milton Keynes UK
UKHW020909100822
407113UK00006BB/1323

9 780984 379057